Technology Fear

"To build a better future, we have to believe in a better future. This means reversing today's anti-tech mindset and restoring America's faith in scientific advancement. This book does both."
—Marc Andreessen, *Founder of Netscape and Cofounder of Andreessen-Horowitz*

"Atkinson and Moschella deliver a much-needed reminder that technology, data and innovation can be criticalingredients for solving society's biggest problems - from accelerating a clean energy revolution, delivering amore equitable healthcare system, to a more open and dynamic economy that rewards entrepreneurship."
—Aneesh Chopra, *President of CareJourney, former US Chief Technology Officer, and author of Innovative State*

"Debates over AI and digital media swing between utopian (technology will cure everything!) and dystopian (too many uncontrollable harms!). Luckily, this insightful new book helps experts and the public alike find the research-based middle ground beyond the hype at both extremes: how to embrace the opportunities while reducing the hazards."
—Rosabeth Moss Kanter, *Ernest L. Arbuckle Professor of Business Administration at Harvard Business School and author of* Think Outside the Building

"This is an excellent collection of essays on U.S. technology actions, policies, and proposals. I strongly endorse this book. It is ideal for wide audiences, and I believe universities and high schools will greatly benefit from the chapters included."
—Albert N. Link, *Virginia Batte Phillips Distinguished Professor of Economics at University of North Carolina at Greensboro, Series Editor of Palgrave Advances in the Economics of Innovation and Technology, and coauthor of* Innovative Activity in Minority-Owned and Women-Owned Business

"It's odd that we need a book defending technology and debunking today's many myths. Odd because so much good comes from advances in science and technology. But there are so many complaints about tech these days that debunk we must, and Rob and David do it very well."
—Robert Metcalfe, *inventor of Ethernet and Winner of the 2022 Turing Award*

"Technological progress is our best hope for a future of peace and prosperity, especially in changing the trajectory of climate change. Fortunately, there are a wide array of technologies that can help people achieve those hopes. Unfortunately, there are also a large number of myths that diminish public support for those technologies. Atkinson and Moschella take these myths head on. *Technology Fears and Scapegoats* is a profound antidote to pessimism about the future and opens the door to a brighter day."

—Peter Schwartz, *Chief Future Officer at Salesforce and author of* The Art of the Long View

"Atkinson and Moschella have written an important book on something that should matter to every American: success and innovation in our tech industry. They tackle hard questions head on and provide deep insight."

—Dan Scheinman, *technology executive, investor, and advisor*

"Throughout history, emerging technologies have been blamed for societal ills. Recently, we've seen the shift from Techlash around social media to hysteria over 'human extinction from AI.' Making sweeping negative generalizations based on inconclusive evidence is easy. Adding scary media narratives on top of it is even easier. The hard task is debunking them. *Technology Fears and Scapegoats* does an excellent job of battling well-known misconceptions. It's, therefore, a must-read for policymakers."

—Nirit Weiss-Blatt, *author of* The Techlash and Tech Crisis Communication

Robert D. Atkinson · David Moschella

Technology Fears and Scapegoats

40 Myths About Privacy, Jobs, AI, and Today's Innovation Economy

Robert D. Atkinson
Information Technology and Innovation
Foundation
Washington, DC, USA

David Moschella
Information Technology and Innovation
Foundation
Boston, MA, USA

ISBN 978-3-031-52348-9   ISBN 978-3-031-52349-6   (eBook)
https://doi.org/10.1007/978-3-031-52349-6

This Palgrave Macmillan imprint is published by the registered company Springer Nature Switzerland AG
The registered company address is: Gewerbestrasse 11, 6330 Cham, Switzerland

Paper in this product is recyclable.

Acknowledgments

At the *Information Technology and Innovation Foundation*, we try to think critically and independently about technology and its economic and societal impact. Sometimes this means being in the minority while almost everyone else is conveying safe answers, the party line, and/or the conventional wisdom. To challenge entrenched assumptions across a broad range of topics you need people with specialized expertise who are willing to take a non-partisan stand. We want to thank everyone at ITIF who contributed to the research, analysis, and opinions in this book, especially Daniel Castro, Nigel Cory, Jessica Dine, Ashley Johnson, Robin Gaster, and Trelysa Long.

David would also like to thank his former colleagues at DXC's Leading Edge Forum. It was at LEF in 2017 that he first became concerned about *the techlash*, and started pushing back against many of the most exaggerated Big Tech critiques. LEF supported this work for several years even though it was largely tangential to its core mission of improving the use of technology by large enterprises.

We also need to thank ITIF's Randolph Court for his indispensable editorial guidance and wisdom for both this book and ITIF's *Defending Digital* series where earlier versions of many of this book's analyses were first published. Special thanks also to Nicole Duca for her editorial and production support. Finally, many thanks to the team at Palgrave, especially

Bronwyn Geyer, for her enthusiastic backing of this project over these many months.

Robert D. Atkinson
David Moschella

Contents

About the Authors

Robert D. Atkinson is the founder and president of the Information Technology and Innovation Foundation (ITIF). His previous books include *Big is Beautiful: Debunking the Myth of Small Business* (The MIT Press, 2018), *Innovation Economics: The Race for Global Advantage* (Yale, 2012), *Supply-Side Follies: Why Conservative Economics Fails, Liberal Economics Falters, and Innovation Economics is the Answer* (Rowman Littlefield, 2007), and *The Past and Future of America's Economy: Long Waves of Innovation That Power Cycles of Growth* (Edward Elgar, 2005). He holds a Ph.D. in city and regional planning from the University of North Carolina, Chapel Hill.

David Moschella is a nonresident senior fellow at ITIF, in charge of its *Defending Digital* project. For more than a decade, David was head of worldwide research for IDC, the largest market analysis firm in the information technology industry, responsible for the company's global technology industry forecasts and analysis. His previous books include *Seeing Digital— A Visual Guide to the Industries, Organizations, and Careers of the 2020s* (DXC Technology, 2018), *Customer-Driven IT* (Harvard Business School Press, 2003), and *Waves of Power* (AMACOM, 1997). He has lectured and consulted on technology trends and strategies in more than 30 countries.

List of Figures

Introduction: The Roots and Risks of Today's Techno-Mythologies

Technological innovation is the most important factor determining not only America's future, but the world's. For the last 200 years, innovation has powered dramatic increases in living standards and the quality of life. Given twenty-first-century challenges such as economic inequality, climate change, aging populations, government indebtedness, resource shortages, lagging productivity, and intensifying global competition, this progress must continue. Only technology can deliver the necessary growth, productivity, and scale to create a world with higher wages, clean and inexpensive energy, advanced health care, 24*7 support for the elderly, enhanced education for the young, and so much more.

Who wouldn't want this future? Well, as it turns out, a lot of people. The biggest barrier to achieving today's technological imperative is the growing animus against an innovation-driven future. This animus can be seen in the many falsehoods that demonize advanced technology and the people and companies that bring it to market. Today's conventional wisdom holds that technology destroys privacy, spreads misinformation, undermines trust and democracy, eliminates jobs, discriminates by race and gender, increases inequality, rips off consumer, harms children, and even threatens the human race. Companies are also routinely attacked for a wide range of alleged market failures, including excess profits, a shrinking middle class, overly concentrated industries, and monopoly pricing power.

Unless these, and many other, fears are exposed as the myths, exaggerations, and scapegoats they are, it will be increasingly difficult for the West to restore the kind of optimism and spirit needed for a robust innovation ecosystem. This book seeks to support this restoration by identifying and

© The Author(s), under exclusive license to Springer Nature
Switzerland AG 2024
R. D. Atkinson and D. Moschella, *Technology Fears and Scapegoats*,
https://doi.org/10.1007/978-3-031-52349-6_1

debunking 40 prominent myths that stand in the way of a technology-enhanced future.

The Innovation Formula

The recipe for hi-tech innovation is no secret. History has shown that the key ingredients are: science and engineering research, STEM and entrepreneurial skills, effective mass education, modern infrastructure, and the success of technology firms of all sizes, including large, dominant ones. Innovation also requires smart, supportive government policies that put accelerating the rate of progress at the center of economic thinking. Unfortunately, this formula often seems to better describe modern China than today's United States.

Both innovation and innovation policy must be grounded on a bedrock of aspiration and optimism. If society sees innovation as a necessary force for good, and government as a key enabler, there will be better innovation policies and more innovation. But if the dominant narrative is that technology is an out-of-control force for harm, there will be detrimental policies and less innovation. This latter situation is where the United States and many other Western nations find themselves today. Important technologies such as AI, robotics, analytics, satellites, drones, sensors, personalization, facial recognition, speech syntheses, advanced cryptography, algorithms, automated operations, and genetic profiling are seen as inherently suspect and problematic. Like Gulliver, they are threats to be tied down, not the likely pillars of an advanced technological society.

These attitudes reduce both the enthusiasm for innovation and the efforts by government needed to spur it. Too often, America has shifted its focus from delivering technological wonders to preventing "harmful" change. This mindset has led to technology bans, counter-productive taxes, overly stringent and conflicting federal and state regulations, excessive approval cycles, limitations on data usage, resistance to automation, under-utilization of domestic resources, foreign dependencies, efforts to block mergers and acquisitions, unwarranted antitrust charges, extensive litigation, slower adoption, project delays, cost overruns, and an overall fear of the future. Once widely seen as a savior of humanity, technology is increasingly used as a scapegoat for just about every societal ill. The knowledge of Athena now gets treated more like the curse of Eris, the goddess of discord.

These overly negative attitudes are leading America to increasingly retreat from the future, at risk of ceding important innovation areas to its global rivals. While Chinese leader Xi Jinping proclaims: "The Internet Age will promote the development of human life, production and productivity," President Biden, reflecting the view of many Western leaders, recently wrote with regard to artificial intelligence: "We must be clear eyed and vigilant about the threats."[1] Unless such narratives are rejected and replaced with more hopeful ones of the kind that enabled the West to become the most advanced region in the world, we can expect slower rates of progress, declining competitiveness and the eventual loss of global leadership.

Such a loss risks transforming America into a different kind of nation: fearful, static, and increasingly angry. In this sense, technological pessimism and opposition is like a dry rot eating away at the foundations of the West. Today, it is most advanced in Europe, but it has also spread widely across the United States. America needs to clean out the rot and return to its much more optimistic, dynamic, and appreciative technology roots.

This book seeks to defend the essential value of technology and rebalance a series of debates that have become almost completely one-sided. Each chapter examines a common myth, explains why it is either wrong or significantly overstated, and describes what the real situation is. We don't pretend that this one work can defuse today's negative narratives. These *techno-mythologies* are too deeply embedded in the popular consciousness, repeated endlessly by anti-tech advocacy groups, the elites, and a mass media that often uses scaremongering and misinformation to attract "eyeballs." Bad news, after all, still sells.[2]

Likewise, this isn't to say that tech companies and their innovations are a panacea, and that there are no problems or role for regulators. This is not a call for a libertarian free-for-all. Many of the promises of the information age such as the transformation of health care, education, and transportation have yet to be fulfilled; criticism of tech company shortcomings and business practices is sometimes warranted, and there are important support and oversight roles for the state. But when technology's detractors are so blinded by hostility that they exaggerate the downsides and ignore the many things these companies do right, their critiques cease to be part of a productive debate, and take on the character of an angry mob. Perhaps even more importantly, by blaming so many societal problems on technology, it's all too easy to avoid the real drivers of polarization, distrust, manufacturing job losses, inequality, and many other current maladies.

We hope that this book can serve as a corrective for those who are open to a more positive and balanced perspective on technology's impact on society. More broadly, we believe this work can help America and the West rediscover what used to be a deep-seated optimism about innovation, progress and the future, as well as the role of government in promoting it. For if the West drifts too far from these roots, at a fundamental level it will cease to be the West as we have known it since the Enlightenment—a place and an attitude that mostly welcomes change and progress.

Familiar Tech Fears

Zog probably objected to Grog's discovery of fire because it would lead to less demand for fur, and that the invention of the wheel would undermine the importance of physical strength. Socrates complained that writing was a poor way to communicate knowledge. Religious leaders warned about the printing press, and translating from Latin. The Luddites smashed textile machines. An 1861 article argued that the telegraph was a step down from steamer ships carrying mail because "it has led to no improvement."[3] An 1897 article about cameras stated that "photographs are made to lie."[4] Doctors worried that bicycling could lead to insanity in women.[5] Radio waves were said to cause hurricanes.[6] Experts warned that television would lead to the end of privacy.[7] In 1981, we were told that Sony's "Walkman" devices were "mind altering."[8] And in 2020, we were warned that 5G cell towers and Covid-19 cases were related.[9]

In hindsight, these techno-panics are amusing and seem like human nature: "What were these people thinking?" Hopefully in 30 to 40 years, the myths we describe in this book will be seen as similarly silly. How could so many educated people possibly believe that AI would destroy human worth? Where did we get the idea that Big Tech exploits low-income nations by providing free services? Why did we think that personalized information services are a bad idea? What made us expect private companies to tell us what is true and what is false? How could so many experts have believed that technology would soon lead to the *end of work?*

But Western societies are very different today than they were 40 years ago. They are less optimistic, more fearful, and more divided. Anti-technology forces are also much stronger and institutionalized, with financial support from well-endowed foundations and wealthy former tech entrepreneurs. Ideological extremes—which thrive on myths the way the *National Inquirer* thrives on celebrity gossip—are much wider and more entrenched. In short, today's anti-tech headwinds are powerful.

America's Pro-Technology Past

For most of U.S. history, the narrative about technology was not only positive, it was often ecstatic. Americans of earlier generations remembered all too well the hardships of the past; they mostly saw technology as a blessing, and celebrated both inventors and the companies that employed them. There was a deep belief in the United States in the inevitability, and desirability, of economic and technological progress. Indeed, the enlightenment era was largely built on this idea. As Harvard Economist Benjamin Friedman wrote in *The Moral Consequences of Economic Growth*, "the idea that progress, including worldly progress, not only existed, but was inevitable, was a major step toward Enlightenment thinking."[10]

The historian Merritt Roe Smith highlights a sample of books from the 1860s to the early 1900s with titles such as:

- *Eighty Years' Progress of the United States* (1861).
- *Triumphs and Wonders of the 19th Century, the True Mirror of a Phenomenal Era* (1901).
- *The Marvels of Modern Mechanism and Their Relations to Social Benefit* (1901).
- *Our Wonderful Progress; The World's Triumphant Knowledge and Works* (1902).
- *The Wonder Book of Knowledge, the Marvels of Modern Industry and Invention* (1919).
- *Modern Wonder Workers; A Popular History of American Invention* (1924).

This optimistic outlook was reflected not just in story, song, and mass media, but in the writings of leading intellectuals who celebrated the notion of progress and saw technology as a force for liberation and enlightenment. Economist Benjamin Anderson wrote in the 1930s that, "on no account, must we retard or interfere with the most rapid utilization of new inventions."[11]

Importantly, it wasn't just capitalist intellectuals who saw the potential of new technologies. Socialist Jack London warned the working man: "Let us not destroy these wonderful machines that produce efficiently and cheaply. Let us control them. Let us profit by their efficiency and cheapness. Let us run them by ourselves. That, gentlemen, is socialism."[12] Socialists, communists, and others on the left embraced technology because they believed that liberation could come about only when the problem of production had been solved, and that could only be achieved through mechanization and innovation. Even the Catholic Church praised the wonders of technology. In 1967, Pope Paul VI stated:

> The introduction of industrialization, which is necessary for economic growth and human progress, is both a sign of development and a spur to it. By dint of intelligent thought and hard work, man gradually uncovers the hidden laws of nature and learns to make better use of natural resources. As he takes control over his way of life, he is stimulated to undertake new investigations and fresh discoveries, to take prudent risks and launch new ventures, to act responsibly and give of himself unselfishly.[13]

Compare this to a recent complaint from Pope Francis:

> Artificial intelligence and the latest technological innovations start with the notion of a human being with no limits, whose abilities and possibilities can be infinitely expanded thanks to technology. In this way, the technocratic paradigm monstrously feeds upon itself.[14]

He goes on to state:

> It is chilling to realize that the capacities expanded by technology have given those with the knowledge and especially the economic resources to use them, an impressive dominance over the whole of humanity and the entire world.

Of course, the most enthusiastic of these earlier writings tended to come before the Great Depression and two catastrophic world wars, and it was inevitable that any utopian views of technology would erode over time. As Robert Friedel wrote in *A Culture of Improvement: Technology and the Western Millennium*, "The 1970s saw a confluence of forces that collectively cast into doubt the ascendent culture of improvement."[15] These forces included environmental damage, fear of big business power, doubts about corporate life, global and national inequalities, racial divisions, nuclear weapons, and many other concerns. Nevertheless, technological optimism, especially in America, persisted until the second half of the 2010s.

How Myths Harm Innovation

Today's concerns about artificial intelligence (AI) are illustrative of this loss of faith and confidence. Long the Holy Grail of computer science, AI services such as ChatGPT haven't been celebrated for their many potential benefits in science, software, language translation, the arts, and countless other areas; they have mostly triggered a barrage of attacks. AI is racially biased; AI will destroy millions of jobs; AI will kill copyright; AI will undermine democracy; and even that AI is an existential threat to humanity. Given these accusations, anyone getting a Ph.D. in AI must sometimes feel like they're developing nuclear weapons or toxic chemicals. Similarly, when most of the messages around a technology are negative, policymakers don't wonder how they can utilize it, they think about how they should shackle it.

Like AI, many other myths stem from fear. If you fear the loss of privacy, you will be less keen on building the healthcare databases that make new insights possible. If you believe that Big Data biases are inevitable, you will be less tolerant of the early errors that most innovations come with. If you believe the Internet mostly harms teenagers, you might discourage them from learning valuable digital skills, or be less supportive of using computers in and out of the classroom.

Other myths distort policy priorities. If small business is seen as the font of innovation, then policymakers should favor less efficient smaller firms over more efficient larger ones. If automation kills jobs, then governments should develop schemes that tax automation equipment. If productivity gains don't benefit workers, why pursue them? If inequality is out of control, then we should focus on redistribution, not growth. If big is inherently bad, we should break up technology firms regardless of their consumer benefits. If the technology industry is seen as dominated by white males, we devalue the essential contributions of people from India, Asia, and elsewhere, often in America on temporary, and hence revocable, visas.

Still other myths stem from a sense of complacency. If we have all the technologies we need to address climate change, then government should force organizations and individuals to adopt them, instead of developing better and cheaper solutions. If "technology is changing the world as never before" and "China copies but doesn't innovate," there is no need to accelerate innovation, as we are doing just fine already. If you believe that America can get all the IT skills it needs from India, you will be less worried about the decline of America's STEM education.

Finally, some myths are targeted not against innovation, per se, but against government playing an active role to spur it. The views that "government R&D crowds out more productive private sector R&D," and that "industrial policy is not the American way" are both historically wrong and limit support for advanced technology development programs and policies.

Negativity's Roots

So how did all this misinformation about technology, technology firms, and technology policy come about? Why now? Why in America? How did we reach a situation where one of the great innovators of all time is viscerally disliked by so many Americans. In just twenty years, Elon Musk has revitalized the American car, space, solar, and battery industries, used his satellite network to provide vital services to Ukraine, and helped launch OpenAI, all while pushing the frontiers of robotics, brain implants, and space exploration. Yet because many people disapprove of his political views, his very un-CEO-like outspokenness, and/or his turbulent efforts to change the former Twitter into a new X, his extraordinary contributions are minimized and his reputation routinely vilified.

Readers of sufficient age will recall that there was virtually no opposition to the Internet and its leaders when it was first rolled out commercially in the 1990s. It was widely seen as both positive and transformative. *The New York Times'* John Markoff wrote in 1993:

> Forget Elaine's. The Internet is currently the world's most fashionable rendezvous. WHO USES IT: Well-known nerds like Steve Jobs and William Gates, pop folks like Todd Rundgren and Billy Idol, cyberpunks and yuppies, your mom.[16]

This sort of gushing was commonplace, and similar to that of a century ago, complete with many enthusiastic books about the wonders of the coming Information Age. Although one could argue that there was little initial opposition because people didn't see the dark side of the Internet which would only emerge later, this view is unconvincing. AI is at a similarly early stage of development, and yet it is already widely demonized, so there must be something additional going on. While it was the 2016 election of Donald Trump that released the full fury of anti-tech forces, the ten dynamics below laid the necessary groundwork.

1. *Diverse Resentments*

It's only human nature that the extraordinary success of Silicon Valley has led to various resentments. Many people resent the great riches of a handful of individuals and the millions of very high-paying office jobs the technology world has created. Traditional media can't help but resent the way new media now dominates the advertising industry, putting existential pressures on many once powerful firms. Book publishers resent their dependence on Amazon, and the fact that books are less influential than they used to be. Older workers resent the wild success of people barely out of their teens. Politicians and governments resent that they no longer control the dissemination of information. Many citizens without technological skills resent feeling unappreciated. Citizens around the world resent the fact that, outside of China, American tech companies are so dominant. While these same groups enjoy technology's many benefits, there is an underlying unease more than open to technology critiques.

2. *The Need for Scapegoats*

Technology is now blamed for a wide range of societal problems. As techlash scholar Nirit Weiss-Blatt writes "Silicon Valley—once the golden child of American industry—has become a villain."[17] But as this book will show, technology is not the main cause of polarization, distrust, loss of faith in elections, stagnant wages, or the decline in manufacturing. Such claims are mostly a form of scapegoating for a society fundamentally divided on issues such as abortion, immigration, taxes, school choice, police reform, trade, affirmative action, Covid-19 mandates, judicial fairness, support for Ukraine, and much more. It's much easier to blame these divisions on the impact of technology than recognize that America's distrust mostly stems from real institutional failures—be it the wars in Iraq and Afghanistan; unchecked globalization; spiraling national debt; abuses by the police, religious institutions, athletic coaches, the Boy Scouts and other guardians; rising crime; failing schools; media biases; open borders, inflation, and more. Blaming Tech is the easy way out.

3. *Free-Market Ideologies*

Some myths are mostly rooted in philosophy, an overarching belief system so strong that everything is filtered through it. For example, the myth that "industrial policy is not the American way" stems from the dominance, at least on the political right, of the view that free markets are inherently superior to public/private partnerships. Never mind that U.S. state and federal governments have implemented industrial policies since before the Constitutional Convention and they have been a major reason for America's techno-economic dominance.[18] This laissez-faire view can easily lead to the false beliefs that China's reliance on a strong and engaged state is either destined to fail or a form of cheating.

4. *First-Order Thinking*

Type into Google the words "AI impact on jobs," and you will see many links warning of mass unemployment. But this misunderstanding comes from only considering first-order effects. Of course, a company adopting technology to reduce costs will often find that it can produce more output with the same or fewer workers. Unfortunately, for many observers, including many journalists and academics, that's as far as they go with their analysis: Automation leads to fewer jobs, especially in the most immediately affected localities.

But as has been true since at least the emergence of agriculture, when a technology boosts labor productivity, yes, fewer workers might be needed, but because that product or service now costs less, consumers save money, which they can spend something else. If making a car is cheaper because of robotics, people might spend the savings on home improvement or a long-desired boat. If a law firm uses AI to boost productivity and employs fewer legal assistants, legal services can cost less, and people can spend those savings on things like going out to dinner.

These second-order effects explain why even though U.S. labor productivity has increased by more than sevenfold over the last 120 years, the unemployment rate is near an all-time low.[19] Fears that ATM machines, self-service gas stations, self-checkout grocery stores, camera-based toll booths, industrial robots, software, and other forms of automation would result in mass unemployment have proved unwarranted. While *globalization* has led to many job losses, we will show that *automation* is actually part of the higher employment and higher-wage solution, not the problem.

This kind of first-order thinking permeates tech myths: If companies reduce workers, profits must go up, ignoring the second-order effect of competition driving down prices. If a web site places a targeted ad based on your Internet activity, your privacy must be violated, ignoring the second-order reality that neither the advertiser nor the company knows your information, only an algorithm does.

5. *Entrenched Groupthink*

Many myths have gained their strength and endurance through the power of "groupthink." The term was first introduced in 1971 in *Psychology Today* by psychologist Irving Janis. Janis had studied group decision-making under conditions of stress and found that:

... individuals tend to refrain from expressing doubts and judgments or disagreeing with the consensus. In the interest of making a decision that furthers their group cause, members may also ignore ethical or moral consequences. While it is often invoked at the level of geopolitics or within business organizations, groupthink can also refer to subtler processes of social or ideological conformity.[20]

In other words, groupthink is pervasive because it's easier for people to go along with the dominant narrative, and because challenging that narrative can have real personal costs. In many organizations, it can mean being passed over for promotion because one is not seen as a *team player*. As a professional, it can mean being quietly ignored by one's peers. Because someone doesn't hold the "right" views, it's not a good idea to invite them to submit an article, speak on a panel, or come to a roundtable lunch.

This speaks to a central challenge facing the United States. Whether for an individual, a company, or a nation, progress depends on the ability to challenge the status quo. Yet adherence to many of these anti-tech myths is now required for acceptance into polite society. We all *know* that AI is biased. We all *know* that big companies have gotten too powerful and industries too concentrated. We all know that U.S. broadband services lag the modern world. We all *know* that social media is the cause of political polarization. These and similar assertions are no longer seriously debated; they are barely even allowed to be debated. They are the accepted wisdom that elites (and anyone who seeks to be accepted into the elite class) must hold.

6. *The Hype Cycle in Reverse*

Originally coined by Gartner, the key idea is that most new technologies go through phases. After a major new technology is introduced, there is often a phase of "Inflated Expectations" when the technology is seen as game-changing in its potential. No recent innovation has seen a higher peak of expectations than AI and ChatGPT. After years of disappointment, AI is now widely seen as a world-shattering innovation.

In earlier years, technology hype was mostly about the benefits of a new innovation, but today it's more about the potential downsides. As one tech journal wrote: "When a technology is subject to overhype, it is easy for policymakers to assume vast and unexpected impacts, many of which could be or likely will be, negative."[21] If policymakers are inclined to take a precautionary-principle approach (believing that any potential harms must be regulated before any harms might actually occur), technology hype is regulatory rocket fuel. If you believe that AI will take over the world, as opposed to being yet another remarkable and useful innovation, then you will be inclined to bring the regulatory hammer down sooner than later, as suggested by President Biden's October 30, 2023, AI executive order.[22]

7. Anti-Capitalist Longings

Some of the most damaging myths stem from a deep-seated rejection of the Western capitalist system, and a desire to replace it with something more stable, small-firm dominated, and egalitarian. But to justify such an agenda, anti-capitalists must first convince voters that the current system is failing: Corporations are socially irresponsible; prices and profits are too high; beneficial innovations are too rare; privacy is too unprotected; worker wages are too low; etc. They must paint a picture of big firms, particularly in technologically advanced industries, as harming both consumers and small businesses via their single-minded drive to accumulate wealth and power at the expense of "the people."

Although most of these claims are wrong, or at best overstated, that does not stop them from being recycled on social media, in the press, at conferences, and in Congressional hearings, thus laying the groundwork for a set of anti-corporate beliefs and policies that, if implemented, will result in lower economic growth, less innovation, reduced U.S. competitiveness, and fewer opportunities for disadvantaged Americans. The simple reality is that Hi-Tech and Big Tech are often inseparable. You can't really have one without the other.

8. Advocacy Funding Imbalances

For much of the twentieth century, organized labor was the major countervailing force to large corporations. But as the role of organized labor, particularly in the private sector, shrank, the new countervailing force has come from an amalgam of single-issue groups organized around causes such as the environment, poverty, gender, intellectual property, race, privacy, civil liberties, monopoly power, inequality, and the like. The growth of these groups has been fueled by the dramatic growth of left-leaning foundations, and the enormous personal wealth of liberal individuals seeking to "change capitalism" and perhaps *atone* for the sin of getting so wealthy.

According to *The Giving Review*, none of the largest 15 foundations "is principally dedicated to funding recipients pursuing conservative principles or policies. On the contrary, many of these foundations, especially those with policy-related program interests, are clearly dedicated to just the opposite."[23] The authors found that "right-leaning groups' revenues totaled just under $2.2 billion in 2014, but left-leaning groups' totaled more than $7.4 billion."[24] The gap has almost certainly widened since then.

Similarly, the philanthropy consultancy, Blue Tent, has identified over 200 left-leaning foundations in America.[25] These include groups that reject copyright enforcement, seek to hold tech firms "accountable," promote technology *justice*, protect individual privacy, oppose new technologies such as facial recognition and AI, highlight "power imbalances," want to break up large firms, and regulate large telecom providers to bridge various digital divides. The Ford Foundation alone has funded nearly 100 non-profit advocacy groups focused on "public interest technology."[26]

These organizations mostly refuse to fund any work that doesn't advance their "cause;" while they are not new, their number, scope, and influence have increased significantly. As such, they provide a constant drum beat against technology and corporations, and vocal support for policies that rein them in. And in contrast to what most people might think, the technology industry spends relatively little money defending itself. According to Open Secrets, the Internet industry ranked just 13th in lobbying spending in 2022, behind hospitals, electric utilities, and real estate. Technology industry spending is less than $100 million, with Telecom Services spending another $118 million.[27]

9. *Purveyors of Doom*

In contrast to the pro-technology books of the past, *fear of the future* is now the main technology book genre. The titles of the ten works below are typical and are seemingly coming with increasing frequency:

- *The End of Work: The Decline of the Global Labor Force and the Dawn of the Post-Market Era* (1994).
- *Spychips: How Major Corporations and Government Plan to Track Your Every Purchase and Watch Your Every Move* (2005).
- *The Net Delusion—The Dark Side of Internet Freedom* (2011).
- *Our Final Invention: Artificial Intelligence and the End of the Human Era* (2013).
- *The Rise of the Robots: Technology and the Threat of Mass Unemployment* (2016).
- *Ten Arguments for Deleting Your Social Media Accounts Right Now* (2018).

- *The Age of Surveillance Capitalism- The Fight For a Human Future At the New Frontier of Power* (2019).
- *The Shallows: What the Internet is Doing to Our Brains* (2020).
- *Disinformation: The Nature of Facts and Lies in the Post-Truth Era* (2022).
- *Technofeudalism: What Killed Capitalism* (2023).

These and many other books and articles have relentlessly laid the intellectual foundation for the techlash. To the extent that there is a significant counternarrative promoting technology innovation, it mostly comes from consultants writing books about how IT can transform business operations. These works are widely read by corporate leaders and managers, but their impact on academia, policymakers, the media, and the general public has been minimal.

This fear of the future mindset explains why Silicon Valley VC Marc Andreesen's recent "Techno-Optimist" Manifesto was met with such widespread derision.[28] The *Washington Post* called it a "self-serving cry for help."[29] The *Financial Times* declares that "unrestrained technological 'accelerationism' is a bad idea."[30] And *Current Affairs* doesn't mince words, telling us that, "'Techno-Optimism' is Not Something You Should Believe In," because it "simply justifies elite power and promotes indifference to human suffering."[31] Clearly, Andreesen, with toxic statements like, "Technology is the glory of human ambition and achievement, the spearhead of progress, and the realization of our potential," must not only be debated, but ridiculed. This is the nature of today's opposition, and this is why digital technology, and technology more generally, needs defending.

10. *Own Goals*

As noted earlier, the tech industry is not blameless. When NSA contractor Edward Snowden leaked classified information to the media that disclosed that the NSA and other government intelligence agencies had secretly required tech companies to turn over information on its users, many online enthusiasts were shocked.[32] When Cambridge Analytica improperly used Facebook data to target U.S. voters, it fed into the election manipulation narrative. When the major tech companies worked closely with the Biden Administration to control information about Covid-19, trust in open and free online speech was damaged.

There have also been numerous hi-tech scandals—especially the fraud at Theranos and FTX, and the pyramid schemes of many cryptocurrencies and NFTs. Likewise, the tech industry has been unable to fully prevent serious problems such as ransomware, identity theft, malware, denial-of-service attacks, bullying, and children's access to inappropriate content. It can and must do better. Perhaps most troubling, America's technology giants have allowed themselves to become highly dependent on both an increasingly powerful China and an increasingly vulnerable Taiwan. Restoring America's faith in technology innovation will require real progress in all of these areas.

Trump as the Tipping Point

Although all ten of these factors had been simmering for some time, it was the 2016 election of Donald Trump that moved anti-tech forces to center stage.

In the early 2010s, when the Arab Spring uprisings occurred, the Internet was still seen as a liberating force. The media gushed about Iran's "Twitter Revolution," Egypt's "Facebook Revolution," and Syria's "YouTube uprising."[33] In 2010, *Time* featured Mark Zuckerberg as its "Man of the Year" for "connecting people, mapping social relations, creating a new system of exchanging information, and changing how we all live our lives."[34]

Similarly, Netflix was "killing piracy."[35] Spotify would let users stream songs for free.[36] Google had "amazing people," and its founding fathers were among the world's top "tech geniuses."[37] In 2011, the world mourned the loss of Steve Jobs, who had launched the "magical" smartphone.[38] Amazon was seen as providing more choice and convenience to tens of millions of consumers.[39] Massive open online courses were democratizing education.[40] Technologies and Big Tech were widely seen as catalysts for positive and needed change, similar to the progress of earlier eras.[41] President Obama was seen as the first tech-savvy president, early on sporting a Blackberry.

However, when Trump was elected in 2016, it all turned. Trump's victory was such a punch in the face to the elites, especially liberals, that it had to be explained, not as the will of the people, but as a dangerous new form of mass manipulation. The fact that Trump had such a huge social media presence further inflamed this view, as did the many exaggerated claims about the impact of Russian bots and misinformation on the 2016 election (The Brexit vote in the UK, also in 2016, raised many similar concerns and resentments across Europe, made easier by the fact that the leading social media firms were virtually all American).

Rather than acknowledging that many voters were understandably unhappy with forever wars, the 2008 financial crash, the loss of manufacturing jobs, radical cultural changes, and ever-increasing government spending and power, it was much easier to claim that social media is the problem. As Dr. Nirit Weiss-Blatt, a researcher who has studied the techlash writes:

> There were years and years of 'build-up' for the flip, but the flip itself was in the pivotal moment of Donald Trump's victory and the post-presidential election reckoning that followed it. The main discussion was the role of social media in helping him win the election.[42]

In other words, if it wasn't for social media, Trump never would have won. Tech gave us Trump, so tech must be punished! This became the dominant mindset and narrative of the 2016–2022 period in the media, in Congress, and with much of the liberal-leaning public. Whatever one thinks of President Trump, it seems undeniable that hostility to his victory turbo-charged the full range of anti-tech accusations. Long-familiar, but previously manageable, concerns about technology's effects on privacy, monopoly power, trust, equity, speech, polarization, and children were now widely described as growing threats to the social order, even democracy itself. The Covid-19 pandemic further aggravated many of these claims and dynamics, turning much of the political right against technology too. There have been very few defenders.

Hopefully, 2022 marked the peak of the techlash. With Covid-19 seemingly receding and the challenge from China becoming more serious every day, a growing number of policymakers are showing signs of recognizing that this is no time to be weakening many of America's strongest firms. While the eventual impact of the CHIPS and Science Act remains to be seen, its passage is evidence that the national mindset may be changing for the better. Nevertheless, the myths and misinformation described in this book are still pervasive and still need to be confronted. The balance of media and policy discussion is still overwhelmingly negative.

Why Us? Why Two?

This book seeks to rebut the principal charges against both the impact of modern technologies and the companies that provide them in a systematic and non-partisan manner. In each chapter, we will challenge one of the 40 most prominent myths—not because we are instinctive contrarians but because we believe that technological innovation is the single most important factor for human progress, and that these false beliefs are significant barriers to American prosperity and competitiveness. Our goal is to restore a sense of balance that counters the excesses of recent years and supports the view that America turns against advanced technology at its peril.

We decided to do this book together because of our long friendship, our shared perspectives, and especially the vast range of topics to be covered. One of us (Atkinson) has focused on technology and economic policy for his entire career, from work at the National Institute of Standards and Technology (NIST) and the Congressional Office of Technology Assessment (OTA), to founding and leading the world's top-ranked science and technology think tank, the Information Technology and Innovation Foundation (ITIF). Rob has taken the lead on most of this book's economic and policy chapters.

In contrast, Moschella has spent his career in the private sector, leading research at one of the world's largest IT market consultancies (IDC) and elsewhere, while working closely with global IT suppliers and enterprise customers alike. His books and research have focused on the changing nature of technology industry competition, be it from new technologies, Japan in the 1980s, China today, or, more speculatively, India in the 2030s. He also writes extensively about technology's impact on business, consumers, and society. David has been advocating the need to better defend the digital world since 2017 and has taken the lead on most of the cultural and international competition chapters (The primary author is initialed at the end of each chapter).

Both of us remain technology optimists. We admire the hard work and struggles of scientists, engineers, and entrepreneurs seeking to crack the code of change and deliver products and services that make our lives better. We are concerned that so much of today's conventional wisdom is simply wrong, and find it hard to understand how so many smart people can believe that technology is not making the world a much better place. But for those who think otherwise, we hope this book spurs an informed and open debate. Is this too much to ask? We shall see.

Notes

1. Justin Sink and Anna Edgerton, "Biden Says U.S. Must Be 'Clear Eyed and Vigilant' on AI Threats," *Government Technology* (July 2023), https://www.govtech.com/artificial-intelligence/biden-says-u-s-must-be-clear-eyed-and-vigilant-on-ai-threats.
2. Doug Allen and Daniel Castro, "Why So Sad? A Look at the Change in Tone of Technology Reporting From 1986 to 2013" (ITIF,

February 2017), https://itif.org/publications/2017/02/22/why-so-sad-look-change-tone-technology-reporting-1986-2013/.

3. "The Overland Telegraph," *The Placer Herald* (November 1861), Pessimists Archive, https://pessimistsarchive.org/list/telegraph/clippings/1861/m-sc-32-39.

4. "Photographs are Made to Lie (1897) and Bicycle Insanity (1896)," Pessimists Archive, https://pessimistsarchive.org/list/photography.

5. Ibid.

6. "Radio Blamed For the Storms," *Indiana Gazette* (October 1926), Pessimists Archive, https://pessimistsarchive.org/list/electricity/clippings/1926/m-sc-480-255.

7. Will Rogers, "Will Envisions Some Troubles of Television," *Wisconsin State Journal* (April 1927), Pessimists Archive, https://pessimistsarchive.org/list/television/clippings/1927/sc-485.

8. Bob Greene, "Walkman Earphones: Mind-Altering Devices," *The Daily Times* (August 1981), Pessimists Archive, https://pessimistsarchive.org/list/walkman/clippings/1981/sc-670.

9. Flaherty, Eoin et al. "The Conspiracy of Covid-19 and 5G: Spatial Analysis Fallacies in the Age of Data Democratization," *Social Science & Medicine (1982)*, vol. 293 (2022), https://www.ncbi.nlm.nih.gov/pmc/articles/PMC8576388/.

10. Benjamin M. Friedman, *The Moral Consequences of Economic Growth* (New York: Vintage Books, 2005), 34.

11. Bix, Amy Sue, *Inventing Ourselves Out of Jobs? America's Debate over Technological Unemployment, 1929–1981* (Baltimore: Johns Hopkins University Press, 2000)

12. David Noble, *Progress Without People: New Technology, Unemployment, and the Message of Resistance* (Between the Lines, 1995), 12.

13. Populorum Progressio, Encyclical of Pope Paul Vi on the Development of Peoples (Excerpts), March 26, 1967, https://www.kateri.org/saint-paul-vi-part-ii/.

14. "Apostolic Exhortation, Laudate Deum of the Holy Father Francis, to All People of Good Will on the Climate Crisis," Given in Rome, at the Basilica of Saint John Lateran, October 4, 2023, https://www.vatican.va/content/francesco/en/apost_exhortations/documents/20231004-laudate-deum.html.

15. Robert Friedel, *A Culture of Improvement: Technology and the Western Millennium* (Cambridge, Mass.: MIT Press, 2007), 537.

16. John Markoff, "THING; The Internet," *The New York Times* (September 1993), https://www.nytimes.com/1993/09/05/style/thing-the-internet.html.

17. Nirit Weiss-Blatt, *The Techlash and Tech Crisis Communication* (Leeds, UK: Emerald Publishing, 2021), https://www.emerald.com/insight/publication/doi/10.1108/9781800430853.

18. Robert D. Atkinson, "How 'National Developmentalism' Built America" (The American Conservative, March 2023), https://www.theamericanconservative.com/how-national-developmentalism-built-america/.

19. Jutta Bolt, Marcel Timmer, Jan Luiten van Zanden, "GDP per capita since 1820" in *How Was Life?: Global Well-being Since 1820* (OECD Publishing, Paris, 2014), https://dspace.library.uu.nl/bitstream/handle/1874/306235/3014041ec007.pdf.

20. "Groupthink," *Psychology Today*, https://www.psychologytoday.com/us/basics/groupthink.

21. Janna Anderson and Lee Raine, "3. Themes: The Most Harmful or Menacing Changes in Digital Life that are Likely by 2035" (Pew Research Center, June 2023), https://www.pewresearch.org/internet/2023/06/21/themes-the-most-harmful-or-menacing-changes-in-digital-life-that-are-likely-by-2035/.

22. Fact Sheet: President Biden Issues Executive order on Safe, Secure, and Trustworthy Artificial Intelligence" (White House, October 30, 2023), https://www.whitehouse.gov/briefing-room/statements-releases/2023/10/30/fact-sheet-president-biden-issues-executive-order-on-safe-secure-and-trustworthy-artificial-intelligence/.

23. Michael Hartmann, "Philanthropy on the Defensive" (American Affairs Journal, April 2022), https://americanaffairsjournal.org/2022/04/philanthropy-on-the-defensive/.

24. Michael Hartmaann, "Philanthropy on the defensive," *The Giving Review* (April 2022), https://www.thegivingreview.com/philanthropy-on-the-defensive/.

25. "Progressive Foundations," Blue Tent, https://bluetent.us/funding/progressive-foundations/.

26. Ibid.

27. To be fair this includes only direct lobbying funding, not other funding for advocacy; "Lobbying Industries," Open Secrets (2022), https://www.opensecrets.org/federal-lobbying/industries?cycle=2022.

28. Marc Andreessen, "The Techno-Optimist Manifesto," *a16z* blog post, Andreesen Horowitz, October 16, 2023, https://a16z.com/the-techno-optimist-manifesto/.

29. Adam Lashinsky, "Marc Andreessen's New Manifesto is a Self-serving Cry for Help," *Washington Post* (October 19, 2023), https://www.washingtonpost.com/opinions/2023/10/19/marc-andreessen-manifesto-silicon-valley/.

30. Jemima Kelly, "I Read Andreessen's 'Techno-optimist Manifesto' So You Don't Have To," *Financial Times* (October 22, 2023), https://www.ft.com/content/7eeb105d-7d79-4a59-89be-e18cd47be68f.

31. Jag Bhalla and Nathan J. Robinson, "'Techno-Optimism' is Not Something You Should Believe In," *Current Affairs* (October 20, 2023), https://www.currentaffairs.org/2023/10/techno-optimism-is-not-something-you-should-believe-in.

32. Shira Ovide, "The spying that changed Big Tech," *New York Times* (September 2021), https://economictimes.indiatimes.com/tech/technology/the-spying-that-changed-big-tech/articleshow/86285010.cms.

33. Gadi Wolfsfeld, Elad Segev, and Tamir Sheafer, "Social Media and the Arab Spring: Politics Come First," The International Journal of Press/Politics, 18(2) 115–137 (2013), https://doi.org/10.1177/1940161212471716; Sahar Khamis, Paul B. Gold, and Katherine Vaughn, "Beyond Egypt's 'Facebook Revolution' and Syria's 'YouTube Uprising:' Comparing Political Contexts, Actors and Communication Strategiesf [sic]," Arab Media & Society, March 28, 2012, https://www.arabmediasociety.com/beyond-egypts-facebook-revolution-and-syrias-youtube-uprising-comparing-political-contexts-actors-and-communication-strategies/.

34. Josh Halliday and Matthew Weaver, "Facebook's Mark Zuckerberg named Time magazine's person of the year," *The Guardian* (December 15, 2010), https://www.theguardian.com/technology/2010/dec/15/mark-zuckerberg-time-person-of-the-year.

35. Farhad Manjoo, "How Netflix is Killing Privacy," *Slate* (July 26, 2011), https://slate.com/technology/2011/07/netflix-streaming-is-killing-piracy.html.

36. Steve Kovach, "How To Use Europe's Amazing Free Music Service Spotify In the US," *Business Insider* (January 4, 2011)), https://www.businessinsider.com/how-to-use-spotify-in-the-us-2011-1?r=US&IR=T.

37. Nicholas Carlson, "Google: Where a Genius Feels Average," *Business Insider* (February 1, 2010), https://www.businessinsider.com/google-where-a-genius-feels-average-2010-2?r=US&IR=T; Christopher Null, "Twenty Tech Geniuses that Changed the World," *itbusiness.ca* (May 21, 2008), https://www.itbusiness.ca/news/twenty-tech-geniuses-that-changed-the-world/2241.

38. Mark Memmott, "The Word For Steve Jobs: Visionary" (National Public Radio, October 6, 2011), https://www.npr.org/sections/the two-way/2011/10/06/141105015/the-word-for-steve-jobs-visionary? t=1566478135752; "Apple's 'Magical' iPhone Unveiled," *BBC News* (January 9, 2007), http://news.bbc.co.uk/2/hi/technology/624606 3.stm.

39. Purvaja Sawant, "E-shopping made easy," *Times of India* (October 24, 2014), https://timesofindia.indiatimes.com/life-style/home-garden/E-shopping-made-easy/articleshow/39545171.cms.

40. Douglas Belkin and Caroline Porter, "Job Market Embraces Massive Online Courses," *The Wall Street Journal* (September 26, 2013), https://www.wsj.com/articles/no-headline-available-1380222900.

41. Coy Christmas, "Living in the Post-Internet World: How Technology has Liberated Us from the Network" (Business 2 Community, August 25, 2015), https://www.business2community.com/tech-gadgets/liv ing-post-internet-world-technology-liberated-us-network-01311600.

42. Nirit Weiss-Blatt, "Donald Trump Caused The Techlash," *Techdirt* (April 2021), https://www.techdirt.com/2021/04/14/donald-trump-caused-techlash/.

Society & Culture

Myth 1: Technology is Changing the World as Never Before

The technologies of the first half of the twentieth century transformed society far more than the many changes of the digital era. It's not even close. The belief that our own times are special seems to be human nature, but today it is creating unnecessary fears and anxieties.

Rapid improvements in artificial intelligence have triggered the claim once again. How many times have you heard someone say that technology is changing the world as never before? Have you ever asked anyone to prove it?

There is no such proof, not even a reasonable case to be made. Without in any way disparaging the value of today's technologies, even a cursory look demonstrates that the innovations that occurred between 1900 and 1960 had a much more profound effect on society than those of the following years. While no one knows what the next sixty years will bring, we can say with certainty that our own times have been a relative lull in terms of transforming the way we live and work. Consider the comparisons in the eight innovation areas below:

1. **Transportation**. Which were more important cars, trucks, subways, high-speed trains, airplanes, jet engines and rockets, or recent advances such as Uber, GPS navigation and the early days of smart roads, electric vehicles, self-driving cars, and space tourism?
2. **Infrastructure**. The impact of broadband cable, cellular networks, Wi-Fi, and Bluetooth pales in comparison with that of electrification, lighting,

© The Author(s), under exclusive license to Springer Nature Switzerland AG 2024
R. D. Atkinson and D. Moschella, *Technology Fears and Scapegoats*,
https://doi.org/10.1007/978-3-031-52349-6_2

clean running water, sewerage systems, roads and highways, airports, and more.

3. **Housing**. Internet connectivity, on-demand entertainment, smart products, and working at home have many benefits, but they don't come close to matching the combined importance of home heating, electricity, plumbing, air conditioning, ovens, refrigerators, freezers, washers/dryers, and other household appliances.

4. **Communication**. While the Internet, mobility, text messaging, satellites, and social media are of profound value, have they really changed society more than telephones, radio, television, and motion pictures, all of which were seen as nearly magical at the time? (This one is at least fairly close).

5. **Health**. Has anything in digital health care matched the importance of pre-1960 advances in X-ray machines, vaccines, surgery, dentistry, antibiotics, painkillers, and sterilization?

6. **Culture**. The birth control pill (developed in 1950) arguably changed the world more than any other innovation. It's inseparable from the feminist movement, the rise of women into the workforce, changing gender relations, declining societal birth rates, the nature of the family and many other important social, cultural, and economic dynamics. Digital technology hasn't reshaped society in any comparable way.

7. **Warfare**. Nothing has changed geopolitics more than the atom bomb and the fear of Mutually Assured Destruction. Fighter planes, bombers, aircraft carriers, submarines, tanks, and missiles are also all from the first half of the twentieth century. These systems still substantially outweigh the power of satellite imagery, cyber warfare, robots, and even today's powerful drones.

8. **The Environment**. Our major environmental concerns—air and water pollution, chemicals, non-degradable plastics, nuclear waste, the destruction of species and habitats, and climate change—all have their roots in the industries of the pre-digital era. These environmental challenges vastly outweigh the damage caused by information technology manufacturing, usage, and disposal.

And let's not forget that during the first half of the twentieth century citizens suffered through two cataclysmic world wars, a devastating influenza pandemic, a decade-long global depression, mass atrocities, the uncertain struggle between capitalism, communism, socialism and fascism, the specter of nuclear annihilation, collapsing colonial empires, and brutal racial, religious and ethnic discrimination, among other dangerous and unjust dynamics. So, the next time you hear anyone say that we live in uniquely challenging, fast-moving, and stressful times, it's okay to laugh. Nothing could be farther from the truth.

Familiar Human Foibles

Given that previous innovations were so much more important, why would anyone believe that our own times are so special? It seems to be human nature to appreciate the complexities and uncertainties of the present, while diminishing those of the past. It's all too easy to think that historical outcomes were much more inevitable than they actually were. This same preference for the present explains why so many people deem each election to be "the most important of our lifetime," even though they know that they've said the same thing before. It's also why people often claim that a recent sporting event or team is the most exciting or greatest ever.

In this sense, these recency biases seem harmless enough, and often they are. But they also contribute to unnecessary anxiety about the future. If you believe that every election is the most vital, it will tend to make you less tolerant of those who vote differently. If you believe that today's technologies are more impactful than those of the past, the fact that previous technologies have been overwhelmingly beneficial is less reassuring. If you believe that the pace of change from technology is unprecedented, then calls for slowing down AI innovation seem more understandable. Indeed, the belief that we live in uniquely fast-changing and precarious times is an essential pillar for much of today's technology resistance. It's a belief best gotten rid of.

—*DM*

Myth 2: Technology Is Destroying Individual Privacy

Politicians and the media constantly warn us about the privacy risks that come with modern digital technologies, but they completely ignore the many ways that the Internet and smartphones have built unprecedented privacy into our everyday lives. This extreme imbalance damages perceptions and leads to unnecessary fears and resentments. The reality is that technology has created far more privacy than it has destroyed. The challenge is to keep it that way.

That technology is destroying individual privacy is one of the few things the Washington world seems to agree on. Policymakers and media across the political spectrum warn of a future where faces are identified; movements, actions, and speech are tracked; personal data is used and sold in byzantine ways; data is retained forever; algorithms are manipulative; profiling is discriminatory; targeting is intrusive; and deep fakes are damaging reputations, all in the name of making money. China shows us what a surveillance state could look like. It's scary stuff.

But although there are many legitimate concerns in these and other areas, the ways in which digital technology has increased our privacy are so obvious and so pervasive that they are almost never mentioned. Put simply, we often prefer to share our most sensitive information interests and needs with distant computers rather than nearby humans. We take a calculated risk that whatever the computers of Alphabet, Amazon, Meta, or others digitally "know" about us is less likely to come back to haunt or embarrass us than the physical world alternatives. Thus far, with a few high-profile exceptions, this has been a winning bet. Consider the following ten areas where digital technologies provide us with vastly more privacy than we had during the pre-Internet era.

© The Author(s), under exclusive license to Springer Nature Switzerland AG 2024
R. D. Atkinson and D. Moschella, *Technology Fears and Scapegoats*, https://doi.org/10.1007/978-3-031-52349-6_3

1. **Health Issues.** Before the Internet, how did we learn about diseases, symptoms, or conditions without going to see a medical professional? Sure, there were books and magazines, but we had very limited access to accurate, specific, and confidential medical information and advice.

2. **Gender and Sexuality Issues.** Many people are understandably reluctant to talk to their friends and family about their relationships, preferences, and problems, while history has repeatedly demonstrated the limitations of receiving sex education from parents, friends, churches, schools, and similar entities. Fortunately, technology has greatly increased both societal knowledge and individual privacy in these often highly sensitive areas.

3. **Legal Issues.** Before the Internet, how did people inform themselves about issues such as indebtedness, bankruptcy, divorce, and child custody rights, or simply determining whether something is legal or not? Many people want to learn as much as they can before they talk to an expensive lawyer, but they'd rather not ask people they know. Technology provides both important information and greatly valued privacy.

4. **Values and Beliefs.** Perhaps you want to determine the best way to participate in a protest, or check out a controversial organization, activity, or cause. Maybe you are considering changing your political, religious, or ethical beliefs. In many such cases, confidentiality is a high priority, and the Internet provides it.

5. **Shopping.** People don't use Amazon just for convenience. Compared to traditional retail stores, the ability to go online and confidentially read about a product, see its reviews, purchase it, and have it delivered in a generic package is also of great value in areas such as health, nutrition, fitness, and entertainment, or just wanting to surprise someone with a gift.

6. **Reading, Watching, and Listening.** There are many books, magazines, and journals that you might not want your fellow subway riders, family members, or friends and colleagues to see you reading, just as there are many videos you might not want to rent at a video store, or podcasts you might not want everyone to know you are listening to. Headphones, streaming videos, and eBooks effectively address these concerns.

7. **Work Life.** Before email and cell phones, do you remember how awkward it was to cope with confidential family or other personal matters while at work or school? By enabling instantaneous and largely private communication, technology has helped countless people better balance their work and non-work obligations.

8. **Home Life**. Covid-19 demonstrated the importance of privacy even within our own homes—so that we don't overhear each other's conversations, Zoom calls, or entertainment. Individually owned keyboards, headphones, and screens are the building blocks of personal privacy, whether in computer, tablet, or smartphone form. Shared devices, although often necessary economically, are inherently less private.

9. **Small Town Life**. In many small communities, there was little to no privacy as the local librarian, postal worker, pastor, lawyer, doctor, policeman, or bookstore clerk (if there even was one) may well have known about your activities in the above areas for much of your life. (Urban areas have fewer such problems.)

10. **Anonymity**. As the bad behavior on X proves every day, there are downsides to allowing people to use pseudonyms, but the ability to post comments anonymously is also liberating and can help hold corporations, governments, and other institutions accountable. In this sense, Internet anonymity enables private expression in much the same way that voting, donating, or whistleblowing anonymously do.

Weighing the Balance

How should we compare these proven benefits to today's highly publicized privacy risks? There are at least six main dimensions to consider.

1. **The Threats**. As China has shown, the biggest privacy risks tend to come from potential government abuses, with people having legitimate concerns about the government knowing where they have been, who they are associating with, what they are saying, and where they have spent their money. Recent events have shown that America is not immune to such forces and must remain on guard, although the Constitution and a large array of civil liberties groups should provide strong protection.

2. **The Numbers**. The ten items above illustrate how modern information technologies provide substantial privacy benefits to just about every American who uses them. This translates to hundreds of millions of people in the United States and billions worldwide. Although it is difficult to quantify the total number of U.S. residents who have experienced material consumer privacy harm online, it seems clear that this figure is relatively small, and can remain so if data anonymization and masking are used properly.

3. **The Intentions.** Most of the privacy benefits above stem from the intended use of technology products and services: In contrast, most privacy risks—identity theft, targeted scams, hidden surveillance, false information, objectionable profiling, and data breaches—stem from errors, misuse, or outright illegal acts. The intended benefits will surely continue; the misuses can at least in theory be minimized over time, especially if regulators spend more time on fighting actual harms.

4. **The Major Players.** There is a tendency to treat Big Tech's impact on privacy in a monolithic way, but this is misleading. Companies such as Apple, Amazon, Microsoft, and Netflix mostly sell their products directly to their customers for a price, and thus are much less reliant on advertising revenues. In contrast, Alphabet and Meta rely heavily on selling targeted advertising services. This puts privacy concerns at the heart of their business model. Both companies have a huge incentive to safely and effectively provide targeted services in an anonymized manner. In almost all cases, software systems determine what ads to put in front of what people; the advertiser does not get personally-identifiable information.

5. **The Wider Ecosystem.** Although privacy watchdogs often see Alphabet and Meta as rich and tempting targets, they are only part of the vast consumer data industry. Credit card issuers, loyalty card programs, government records, data brokers such as Acxiom and Equifax, third-party apps, and countless specialized information and service providers all play important roles within the murky data-sharing ecosystem. Focusing just on Big Tech gets headlines, but it won't solve many privacy problems.

6. **The Present vs. the Future.** The privacy benefits of digital technology have been greatly valued by consumers since the earliest days of the Internet and smartphone eras. In contrast, many privacy fears are still somewhat speculative in nature. And while one can imagine an American version of a surveillance and social credit society, China's system only exists because the Chinese government wants it to. Hopefully, the United States doesn't, and its courts and regulatory systems, along with consumer demands and expectations, can avoid widespread surveillance, de-banking, de-platforming, and other Orwellian scenarios. Hopefully.

The Privacy Agenda Going Forward

None of the above is meant to minimize the potential risks to individual privacy nor today's complex privacy challenges. But policymakers should maintain a balanced and less alarmist perspective which recognizes that collecting and using data is an important source of innovation and value—to individuals, organizations, and society as a whole. In many areas, including education and health care we need vastly more data, not less if we are to make needed improvements. Calls to drastically cut back on such activities reflect a fundamental—and still unwarranted—pessimism about the future of technology and the information age.

That said, both American consumers and technology providers would benefit greatly from effective privacy policies and practices such as: having national privacy standards instead of state and local rules; establishing clear encryption policies; giving consumers a path to opt out of data collection; providing a better process for correcting damaging and inaccurate misinformation; conducting greater scrutiny of third-party data brokers; and putting in place more transparent and secure data usage, retention, and anonymization practices.

Addressing these issues requires smart government policies, effective industry self-regulation, and more informed and empowered consumers, three ingredients that are often in short supply. But we need to keep the bigger picture in mind. The public Internet is nearly 30 years old, and there have been warnings about the imminent loss of privacy during this entire time. Yet, thus far, technology hasn't reduced privacy; it has increased it substantially. How can we keep it that way?

Here's one suggestion: Imagine if the next time the so-called Big Tech CEOs testify on Capitol Hill about privacy, the committee chairperson opens the hearing by saying, "We thank the technology industry for the many valuable forms of consumer privacy it has enabled so far, but there are a number of very important areas that we need to work on together…" We might have a much more productive digital privacy conversation.

—DM

Myth 3: Social Media Is Polarizing America

Compared to the many issues dividing America today, social media is a relatively minor factor; it can amplify divisions, but it rarely causes them. In responding to polarization, policymakers should focus on the underlying non-technology factors. They should also focus less on "extremist" online language and more on clarifying what on- and offline behavior is legal, and what is not.

This book of forty myths begs the question: "Of all the complaints about Big Tech today, which is the most exaggerated?"

At or near the top of the list is one of the most currently widespread: that social media and the Internet are polarizing America. This is like saying that littered plastic straws and used Covid-19 masks are ruining the oceans. Sure, they add to pollution and can make for a depressing sight, but compared to the billions of plastic bottles, bags, product packages, and other trash, they are literally a drop in the ocean. So it is with social media.

Sources of Polarization

No one disputes the fact that polarization is now deeply embedded in American society, affecting all of us in one way or another, and that the rise of polarization has coincided with the rise of social media. But although it may be comforting to blame "toxic social media," for today's problems, the causes run much deeper than that. Consider the ten dynamics below, every one of which is more divisive than anything stemming from the digital world.

© The Author(s), under exclusive license to Springer Nature
Switzerland AG 2024
R. D. Atkinson and D. Moschella, *Technology Fears and Scapegoats*,
https://doi.org/10.1007/978-3-031-52349-6_4

1. **All Things Trump.** President Trump remains a uniquely polarizing figure, revered and reviled in roughly equal measure. His supporters are enraged by seven years of accusations and investigations, two impeachment trials, the FBI's "raid" on Mar-a-Lago, and now multiple indictments. Opponents are appalled by Trump's language and behavior, his claims of a stolen election, and the "insurrection" of January 6. Depending upon how compelling the evidence is, any convictions of the former president could further increase these divisions.

2. **Policy Disagreements.** The public has strong but sharply different views on many important issues—abortion, gun control, climate change, school curricula, border security, the use of fossil fuels, police funding, drug legalization, vaccine mandates, transgender sports, voter IDs, mail-in ballots, Ukraine, the Mideast, etc. Differences in these areas have deeply—and sometimes permanently—divided friends, families, communities, schools, workplaces, states, and the nation as a whole.

3. **Institutional Distrust.** Public confidence in the Congress, the courts, the police, the media, and now the FBI, as well as in schools, experts, religious organizations, and election results has declined significantly. This lack of societal trust makes it much more likely that institutional decisions and actions will be resented and/or resisted by one side or the other. Few ideas are more corrosive than the belief—now widely held by both the left and the right—that there are two standards of American justice.

4. **Tribal Politics.** Two-party systems can easily result in a Manichean mindset—us vs. them; we're good, they're evil; if they win, we lose—especially when there are little to no unifying issues (such as there were with foreign policy during much of the Cold War). In a 50/50 environment where every vote is seen as critical, tribal loyalties and tribal rhetoric dominate.

5. **Media Incitement.** CNN, MSNBC, Fox News, and others have put polarization at the heart of their business model. They deliberately select and spin stories that stir up their audiences. Radio—and now podcasts—is also highly polarized. Americans can listen to the soft-spoken liberalism of NPR or the shock-jock descendants of Rush Limbaugh, but there isn't much talk radio in between. Similarly, the most popular podcast in the United States—The Joe Rogan Experience—is also among the most criticized. America's major news organizations, including the Washington Post and New York Times, have also become much more partisan and strident in recent years.

6. **State vs. National "Majorities".** In terms of the number of states and as a share of its overall landmass, America is a conservative nation, but in terms of its overall population it's more liberal. Actions that reflect the will of the majority at a state level often conflict with those of the national majority. Since the boundaries between state and federal power are murky in many areas, jurisdictional tensions are inevitable. Loose talk about Civil War and secession is now commonplace.

7. **Covid-19 Schisms.** During the pandemic, richer Americans stayed at home and got richer, while the less-well-off did most of the dangerous and necessary work. School closures, business lockdowns, mask mandates, travel restrictions, the firing of non-vaccinated workers, and repeated assertions of (evolving) "official truths" vs. "dangerous misinformation" have further raised concerns about both societal fairness and unchecked government power.

8. **Woke Academia.** Once a respected source of expertise and perspective, America's universities are increasingly seen as far left and out of touch. The recent emphasis on intersectionality, "offensive" speech, trigger warnings, safe spaces, microaggressions, white privilege, gender fluidity, pronoun policies, toxic masculinity, defining who is woman, and transgender athlete and bathroom rights are far removed from the day-to-day concerns of most citizens, many of whom believe that these priorities are trickling down into K-12 education.

9. **Race, Crime, and Identity.** Many Americans saw the Black Lives Matter protests and riots of 2020 as entirely understandable and justified; many others saw criminal violence and the suspension of the rule of law. Emotions ran high on both sides, and still do. Massive immigration across the southern U.S. border, rising crime rates, and increased discussion of white supremacy, white privilege and anti-Semitism have also contributed to heightened racial divisions and identity politics.

10. **Shifting Intolerances.** As social tolerance has gone up—for marijuana, gay marriage, LGBTQ lifestyles, and religious beliefs—political and free speech tolerance has gone down. Where once parents worried that their children might be gay or marry someone from another faith or race, now they worry their sons and daughters might love a Republican or Democrat, or say something that one group or another finds offensive.

In short, if every form of social media and every online forum were switched off today, America would still be a highly polarized nation, just as it was during the 1960s when war, riots, protests, racial tensions, assassinations, bombings, drugs, and huge political, cultural, and generational shifts created similar societal divisions, all without any help from digital technology. Happily, that era also resulted in the civil rights, women's, environmental and other movements, as well as some of the finest music the world has ever produced. We should be so lucky this time.

Before Elon Musk took over Twitter (now X), Donald Trump, Dr. Robert Malone, Robert F. Kennedy, Jr, Marjorie Taylor Greene, Steve Bannon, Jordan Petersen, Alex Berenson, James O'Keefe, Michael Flynn, Sydney Powell, Roger Stone, Naomi Wolf, Mike Lindell, Jay Bhattacharya, and others were all banned or suspended. Meta and YouTube engaged in similar practices. But whether you agree with all, some, or none of those decisions, does anyone believe that social media silencing has made for a less divided America? When it comes to polarization, the Internet just isn't that important.

Social Media Scapegoating

Given that there are obviously much more important sources of polarization, why have social media, online forums, and the Internet received so much of the blame? There are at least five reasons, only the last one of which is compelling:

1. **Social Media and Polarization Grew Up Together**. Facebook was founded in 2004, and Twitter in 2006 and their rise to prominence came during the 2010s. Polarization increased sharply during this period. But correlation is not causation.
2. **It's Easier than Looking in the Mirror**. It's hardly surprising that politicians, traditional media, universities, and other major institutions would rather blame new technologies that stir up the unwashed masses than take a close look at their own role. "If only the citizenry would rely more on mainstream institutions, all would be well."
3. **It Simplifies the Problem**. It's much more comforting to believe that all we have to do is curb the excesses of social media than admit that the problem is much deeper and more fundamental than that. "If only we could reform Sect. 230."
4. **There Are Easy to Point to Excesses**. Social media doesn't cause polarization but it does showcase it. People say nastier things when they can do so anonymously, as they can on X. Facebook's own employees have complained about the way the company's algorithms are polarizing.[1] But these two issues are manageable. Only 20 percent of Americans use X at

all, and only about 10 percent regularly. Facebook's algorithms are a small issue in the scheme of things, and the fact that this topic has received such extraordinary media coverage is telling. (While there are concerns about misinformation on TikTok, the company hasn't yet been a major part of the polarization blame game, although that is surely starting.)[2]

5. **The Online World Can Be Linked to High-Profile Criminal Acts**. Unfortunately, digital technologies have played a role in some mass shootings, political riots, threats and attacks against public officials, and other troubling events. As discussed below, this is the main area that public policy should focus on.

The "Extremism" Fudge

Almost by definition, rising polarization tends to increase extremism and radicalization. But the use of those latter two words as pejoratives has pushed policymakers in the wrong direction. Americans are entitled to hold extreme and controversial views. We are free to proclaim that abortion is murder; fossil fuels should be outlawed; the government is hopelessly corrupt, or that visitors from outer space are among us, just as we are free to say we hate Trump or Biden. While one could argue that policymakers should try to distinguish between safe and dangerous extremist speech, in practice this rarely occurs. "Extremism" almost always comes with a negative connotation, despite what Barry Goldwater famously proclaimed.[3]

This is unfortunate because the real problem isn't extremism or radicalization; it's crime. In recent years, politicians and the media have shied away from using the word "crime" in this context because it raises questions that are hard to answer definitively. As listed below, many of these questions are particularly relevant to social media and other online forums.

- To what extent can protestors disrupt business or government activity on or offline?
- When does a fiery speech become illegal incitement?
- Is it ever okay to tear down a statue or destroy/disable public or private property?
- At what point does online hatred and "veiled" threats become criminal?
- Is it legal to block a highway, or publish videos of visitors to an abortion clinic?
- Is it okay to post the residential addresses of government officials, or harass them in public or at home?

- What limits should be placed on the purveyors of violent online content?
- How do we determine if an angry activist group is actually engaged in a criminal conspiracy?
- Under what circumstances, if any, can law enforcement use profiling to predict who might become a mass shooter, a terrorist, or similar public risk?

By using the word extremism instead of the word crime, we essentially fudge these issues, conflating the legal right to express controversial views with the illegal acts they may or may not lead to. This now widespread practice has only added to polarization, as it can demonize those with strongly held views regardless of whether there is any criminal intent or action.

To avoid this conflation, policymakers should talk much less about extremism and much more about what is legal and what is not at the federal, state, and local levels. If people know the laws and rules, they are less likely to break them, especially if those rules are enforced consistently and even-handedly. While there have been many debates about the nine questions above, there is still no clear set of widely understood and enforced guidelines. But this is what is needed to help social media firms, law enforcement, and the citizenry alike. Legal clarity and consistency won't end the worrisome divisions within America today, but they might reduce polarization's more dangerous effects until the national mood calms down, whenever that might be.

—*DM*

Notes

1. Meltem Odabas, "10 facts about Americans and Twitter" (Pew Research Center, May 5, 2022), https://www.pewresearch.org/fact-tank/2022/05/05/10-facts-about-americans-and-twitter/.
2. Tiffany Hsu, "On TikTok, Election Misinformation Thrives Ahead of Midterms," *The New York Times* (August 14, 2022), https://www.nytimes.com/2022/08/14/business/media/on-tiktok-election-misinformation.html.
3. Senator Barry Goldwater (R-AZ) accepted the Republican Party's nomination for president of the United States on July 16, 1964. In his acceptance speech, Goldwater said, "I would remind you that extremism in the defense of liberty is no vice! And let me remind you also that moderation in the pursuit of justice is

no virtue!" See: https://www.c-span.org/video/?320250-1/reel-america-barry-goldwaters-1964-acceptance-speech.

Myth 4: Technology Is Driving Today's Societal Distrust

Technology is way down the list of the forces undermining societal trust. But because the next phase of digital innovation requires confidence in technologies that will operate mostly in the public sphere, America's declining societal trust is harming its innovation ecosystem and overall competitiveness.

Between the scandals of Theranos and FTX, the collapse of many cryptocurrencies and NFTs, the content suppression at Twitter, Meta, and elsewhere, the voting machine malfunctions in Maricopa County, and the failure of the Federal Aviation Administration's computer systems, the last few years haven't been good ones for trust in digital technologies.

These high-profile events have only added to long-standing technology security challenges such as denial-of-service attacks, malware, ransomware, fraud, identity and intellectual property theft, misinformation, hacktivists, privacy violations, data loss, AI *hallucinations,* and more. As has often been noted, the Internet was not designed with digital security in mind. Quite the opposite, it was optimized for the openness and decentralization needed for scientific collaboration and resiliency.

But we shouldn't exaggerate the extent of these problems. Citizens around the world have become comfortable managing their finances, careers, health, and relationships through various online intermediaries, and this implies that there is a solid foundation of digital trust. To most Americans, the products and services from companies such as Amazon, Alphabet, Microsoft, Meta, and Apple have offered clear value and rarely seem to break or fail. Businesses also trust the Internet for everything from simple communications to complex global transactions.

© The Author(s), under exclusive license to Springer Nature Switzerland AG 2024
R. D. Atkinson and D. Moschella, *Technology Fears and Scapegoats,*
https://doi.org/10.1007/978-3-031-52349-6_5

Thus, while efforts to improve digital trust must continue, the bigger challenge is that declining societal trust will limit America's ability to innovate in digital technologies. Advanced applications will increasingly operate in the public sphere and thus depend on societal confidence much more than just consumer demand. Nations with high levels of societal trust will have distinct advantages in deployment and acceptance. As a high-innovation, but currently low-trust nation, America's position is more strategically precarious than it currently appears. Improving this situation requires both a digital trust and a societal trust agenda. But it's the latter that's both more important and more difficult.

Snowballing Societal Distrust

As many have noted, within just a few generations the United States has shifted from a relatively high-trust nation to a relatively low one, now ranking 30th according to *U.S. News and World Report*.[1] It's widely said that this shift began gathering significant momentum in the 1960s and 1970s, driven by President Kennedy's assassination, false government claims about the Vietnam War, pervasive air and water pollution, the impeachment of President Nixon, oppressive race and gender attitudes, and a self-identified "counterculture" that openly questioned traditional sources of official and cultural authority. Much of this distrust was warranted and long overdue, so in this sense distrust can lead to much-needed improvements.

But America has lived through a series of events in the twenty-first century that have shaken just about every traditional pillar of societal trust:

- the false claims of weapons of mass destruction used to justify the Iraq war;
- the recklessness of the financial services industry, and failure of regulators that led to the 2008 financial crash;
- the sickening child abuse covered up by the Catholic Church, the Boy Scouts, gymnastic coaches, and others;
- the National Security Agency's mass surveillance of American citizens as revealed by Edward Snowden;
- the OxyContin scandal at Purdue Pharma;
- widespread questioning of the 2000, 2016, and 2020 presidential elections;
- the death of George Floyd and other examples of police abuse;
- an FBI seen by many as overly politicized and a Supreme Court seen by many others as overly conservative;

- teachers unions blamed for keeping schools closed for too long during Covid-19;
- a Congress that has run up more than $34 trillion in national debt;
- a scientific community that suppressed and demonized peers who challenged the official views regarding the origins and management of Covid-19;
- the chaotic U.S. military withdrawal from Afghanistan;
- ongoing failure at America's southern border;
- the weakening of academic standards at seemingly every educational level;
- a biased and polarized national media; and
- a citizenry increasingly wary and intolerant of those it disagrees with.

Unlike the 1960s, the benefits of this era of distrust are hard to discern. The Internet may have made it easier to talk about and amplify these issues, but it did not cause them. Indeed, the loss of societal trust has had very little to do with technology. While many commentators have blamed today's societal divisions on misinformation, the examples above show the opposite. The most serious losses of trust occur when people learn the truth about what has actually happened. Whether these truths emerge first from online or offline sources is a relatively minor factor.

Improving Digital Trust

Compared to the challenge of making America a high-trust nation again, the task of increasing trust in digital technologies is much more straight-forward. Whereas societal divisions can seem irreparable and often involve participants who fundamentally disagree about what should be done, there is a broad-based consensus that the digital world needs to be safer and more stable. The main debate is about how to do this, whether industry evolution or government regulation is the best path forward, and if it's the latter, then how onerous and prescriptive this regulation should be.

In order to systematically assess and enhance the state of digital trust today, it's useful to segment the challenge into relatively discrete categories:

1. **Product Trust**. Do digital products and services perform as advertised? The industry tends to do pretty well here, but artificial intelligence presents new product trust challenges going forward.
2. **Company Trust**. Do the leading technology companies behave in a socially responsible way? The revelations of the Twitter Files and similar

actions have been damaging to Internet content providers, but most established Internet businesses are trusted by consumers, especially in e-commerce.[2]

3. **Transaction Trust**. Is there sufficient security, fraud detection, oversight, and recourse? The FTX scandal is of historic and lasting proportions, but most digital transactions, especially with the major players, are trustworthy.

4. **Personal Trust**. Are citizens' digital property and accounts sufficiently secure and protected? Ransomware remains particularly difficult to fully prevent.

5. **Technology Trust**. Are core technologies such as identification, encryption, backup, and recovery working effectively across systems? Good progress has been made here but deep fakes present important new challenges.

6. **Privacy Trust**. Is there a right to correct or forget, and an effective range of settings and permissions? Europe continues to be active here, but the U.S isn't, at least at a national level.

7. **Fairness Trust**. Are there accepted principles of data usage, fair use, fair compensation, and fair competition? The debate continues, both for traditional news media and now the use of Internet data in training large language models.

8. **Environmental Trust**. Is the technology industry sufficiently green? There has generally been too much focus on the tech industry's energy usage and not enough on the environmental downsides of hi-tech manufacturing and what to do with billions and billions of obsolete tech products.[3] The many ways that the digitalization of society helps reduce energy use also receive insufficient attention.

9. **Global Trust**. Are the societal norms mentioned above undermined or reinforced by offshore players in today's increasingly multipolar world? The Internet is clearly splintering along national and regional lines, meaning that trust in the above areas will vary significantly by geography.

It's important for the technology industry to effectively manage these issues if it goes through tougher economic times after the long boom of the previous 20 years. Companies behave one way when times are good, and differently when financial pressures mount. Don't be surprised if popular services that are currently free begin to have charges. As always, there are many media outlets and technology critics ready to pounce on any real or imagined mistakes.

Looking ahead, many tech services are becoming core components of functioning societies, and this means that key technologies must maintain relatively high levels of stability and trust. The incentives to continually make technology safer are strong, and this provides grounds for long-term optimism. In contrast, improvements in societal trust seem much less certain.

Co-Evolving Trust

For decades, the idea that businesses, science, the arts, culture, and society itself would increasingly *co-evolve* with information technology has been a useful guiding principle. In this sense, the largely separate evolution of digital and societal trust thus far has been an aberration. But this anomaly won't continue. The first great phase of Internet industry growth was driven by consumers, who could decide for themselves whether a particular product or service was trustworthy and worth using. The next phase of technology innovation will be much more collective in nature.

Important future innovations such as autonomous vehicles, drones, smart grids, charging infrastructure, blockchains, digital cash, voting systems, digital IDs, facial recognition, robotics, data analytics, and AI will often operate in the public sphere, and thus won't be driven by consumer choice alone. They must be developed and deployed in a trusted, cooperative way. It only makes sense that high-trust—often smaller—nations would have advantages in these areas, and from Singapore to Estonia, there are many examples of this being the case.

It follows that America's declining national trust presents a serious challenge to its future technology leadership. Continually improving the safety of digital products and services will always be important, but it won't guarantee leading-edge innovation. Building an advanced, intelligent economy will require a level of societal cohesion that is currently lacking, and without it, anti-technology forces are much more likely to prevail. Digital innovation isn't undermining societal trust, but declining societal trust will eventually undermine digital innovation.

—DM

Notes

1. *U.S. News & World Report*, "These Are the Most Trustworthy Countries," https://www.usnews.com/news/best-countries/rankings/trustworthy.

2. Daniel Castro, "Congress Should Not Break Big Tech to Fix Local News" (Innovation Files, February 11, 2022), https://itif.org/public ations/2022/02/11/congress-should-not-break-big-tech-fix-local-news/; Daniel Castro, "History Shows That the News Industry Does Not Need a Handout from Big Tech" (Innovation Files, August 31, 2022), https://itif.org/publications/2022/08/31/history-shows-that-the-news-industry-does-not-need-a-handout-from-big-tech/.

3. Colin Cunliff, "Beyond the Energy Techlash: The Real Climate Impacts of Information Technology" (ITIF, July 2020), https://itif.org/publicati ons/2020/07/06/beyond-energy-techlash-real-climate-impacts-inform ation-tcchnology/.

Myth 5: AI's Arrival Is an Atomic Bomb Moment

Recent high-profile statements warning of the existential risk of artificial intelligence are unconvincing. Other than deep fakes, most AI fears are still speculative, and many others seem manageable. Unless serious problems actually emerge, AI innovation should proceed and proliferate. Too much regulation too early will be harmful to American innovation and competitiveness.

"Mitigating the risk of extinction from AI should be a global priority alongside other societal-scale risks such as pandemics and nuclear war."

What are we to make of the fact that Geoffrey Hinton, Sam Altman, and hundreds of other leading AI experts lent their names to the one sentence statement above?[1] There's no mention of AI's many benefits, just the word "extinction" and two terrifying analogies certain to excite the media, trouble the public, and cast doubt over America's technological future.

The sentence is worth deconstructing. The priority is "*mitigating the risk of extinction.*" "Mitigate" typically means that a problem can't be eliminated, just reduced in the sense of mitigating pain. It's true that the risks of pandemics and nuclear war can't currently be eliminated, so we need to mitigate those threats as best we can. But it's odd that so many scientists believe that the threat of AI-driven human *extinction* is similarly permanent. The horrors of viruses and atomic bombs are all too real, but most AI risks are still vague and speculative. Others seem quite manageable and much less deadly. Today's alarmists have yet to convince us otherwise. Yet virtually all discussions in the

© The Author(s), under exclusive license to Springer Nature
Switzerland AG 2024
R. D. Atkinson and D. Moschella, *Technology Fears and Scapegoats*,
https://doi.org/10.1007/978-3-031-52349-6_6

OECD nations about AI policy are focused on limiting potential AI harms, rather than fostering benefits.

Flawed Analogies

The pandemic analogy is flawed because AI is not a virus like Mydoom or WannaCry that must be contained or eradicated; it's an extremely valuable tool that we want to use. Nor was Covid-19 successfully "mitigated"; supplies were not available; national decisions were chaotic; and many millions died or suffered. Neither the World Health Organization nor the Center for Disease Control acquitted themselves well. The former gave in to political pressures, while the latter sent mixed messages, and lost the trust of many Americans. Do we really want similarly powerful organizations—or Congress—to oversee the diverse and fast-moving AI field?

The nuclear weapons analogy is also flawed because AI isn't primarily a military technology. Should we really try to stop AI proliferation in the same way we have tried (and sometimes failed) to prevent nuclear proliferation? Of course not. Additionally, the risk of nuclear war has long been mitigated only by the reality of Mutually Assured Destruction. AI-enabled missiles, submarines, drones, etc., will surely become part of the MAD calculation, but this makes AI mostly an extension of today's military status quo. The big AI-driven changes will be in business and society where competition and consumer demand have always led to innovation and change, not the wary standoffs of MAD.

And One Missing One

It's curious that the statement didn't mention climate change as a societal-scale risk, even though this is a much more accurate analogy than either viruses or bombs. Like fossil fuels, AI is widely used, has a great many benefits, and comes with both real and potential downsides.[2] Whereas pandemics spread quickly, and nuclear bombs can be detonated at any time, the risks of AI—like climate change—typically build up over time. By raising the specters of Covid-19 and nuclear war, the statement creates a sense of urgency. In contrast, the climate change challenge has been characterized by two decades of warnings, scientific panels, and political summits that have resulted in gradual business and societal change. The AI world is already supporting similar groups and forums, most likely with similarly gradual results. This seems the best and most likely path forward.

All Too Familiar Fears

That great AI progress has generated great AI fears is hardly surprising. From Dr. Frankenstein's monster to HAL in the movie *2001: A Space Odyssey*, there have always been warnings that human-like inventions would eventually spin out of control and turn on their creators. Today's AI concerns can be grouped into the broad categories below:

1. AI-based automation will eliminate millions of white-collar jobs.
2. AI systems are inherently biased and discriminatory.
3. AI systems and algorithms are unaccountable and unexplainable.
4. AI will destroy privacy and lead to a surveillance state.
5. AI will lead to further increases in societal inequality.
6. AI-based deep fakes will undermine trust and disrupt politics and society.
7. Autonomous AI systems and weaponry will destabilize international relations.
8. Hostile powers will seek to dominate the world through AI.
9. AI lacks human values and ethics.
10. General AI intelligence will soon surpass that of humans.
11. AI will diminish human worth.
12. AI systems will go rogue, take control of society, and make humans expendable.

Specific Solutions

The fears above are all important issues to consider. But they can also be used to help us see how AI becomes less scary once each threat is addressed separately, especially if their potential impact is well out into the future. Consider the way the twelve scenarios above might prove largely manageable over time:

1. As discussed throughout this book, technology has never led to long-term unemployment and AI will likely be no different. Fears that automation will result in *the end of work* have always been proven wrong for the simple reason that automation reduces costs, which enables more demand, which leads to additional need for workers.

2. AI biases can be corrected over time by improving the underlying data sets, better understanding how these systems work, and closely overseeing their output in important areas. As we have long argued, machines will ultimately prove to be much less biased than people.[3]

3. Whether the output of an AI system is fully explainable or not, organizations that develop and deploy AI will surely be held accountable, just as they are for their use of software, machines, robots and other tools, materials, and processes. Of course, terrorists, the criminal underworld, and other anonymous entities will use new technologies such as AI to commit crimes and/or cause mayhem. It has ever been thus.

4. It's America's—and every nation's—choice whether to become more like China's surveillance state or not. Loss of privacy is not the inevitable result of AI, although it's always a real concern. But as China has also shown, widespread societal surveillance can occur with or without advanced AI.

5. Only time will tell whether AI becomes a major driver of income inequality, but fears that AI will be controlled by a few big companies seem dubious as usage is already widespread around the world, and as open source and specialized offerings proliferate.

6. Deep fakes are a serious problem, but technical, legal and behavioral solutions are possible. People will surely become more skeptical, "zero trust" viewers, just as they have because of Photoshop. Similarly, AI-based plagiarism in schools can be reduced by using automated tools and testing students in an offline room. The proliferation of deep fakes might even lead to people to rely more on known/trusted sources. Fears that AI will undermine election integrity have thus far proven to be highly exaggerated.

7. Just as the major nuclear powers have—or should have—hot lines to manage crisis situations, they will hopefully develop similar ways to control autonomous weaponry. It's in everyone's interest to avoid accidental and/or escalating conflicts.

8. Values and ethics can be built into many AI systems and applications, although whose values and whose ethics will always be an issue, especially in today's highly polarized times. As with social media, agreeing on what is true, fair and/or responsible will never be easy or straightforward.

9. Given the way research is shared globally, it will probably be impossible for any one country to maintain a decisive AI edge in terms of data and algorithms, unless some countries intentionally opt out of advanced AI competition. China surely won't.

10. Generalized machine intelligence that surpasses humans won't happen for a very long time, if ever. There will be time to gauge the best path forward. Human oversight and quality checking for AI is still essential in important applications.
11. Even though humans are no match for computers, people still greatly value playing each other at Chess, Go, and other games. Human strength and speed are still valued even though machines are vastly stronger and faster.
12. The idea that AI systems will turn against humans remains the stuff of science fiction. While it's made for some great movies, there's little evidence to support such fears.

Given the above, why are so many experts so alarmed, and even feeling guilty about their life-long work? Our initial reaction was that they must be seeing something that we don't. But many of the statement's signatories have taken to the airwaves to explain their concerns, and we haven't heard anything beyond the familiar fears mentioned above. It is surprising how many experts cited the student essay issue, as if plagiarism is a new problem and there are no effective remedies. Deep fakes are also mentioned a lot, but there is little mention of how this problem could be *mitigated* by the marketplace, the law and consumer awareness. In the end, the alarmism isn't convincing.

Covid-19 demonstrated the risks of making major policy decisions rapidly and under great pressure, which is why governments should be patient in responding to AI. The starting point should always be how well existing laws in health care, financial services, media, political campaigning, privacy, fraud, copyright and other areas apply to AI. Additional AI *guardrails* such as auditing algorithms, requiring ethics training, licensing/credentials, review boards, privacy and copyright policies, and the like can all play a role. But over time, we'll have a much better sense of which AI areas require significant regulatory intervention and which do not. Focusing on a small number of actual problems is much easier than trying to anticipate what will happen across a wide range of complex AI domains. Right now, we would mostly be guessing.

—DM

Notes

1. Center for AI Safety, "Statement on AI Risk," accessed June 7, 2023, https://www.safe.ai/statement-on-ai-risk.

2. David Moschella, "Data Isn't the New Oil; That Might Be a Good Thing" (ITIF Defending Digital Series, no. 18, May 30, 2023), https://itif.org/publications/2023/05/30/data-isnt-the-new-oil-that-might-be-a-good-thing/.

3. David Moschella, "AI Bias Is Correctable. Human Bias? Not So Much" (ITIF, Defending Digital Series, no. 5, April 25, 2022), https://itif.org/publications/2022/04/25/ai-bias-correctable-human-bias-not-so-much/.

Myth 6: Social Media Is the Leading Source of Misinformation

There is now a great deal of misinformation about misinformation. The most widespread and divisive false information in recent years has been primarily spread by traditional media organizations. The Internet has been mostly an amplifier.

Hostility toward the Internet and social media began escalating on Capitol Hill and in the news media in 2016, when Russian hacking, content, and bots were blamed for Donald Trump's surprising victory over Hillary Clinton. While those claims are highly debatable, the belief that the digital world is a dangerous source of misinformation soon became deeply rooted in conventional wisdom.

Yet a review of events over the last few years shows that these fears are largely unfounded, and mainstream media should be less focused on dissing its Internet competitors and more concerned with getting its own information house in order. Consider that America's major television networks, cable channels, and leading news organizations have all served as super spreaders for the following ten examples of damaging, high-profile misinformation:

1. In Ferguson, Missouri, widespread press reports that Michael Brown had his hands up, while saying "Don't shoot!" led to riots, and the phrase became a popular cultural meme. But subsequent investigations by the U.S. Justice Department confirmed that this did not happen. Mr. Brown fought the officer, tried to take his gun, and was moving back toward the officer who then shot him.[1]

© The Author(s), under exclusive license to Springer Nature Switzerland AG 2024
R. D. Atkinson and D. Moschella, *Technology Fears and Scapegoats*, https://doi.org/10.1007/978-3-031-52349-6_7

2. The Steele dossier, with its allegations of Donald Trump's salacious conduct and cooperation with Russia, was widely reported to have come from a "highly credible" former British intelligence source. But the document was actually opposition research that turned out to consist of unsubstantiated and even fabricated information.

3. A social media video appeared to show Nicholas Sandmann and a group of fellow students from Covington High School on a field trip to the National Mall in Washington D.C. taunting a native American elder while chanting "Build that wall!" Most mainstream media outlets ran with and highlighted this story, making it into a huge national issue. But subsequent reporting revealed that the students did no such thing.

4. The Black Lives Matter protests during 2020 were widely described as "mostly peaceful." But while analyses have found that 94 percent of the protests were peaceful, the media downplayed the remaining 6 percent which were the most violent protests across the United States since the 1960s. Over 2,000 police officers were injured, with 2,385 cases of looting, 624 cases of arson, hundreds of police vehicles burned or seriously damaged, and an estimated $2 billion in property damage in 140 U.S. cities.[2] Describing this as "mostly peaceful" is like describing the south side of Chicago as "mostly safe" because 94 percent of the residents haven't been shot.

5. It was widely reported across major media that Russia put "bounties" on U.S. soldiers in Afghanistan, and that President Trump did nothing in response. But the CIA later admitted that it had only "low to moderate confidence" in such bounties. The story quickly vanished.[3]

6. Claims that Covid-19 may have begun in a laboratory in Wuhan, China, were widely described as a "racist conspiracy theory" until many scientists and federal government agencies stepped forward to say that a lab accident was a likely possibility. While China, and some U.S. government officials, continue to stonewall against any and all such inquiries, support for the lab theory continues to grow.

7. The discovery of a laptop that Hunter Biden allegedly left with a computer repair shop was quickly dismissed as "Russian disinformation" when it provided information about the Biden family's business dealings in Ukraine, China, and elsewhere. Both the laptop and its contents were later confirmed to be authentic.

8. *The New York Times* and many others reported that officer Brian Sicknick was beaten to death with a fire extinguisher by rioters during the January 6 attack on the U.S. Capitol. That story was subsequently corrected to

note that Officer Sicknick died the following day from natural causes. There was no such beating.[4]

9. Interest in using the antiparasitic medication ivermectin to treat Covid-19 surged after Australian researchers observed that it killed the virus in a lab setting. Rather than simply stating that the medical consensus is that the drug is not effective for Covid-19, the mainstream press dismissed the drug as a "horse de-wormer." But Ivermectin is not just for animals. It has been safely used by humans for nearly 40 years. Because it has all but eliminated river blindness in many countries, it's on the World Health Organization's list of "essential medicines"; its developers won the 2015 Nobel Prize for Physiology or Medicine. Many doctors and scientists still believe it is effective in treating Covid-19. Even worse, it was the act of making ivermectin unavailable for Covid-19 treatment that led a small number of people to dangerously take the animal dosage.

10. After videos emerged that seemed to show border patrol agents using whips to stop migrants at the Mexican border, mainstream news coverage exploded, with additional outrage coming from the White House and Congress. After an extensive investigation, it was determined that no such whipping occurred.

These were not minor stories; they dominated the news cycle of their time. Even worse, this deeply divisive misinformation was generally not the result of innocent errors; it often stemmed from a mainstream media and national government too keen to assume the worst of those it disagrees with, even in volatile areas such as racial relations, presidential elections, national security, and a global pandemic.

Of course, many news organizations eventually amended their articles and posted corrections. But the damage to society and specific individuals was done. The original stories were aggressively pursued for weeks, months, and even years, and were seen and discussed by tens of millions of people, shaping much of the national dialog. Corrections are typically published once and discussed as briefly as possible. Many Americans still believe the original versions.

The falsehoods above were not just presented as the majority views, they were often accepted as if they were the official truth, and those who publicly challenged them risked being defamed, harassed, ostracized, censored, boycotted, and/or fired. The resulting societal distrust dwarfs that from social media. The sad reality is that if mainstream media insists something is true, many people are now reflexively skeptical in the same way many others are skeptical of anything coming from Fox News.

Dynamics and Incentives

Given this situation, policymakers should seek a more balanced view of the many causes of societal misinformation. In pushing back against the conventional wisdom, it's helpful to keep the following five points in mind:

- **The Internet Hasn't Been the Most Important Source of Government Distrust.** Neither the resistance to lockdowns nor the claims of election fraud started on social media. The former was led by the thousands of scientists signing the *Great Barrington Declaration*; the latter was led by President Trump.
- **Mainstream Media Is Still Far More Influential as a Source of News than Social Media.** The Pew Research Center's 2021 finding that 48 percent of Americans "either sometimes or often get news" from social media (just 19 percent often, 29 percent sometimes) is frequently cited as evidence of social media's vast influence.[5] But the majority of Americans continue to get most of their news from television, radio, and the print media in either their traditional or online versions.
- **Many Social Media Critics Have a Fundamental Conflict of Interest.** The time that consumers spend on online attracts billions of advertising dollars that once went to traditional media businesses. Thus, it's often in the interest of publishers and television networks to tarnish social media's image and curb its influence. Indeed, an alternative title for this chapter could have easily been: "Old Media Agrees: New Media Is the Problem."
- **Using Data to Give Consumers More of What They Like is What Media Companies Do.** Whether it's MSNBC vs. Fox News, The Atlantic vs. The National Review, or countless magazines, websites, blogs, and individual social media accounts, everyone tracks what readers respond to. That social media relies more on algorithms just means it uses automated tools instead of traditional focus groups, reader surveys, page views, likes, shares, and editorial gut feel. The goal of increasing "engagement" is the same.
- **No Company is Capable of Being an Effective "Arbiter of Truth".** While social media is partly like a telephone company and partly like a publisher, it's fundamentally more like the former. Social media firms should block speech that is also illegal offline—harassment, threats, fraud, terrorism, direct incitement, child pornography, etc. Simply being "wrong" is not among these illegalities, and there are just too many examples of something being deemed true today, but false tomorrow, or vice versa. In cases where information is highly dubious and involves public health or safety,

companies would be better off using some sort of rating system than trying to definitively say what is true and what is false.

Among 46 nations surveyed recently by Reuters, the United States ranked last in media trust. Only 29 percent of Americans agreed with the statement "I think you can trust most news most of the time."[6] Mainstream media—newspapers, magazines, radio, and television—and many U.S. policymakers like to blame this distrust on President Trump, Fox News, and social media, but mainstream media itself is also a significant part of the problem. Policymakers who want to assign blame for societal misinformation (and regulate social media) need to examine both new and old media—conservative and liberal alike. To put so much of the focus on one type of media or one type of company is both unfair and unwarranted.

—DM

Notes

1. Jonathan Capehart, "'Hands Up, Don't Shoot' was Built on a Lie," *Washington Post* (March 16, 2015), https://www.washingtonpost. com/blogs/post-partisan/wp/2015/03/16/lesson-learned-from-the-sho oting-of-michael-brown/; U.S. Department of Justice, Civil Rights Division, Investigation of the Ferguson Police Department, March 4, 2015, https://www.justice.gov/sites/default/files/opa/press-releases/ attachments/2015/03/04/ferguson_police_department_report.pdf; U.S. Justice Department, Department of Justice Report Regarding the Criminal Investigation Into the Shooting Death of Michael Brown by Ferguson, Missouri Police Officer Darren Wilson, March 4, 2015, https://www.justice.gov/sites/default/files/opa/press-releases/att achments/2015/03/04/doj_report_on_shooting_of_michael_brown_1. pdf.
2. Major Cities Chiefs Association, Intelligence Commanders Group, "Report on the 2020 Protests & Civil Unrest," October 2020, p. 10, https://majorcitieschiefs.com/wp-content/uploads/2021/01/MCCA-Report-on-the-2020-Protest-and-Civil-Unrest.pdf; L.S. Howard, "As Strikes, Riots and Civil Commotion Risks Increase, Insurers Respond With Exclusions," *Insurance Journal* (October 27, 2021), https://www. insurancejournal.com/news/international/2021/10/27/639323.htm.

3. Nick Niedzwiadek, "White House Dials Down Likelihood Russia Offered Bounties in Afghanistan," *Politico* (April 15, 2021), https://www.politico.com/news/2021/04/15/russia-afghanistan-bounties-psaki-481990.
4. Bethania Palma, "Did US Capitol Police Officer Brian Sicknick Die After Hit With a Fire Extinguisher?" *Snopes* (May 6, 2021), https://www.snopes.com/fact-check/brian-sicknick-fire-extinguisher/.
5. Mason Walker and Katerina Eva Matsa, "News Consumption Across Social Media in 2021" (Pew Research Center, September 2021), https://www.pewresearch.org/journalism/2021/09/20/news-consumption-across-social-media-in-2021/.
6. Rick Edmonds, "US Ranks Last Among 46 Countries in Trust in Media, Reuters Institute Report Finds," *Poynter* (June 24, 2021), https://www.poynter.org/ethics-trust/2021/us-ranks-last-among-46-countries-in-trust-in-media-reuters-institute-report-finds/.

Myth 7: Your Data Is Gold

Claims that "your data" is a modern form of gold, and that Big Tech makes too much money off of it are wrong in two fundamental ways: The data about most individuals isn't worth very much, and when consumers use a business service, the resulting data isn't "theirs." Claiming otherwise only builds up unnecessary resentments.

We hear it so often that it's easy to assume it must be true. "Our data is super valuable, and we should be compensated for it." These two statements basically tell consumers that they are being taken advantage of, even ripped off by Big Tech. Not surprisingly, this has led to resentment and calls for action. But there is just one problem: Both assertions are much more wrong than right. Today's leading technology companies have been extraordinarily profitable, but this is far more due to the unique nature of information economics than any data ownership or usage abuses.

How Much Is Your Data Worth?

In recent years, there have been numerous efforts to determine how much our individual data is worth. Some studies have looked at Big Tech's revenue per user; others focus on the market capitalization per user. We think profits per user is the best starting point because any ongoing payments to individual consumers would come directly out of a company's bottom line.

Calculating profits per consumer is much easier to do at a global as opposed to national level because that's where the best publicly reported

© The Author(s), under exclusive license to Springer Nature
Switzerland AG 2024
R. D. Atkinson and D. Moschella, *Technology Fears and Scapegoats*,
https://doi.org/10.1007/978-3-031-52349-6_8

financial data is most consistently available. We can further simplify the task by just assessing Alphabet and Meta (We don't need to include X because it's relatively small and has mostly lost money over the years).

Let's begin with Alphabet. According to Alphabet's annual 10K filing, for the year ending December 31, 2021, the company had revenues of $257 billion and a net income of $76 billion. (We use 2021 data because that was the year of peak profitability. Both Alphabet and Meta saw sharp profit declines in 2022). Advertising revenues accounted for $209 billion, or 81 percent of total revenues. As ads are Alphabet's cash cow, let's assume that 90 percent of its profits were also ad-based. This translates into $68 billion in advertising profits in 2021. Now let's suppose that, for whatever reasons, Alphabet makes the extraordinary gesture of giving half of this ($34 billion) back to its data sources.

Since Alphabet gets valuable data from both the users of its services as well as Internet, publishers, and other content providers, let's say that it gives both groups half of the $34 billion, or $17 billion each. How should we divide up this $17 billion? Alphabet says that it has nine businesses with more than a billion users—Search, Chrome, Gmail, Android, YouTube, Maps, Google Play, Google Drive, and Google Photos. Best estimates are that roughly 4 billion people use at least one Alphabet product. Using the same 81 percent share above, let's say that some 3 billion people use its ad-based services. If we divide $17 billion by 3 billion users, we get $5.60 per consumer during 2021, more like a cup of artisan coffee than a pot of gold.

We did the same analysis for Meta, using its 10K. The company's 2021 revenues were $118 billion, with a net income of $39.4 billion, virtually all of which was driven by advertising. Once again, let's assume Meta keeps half of its profits for itself and splits the other half ($19.7 billion) between its consumers and content providers. However, as Meta is much less reliant on outside content providers than Alphabet, let's give just one-quarter of this split ($4.9 billion) to providers and three quarters ($14.8 billion) to Meta's estimated 2.9 billion consumers. Dividing $14.8 billion by 2.9 billion customers translates to $5.10 per user, remarkably similar to Alphabet's $5.60.

If the Alphabet and Meta payments to consumers are added together, you get $10.70 per customer per year for 2021. If you include half of the advertising-based profits of Microsoft, Amazon, and Apple, you'd get a little more than $12. But remember: This is making the colossal assumption that all five of these companies give up half of their advertising-based profits. If they only gave back 10 percent, then the total annual payment would be about two bucks per user per year.

Although these numbers might grow in the future, they might not. Either way, they won't add up to much anytime soon. Moreover, the effort needed to calculate and disperse small individual payments would be enormous. Perhaps most fundamentally, who among us thinks that the services these companies provide for free aren't worth more than $12 per year? By this metric, it's one of the great bargains in economic history, which is why these companies are so successful.

Of course, one could argue that some people's data is worth a lot more than $12. This is surely true. But the data that is worth the most tends to come from the most affluent among us. Do we really want to argue that Alphabet and/or Meta's most affluent customers should get a lot more than $12, knowing that this would mean that everyone else would get a lot less? The same is true geographically. Per-user profits in the United States and Europe for both Alphabet and Meta are higher than in the developing world, but do we really want consumers in less developed nations to get very little compared to customers in wealthier countries?

These low payment numbers, high implementation costs, and fairness sensitivities explain why Big Tech will likely remain reluctant to support such schemes in any major way, even though they would really just be the digital version of a traditional loyalty program. These operational challenges also explain why the Data Dividend Project and related start-ups haven't caught on at the time of this writing. It's entirely possible that, eventually, some combination of blockchains, peer-to-peer architectures, avatars, virtual agents, NFTs, cryptocurrencies, and new data collection and usage norms will spawn a generation of important data intermediaries, but today such efforts are still in their very early stages.

It's Not Your Data Anyway

The principles of customer data ownership are as familiar as business record-keeping. Credit card issuers itemize our purchases; cable TV operators know what stations we receive; telecom companies know what numbers we've called; loyalty-card issuers track what we buy; healthcare providers store our medical records; schools know what we studied and what our grades were; governments record what real estate we own, what countries we've visited, and so much more. No one doubts that these organizations own this data. We might be able to see it, challenge its accuracy, or limit its use, but in no way is it "ours."

The rules governing the use of this type of data are based on either explicit or implied understandings between consumers and providers, with each industry having its own set of norms, obligations, and limitations. Although consumers can decide whether to keep a record of the products and services they use, most of us don't bother. Providers, however, have no such choice. Detailed data collection is typically required for legal, accounting, billing, customer service, and many other purposes. The only question is how this data is or isn't to be used. It's the same situation with Big Tech.

If anything, the rights of providers are even stronger when services are supported by advertising and thus provided for free. Consumers As the old saying accurately goes, if you are not paying for a product, you are the product, as advertisers are paying for your attention. Additionally, technology consumers often have more choices than in many of the industries listed above. Most people don't have to use Facebook; it's easy to switch from Google search to Microsoft's Bing or DuckDuckGo, or use one of the many alternatives to Gmail. These Big Tech alternatives will likely continue to gain momentum going forward. Consider the stunning growth of TikTok, ChatGPT, and the way Amazon's Alexa uses Bing as its search engine.

None of this is meant to argue that consumers and policymakers can't or shouldn't try to improve the terms of their data-usage deals. Today's end-user license agreements, privacy settings, anonymity implementations, customer-profiling services, and many other practices are byzantine in nature, and even sophisticated consumers often can't be bothered to understand or tweak them. But even the most worthwhile efforts to improve consumer data protection won't change the fundamental fact that providers own the data, and you don't.

Economics Trumps Analogies

Some readers might counter that although all of the above is true enough, it still leaves us with the problem of Big Tech companies making "too much money." The combined profits of the big five companies reached an astonishing $350 billion in 2021.

The reason today's tech leaders are so profitable has much more to do with information economics than anything to do with data abuses. Although information economics is a term used in a variety of ways, we use it to encompass the unique features of digital technology—nearly infinite economies of scale, powerful network effects, zero marginal costs, perfect reproducibility, and winner-take-all or near-all market share tendencies. Google performs over five billion searches every day, and 300 million photos are uploaded to Meta per day. It is this combination of massive scale and high utility—not advertising abuses or unfair data ownership—that best explains the vast riches of today's tech giants.

This is why analogies with gold or oil—as well as less frequent comparisons to electricity, water, air, and exhaust—typically yield more shade than light. Data is not like gold, which is a scarce commodity with a largely fixed supply and a narrow set of potential uses. The analogy between data and oil is better, as both can power businesses, drive innovation, and create great wealth. However, like gold, oil doesn't have any of the information economics characteristics listed above. Perhaps most fundamentally, data and software are non-rivalrous goods, meaning that my use of a product doesn't prevent you from using it, too. No material goods have this property. These differences explain why efforts to understand the extraordinary success of Big Tech should rely much more on information economics than historical analogies.

In most industries, unusually high profit margins tend to get whittled away over time by competition, market maturation, new business models, technological disruption, expensive but unsuccessful new company ventures, and/or the bloated costs companies' typically take on once they become rich. Odds are that similar economic forces will eventually rein in Big Tech's profits as well.

But as of now, data, information, and knowledge comprise a unique generator of value that historical analogies cannot speak to. One of the wonders of the information age is how data that is worth very little at an individual level becomes extraordinarily valuable when collected at massive scale. It's like a modern form of alchemy. Your data isn't gold; it's not even yours. But when everyone's data is collected and leveraged, the value to companies—and to society—is worth more than all the gold on planet Earth.[1]

—DM

Note

1. Best estimates are that all the known holdings of gold in the world are worth about $10 trillion; the current market cap of just Apple, Alphabet, Microsoft, Amazon, and Meta is over $10 trillion, as of April 2024.

Myth 8: Digital Technology is Dangerously "Addictive"

In today's world, the intensive use of technology is often a practical require-ment. For teenagers, it's also much more like earlier enthusiasms for radio, movies, and television than drugs, alcohol, and tobacco. Describing it otherwise can lead to exaggerated fears, unnecessary policies, and frivolous lawsuits.

The word addiction stems from the Latin word *addicere*, which in Roman law meant "to deliver or hand over formally a person or thing in accordance with a judicial decision." It was essentially the legal language of slavery. Over the centuries, usage evolved to encompass various types of "compulsion," "devotion," and the "giving over of oneself."[1] The connection between slavery and the giving over of oneself to drugs, alcohol, tobacco, or gambling is clear enough.

But in recent years, usage has expanded much further, and people now routinely joke about being addicted to chocolate or *Succession*. In other words, addiction is used to describe everything from severe dependencies that could ruin your life to harmless habits that you enjoy. This unwieldy spectrum should serve as a warning that the seemingly potent phrase *technology addic-tion* has no fixed meaning, and thus can be applied to just about any type of frequent digital usage. This begs the question: Is spending a lot of time online more like eating sweets, watching TV, being hooked on drugs, compulsive gambling, or something different altogether?[2]

© The Author(s), under exclusive license to Springer Nature
Switzerland AG 2024
R. D. Atkinson and D. Moschella, *Technology Fears and Scapegoats*,
https://doi.org/10.1007/978-3-031-52349-6_9

Two Ends of the Spectrum

Critics of Big Tech can show that the heavy use of technology is correlated with increases in depression, anxiety, obsession, isolation, fragility, narcissism, envy, misogyny, pornography, anger, shaming, bullying, self-harm, and violence, as well as decreases in fresh air, sleep, health, fitness, concentration, test scores, empathy, and real-world skills and experience. Whether we are discussing the stereotypes of lonely boys in their parents' basement or anxious girls worried about their social status, there are many troubling cases. The terrible story of the 14-year-old British girl Molly Russel shows how children can be overwhelmed by certain types of targeted content.[3]

As with alcohol, drugs, tobacco, and gambling, many people believe that online services need stricter regulation. Their case is aided by the fact that the digital world often refers to its customers as "users," a term once associated almost exclusively with the use of drugs. It's a metaphor that is hard to ignore. The 2023 suit filed by more than thirty states against Meta alleging that its products are addictive and harmful to children certainly draws upon such language and concerns.

However, putting so much of the blame on online services ignores the way medications, lockdowns, masks, remote learning, shifting gender norms, troubled families, political polarization, economic strains, environmental fears, guns, increased competition to get into colleges, and other pressures have added to the traditional sources of teenage angst. Besides, it's not like people have a lot of choice. The time we once spent with books, magazines, newspapers, maps, games, radios, stereos, televisions, cameras, pens and paper, as well as in schools, libraries, offices, meetings, cinemas, and stores has largely moved to the virtual world. It's not surprising that some children—and some adults—need more time than others to get used to having such unprecedented powers and distractions in the palm of their hand.

Ameliorating Factors

Given that there are valid points on both sides, the impact of the intensive use of technology is somewhere in the middle of our spectrum. But wherever you place it right now, over time technology usage will look less and less like addiction, and more like an essential societal component. Consider the five factors below:

1. The heavy use of technology is the opposite of substance abuse in at least one important way. The technology downsides listed above are concentrated among the young, with the risks diminishing over time. In contrast, the damage from substance abuse tends to accumulate over the years as heavy smoking, drinking, or drug use inevitably take their toll. Long-term dependency is what we have historically meant by addiction; temporary addiction is almost an oxymoron.

2. The fact that technology dependence tends to decline as people enter their 20s, and certainly by their 30s, suggests that today's urge to be online closely resembles previous enthusiasms for radio, movies, television, and music, all of which had very strong appeal to teenagers that many adults found worrisome. And just as the thrill of those older media eventually leveled off, we already see some small drops in the use of social media among the young, and even the adoption of less capable flip phones.[4]

3. Although many people enjoy drugs, drinking, and entertainment media, there is typically little value creation involved. In contrast, the effective use of technology requires many useful skills—operating devices, navigating social media, editing videos, the coordination and concentration needed to excel at video games, the composition skills required to present oneself successfully online, and new means of collaborating, influencing, and networking. The demand for such skills will remain strong for many years. In contrast, there is little demand for people to smoke, drink, listen to music, or watch TV. The many practical benefits of being online are unlike either end of our addiction spectrum, and this will prove to be a decisive difference over time.

4. While the task of blocking harmful content is much more difficult with open online platforms than traditional media, technology service providers know that they must do a better job of protecting children, and are working hard and cooperating with policymakers on this issue. It's the social media industry's single biggest challenge, but it's not primarily a matter of addiction.

5. Looking ahead, it's easy to imagine a future where software agents, speech and voice recognition, artificial intelligence, and/or new human/machine interfaces substantially reduce the time we all spend staring at screens.

Negative Biases

The way we think and talk about technology also tends to push the conversation closer to the addiction metaphor than is generally warranted. Consider these three biases:

1. Reading the technology addiction literature, one might think that dopamine and serotonin are dangerous narcotics. Yes, pleasure hormones are released when we receive likes on social media, just as they are with many recreational drugs, and this can create an almost irresistible urge to check for messages and updates. However, similar pleasures can also be triggered by meditation, exercise, eating, playing an instrument, advances in learning, winning at sports or games, sex, and countless other activities that are only rarely described as addictive. Given the time we spend online, occasional jolts of happiness are nothing to sneer at.

2. There is also a bias in language. "Binge watching" on Netflix, reading a book you can't put down, being passionate about one's field or work, shooting basketballs in the dark, locking yourself in a room to master the guitar, or writing deep into the night are typically seen as fun, useful, or a sign of serious commitment. However, when people make the same time commitment to writing code, making TikTok videos, or competing in online games, the language is almost inevitably more negative, with individuals described as isolated, nerdy, obsessed, narcissistic, or even self-destructive. Back in the 2010s, it was trendy to say that it takes 10,000 hours to become an expert in a particular field or activity. Whether you believe this claim or not, sustained commitment and practice are needed in virtually every field, online activities included.[5]

3. Lastly, there are the familiar biases of age. How many baby boomers used to shake their heads at their children's or colleagues' enthusiasm for personal computers, mobile phones, texting, e-commerce, video games, videoconferencing, and social media, only to become frequent users themselves? Similarly, older people have been complaining about the deficiencies of younger generations since ancient times, to little avail.[6] To cite just one counterexample, because of social media, today's youth tend to be much more comfortable with public speaking and self-presentation than their parents, many of whom dreaded—and struggled in—such situations.

Taken together, these three biases continue to adversely shape the national conversation.

Dueling "Wastelands"

The average American who watches television does so between three and four hours per day, more than any other activity except work and sleep, and far more than the average person spends playing video games.[7] To put this colossal accumulation of time in perspective, consider this: If just 1 percent of the time Americans spend watching TV was focused on building out the Wikipedia, the open-source encyclopedia's six million English language articles could easily have been produced in less than a year.[8] Apparently, adults, like teenagers, also choose to "waste" a lot of time, all while believing they don't have enough "free time."

Although watching a lot of television is also correlated with isolation, depression, obesity, diabetes, over-medication, and other maladies, we rarely hear the phrase TV addiction anymore, even though if people have to miss their favorite shows or sporting events, many suffer from anxieties similar to those that people feel when they don't have their phones with them. As the amount of time spent watching TV has remained relatively stable over the years, it seems to be a habit that's very hard to kick. Yet hardly anyone cares; it's now just normal.

Thus, while it's easy to criticize some of what teenagers do online, we could do the same for adults. Both the Internet and TV can sometimes seem like dueling wastelands. But adults see their viewing habits as understandable and largely benign lifestyle choices, even as they criticize those whose habits differ. Perceptions regarding what constitutes free time, how one spends time, and what amounts to wasting time remain very much in the mind of the beholder. It was ever thus.

The bottom line is that throughout America's post-World War II period, teenagers have struggled with many of the same issues as kids do today. The current pressures may well be greater than they have been in much of the past, partly due to digital technologies but also because of major changes in society overall. During this 75-year period, alcohol, drugs, and new media have often been irresistible outlets for teenage angst. Fortunately, online services are much more like the latter one than the former two, while also having a great many practical benefits. As with television and motion pictures, Internet service providers, and policymakers should focus on age-appropriate content, accurate labeling, and the use of parental controls—not the prohibitions enacted for truly addictive and dangerous substances.

—DM

Notes

1. All the quoted definitions are from the online version of the complete Oxford English Dictionary.
2. For example, the World Health Organization and other medical and psychiatric bodies refer to "gaming disorders," not gaming addiction. See, for example: World Health Organization. Gaming Disorder. FAQ, accessed October 28, 2022. https://www.who.int/standards/classificati ons/frequently-asked-questions/gaming-disorder.
3. Dan Milmo, "'The bleakest of worlds': how Molly Russell fell into a vortex of despair on social media" *The Guardian* (September 30, 2022), https://www.theguardian.com/technology/2022/sep/30/how-molly-rus sell-fell-into-a-vortex-of-despair-on-social-media.
4. Data from Pew Research Center shows that the 18–29 age group is the only one to see a decrease in social media use since 2015. See: Michelle Faverio, "Share of Those 65 and Older Who are Tech Users has Grown in the Past Decade" (Pew Research Center, January 13, 2022), https:// www.pewresearch.org/fact-tank/2022/01/13/share-of-those-65-and-older-who-are-tech-users-has-grown-in-the-past-decade/.
5. Phyllis Lane, 10,000 Hours: You Become What You Practice (CreateSpace Independent Publishing Platform), May 8, 2012, ISBN: 9781475033625.
6. As Horace succinctly put it circa 100 BCE: "Our sires' age was worse than our grandsires' We their sons are worse than they; so in our turn we shall give the world a progeny yet more corrupt."
7. Bureau of Labor Statistics, American Time Use Survey, Table A-1, "Time spent in detailed primary activities and percent of the civilian population engaging in each activity, averages per day by sex, 2021 annual averages," released June 23, 2022, https://www.bls.gov/tus/a1-2021.pdf; Limelight Networks, "The State of Online Gaming 2021," March 1, 2021, https://edg.io/resources/market-research/state-of-online-gaming-2021/; While some teenagers play video games for more than this, many adults watch more than three or four hours per day.
8. 250 million U.S. adults watching 3 hours of TV per day equals roughly 250 billion hours per year, 1 percent of which is 2.5 billion hours. Divided by 6 million Wikipedia articles, this equates to some 400 hours per article, which is almost certainly more than average.

Myth 9: The Internet Is Extinguishing Local Languages

For many years, people have insisted that the Internet would lead to the overwhelming dominance of the English language. But this prediction is now proving more wrong than right. Shifts in economics, geopolitics, and culture, along with major improvements in machine translation are making local languages much more resilient than many expected.

If you Google the question: "Is the internet killing local languages and cultures," you will see a lot of results saying that it is. But if you look more closely, you will see that the most dire warnings tend to be from 2010 to 2017. The more recent results often take the opposite stance: that technology actually helps preserve local languages. It's one of the few areas where perceptions about the impact of the digital world have become more positive. Nevertheless, the myth of widespread language extinction endures.

Advances in machine translation are clearly part of this improvement. But there are also important economic, geopolitical, and cultural forces at work. Languages have always evolved as if in a marketplace. They compete against one another, with shifting winners and losers over time. Having a common cross-country language (Latin, French, English) is useful in that it can facilitate understanding and lower transaction costs, especially as the world becomes more globally integrated. But the roles of local vs shared languages are always shifting, and right now they're tilting back toward the local.

At an individual level, learning languages isn't easy, so the learning process competes with other possible uses of our time. People often criticize Americans for only speaking English. But there's no need to blame this on laziness

© The Author(s), under exclusive license to Springer Nature Switzerland AG 2024
R. D. Atkinson and D. Moschella, *Technology Fears and Scapegoats*,
https://doi.org/10.1007/978-3-031-52349-6_10

or cultural arrogance. The simplest explanation is that Americans have much less incentive to learn another tongue, as some 1.4 billion people speak English all around the world. In contrast, if you are born in, for example, Denmark, learning English opens up a great many career and personal possibilities, as opposed to limiting yourself to the 5 million people who speak Danish. While the global incentives to learn English are still very strong, they are less compelling than they were when American-led globalization was in its ascendancy.

Viewed more abstractly, the world's 7,000 languages can be grouped into three main categories. The 300 most widely spoken ones are used by 90 percent of the world's population. The remaining ten percent span some 6,700 languages, many having little or no written form at all.[1] Obviously, these are two very distinct language "markets" that are best assessed separately. A third group consists of the languages that dominate online. It's estimated that just twenty languages account for some 95 percent of all Internet content, with nearly 60 percent of this content being in English.[2] Machine translation will be a decisive factor in determining how this group evolves going forward.

Peak English?

Even before deep learning, large language models and inexpensive computing power enabled major advances in machine translation, significant changes in language learning incentives were already underway, especially due to the following five forces:

1. **The Rise of China**. The appeal of English was driven by America's global leadership, the dominance of its tech firms, and the lasting influences of the former British Empire. China challenges all three factors. In addition to its economic and technological power, it's developing close bilateral relationships all around the world. In many countries, speaking Chinese is now more valuable (because it is more scarce) than speaking English.
2. **A Divided America**. The flip side of the rise of China is the fact that America's image around the world has been tarnished by wars, mass shootings, crime, drugs, political polarization, January 6, and more. Work and student visa restrictions have also lowered the value of speaking English for many individuals.

3. **Brexit**. Over time, the UK's leaving of the European Union will tend to decrease the role of the English language within Europe. European citizen incentives to learn and use French, German, Spanish, and Italian will increase.

4. **Splinternet**. Countries are increasingly asserting technological sovereignty within their borders in areas such as media ownership, permissible speech and data usage, as well as in e-commerce, transportation services, payments, and other digital applications. This *splintering* of the Internet will tend to increase the use of national languages.

5. **Cultural Preservation**. In every part of the world, there are renewed efforts to protect local languages, often with substantial national and citizen support.[3] For example, requiring at least some teaching and use of indigenous languages in K-12 schools is important for their long-term survival. Such initiatives will sometimes make learning English a third or fourth option.

All of the above have changed the global demand for languages, and explain why the dire warnings of an all pervasive English Internet have receded. Taken together, the five dynamics above suggest that the world has probably passed its *peak English* period (at least for now). For the foreseeable future, English will continue to be the most common language for science, business, entertainment, and many other global activities. Nevertheless, country and regional languages are strengthening.

The Impact of AI

We can use the 20, 300, and 6,700 groupings to better understand the likely economic and cultural impact of greatly improved machine translation. By looking at how AI changes both the competition between languages and incentives to learn one, we can see that the overall impact of technology on local language resiliency is most likely to be positive. AI will reduce—but far from eliminate—the economic value of speaking a common second language, and thus it will reduce—but far from eliminate—the incentive to learn one. Consider the patterns within each group today.

The Top Twenty

Google Translate supports the world's top 20 most widely spoken languages (Fig. 1), and firms such as Baidu have important Chinese translation capabilities, which will be essential both domestically and internationally. The fact that six of these languages are widely used across India, Pakistan, and Bangladesh suggests significant machine translation opportunities in the Indian subcontinent as well.

While the quality of each translation pairing varies, it's fair to say that useful and ever-improving capabilities will be available for pretty much all twenty of these languages. If so, it seems likely that users of web sites, social media and other online content, devices such as Alexa, and even mobile phones will increasingly be able to toggle between languages quite effectively. This will tend to reduce the online competition between languages because one won't have to always choose one language over another. Similarly, from an individual perspective, the knowledge that one can reliably translate

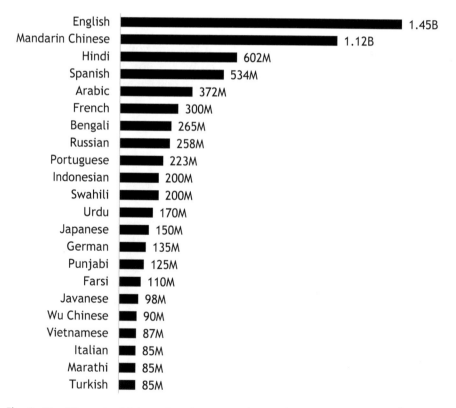

Fig. 1 Top 20 most widely spoken languages by number of speakers, 2023[4]

English language content into one's native tongue could substantially reduce the incentive to become highly fluent in English.

To be clear, the incentives to learn English or another second language won't go away. There are still many important career, cultural, and personal benefits. But on the margin, the necessity of such efforts will likely be less than during the peak English years of 2000–2015, and this bodes well for the vitality of the 20 languages above.

The Core 300… Or is it 1,000?

As noted earlier, 300 languages are used by some 90 percent of the human population, so when thinking about the impact of technology on the world's languages this is obviously the most influential group. It's also the hardest one to predict. Today, Google's translation services support 133 languages. It seems logical that for those languages where quality translation services are available, the dynamics will be similar to those for the top 20 above. On the margin, effective machine translation services will tend to strengthen the use of local languages and reduce the incentive/need to learn new ones.

But for those languages that do not have effective translation services, the logic would seem to run the other way. From a career, cultural, and personal perspective, important forms of content might not be available in one's native tongue, and thus the incentive to learn English or another widely used language would rise. Once the need for a second language increases, competition with the local language intensifies, especially in business. Overall, it seems likely that the future availability and quality of translation for the 170 languages not yet supported by Google will be a decisive factor going forward.

This is why Google's 1,000 language initiative could be so important. While there are other important translation companies—Microsoft, Amazon, DeepL, Systran, Baidu, Youdao, and others—Google is still the market leader. If the company, or one of its rivals, can successfully get to anywhere near 1,000, the machine translation era will have fully arrived, along with all of the dynamics that come with it. To quote from Google's March 2023 press release:

> Last November, we announced the *1,000 Languages Initiative*, an ambitious commitment to build a machine learning (ML) model that would support the world's one thousand most-spoken languages, bringing greater inclusion to billions of people around the globe. However, some of these languages are spoken by fewer than twenty million people, so a core challenge is how to

support languages for which there are relatively few speakers or limited available data. Today, we are excited to share more about the *Universal Speech Model* (USM), a critical first step towards supporting 1,000 languages. USM is a family of state-of-the-art speech models with 2B parameters trained on 12 million hours of speech and 28 billion sentences of text, spanning 300+ languages.[5]

We wish them luck.

Indigenous Preservation

For the 6,700 less used languages, the dynamics are entirely different. Here, there is much less emphasis on the competition between languages. These languages will never be competitive in the sense of largely replacing much more widely used ones. Individual economic incentives are also much less of a factor, as the career benefits of learning rarely used languages are relatively low. What drives efforts in this area is cultural, the sense that these languages are worth preserving regardless of their economic impact. It's a very different mindset.

The main question is whether technology will help or hurt such efforts. As more and more communication takes place online, the lack of digital support for indigenous languages is a significant negative factor, especially for those languages with little to no written form at all. On the other hand, there are many examples of how technology is now helping preserve local languages, including the four below:

1. Local languages no longer have to stay local, as people can move around the world and still be closely connected to a particular language community.
2. Apps, emojis, and dual language stories are being used to better appeal to children who learn languages much more easily than adults.
3. Technology can preserve the past, so that whatever language data is digitally captured—dictionaries, grammar, pronunciations, scripts, stories—is never lost as community elders inevitably pass.
4. Machine learning can leverage whatever data is available to see language patterns that humans either can't or don't have time or energy for. AI is even being used to better understand "dead languages," such as ancient Greek.[6]

But in the end, the preservation of rarely used languages is a primarily matter of will at an individual, local community, and increasingly at a regional and national level. While some indigenous languages will continue to disappear, there is reason for optimism. In this sense, the indigenous language situation resembles efforts to protect and revitalize endangered species, which exhibit a similarly mixed picture of some surviving and others not.

A Boon for Translators

One of the worst language predictions of recent years has been that machine translation services will increasingly eliminate the need for human translators. This is clearly not the case. For documents that require high-quality translation—laws, business and government records, creative expressions, and more—human review and editing is almost always required. Even moderately sensitive content often requires at least some level of human oversight to avoid embarrassing errors. Additionally, the use of AI to produce the first translation draft can make skilled and scarce human translators vastly more productive. The bottom line is that AI greatly lowers the overall cost of translation, and when costs go way down, volumes go way up, with the benefits far outweighing the costs.

—DM

Notes

1. The Rosetta Project, "About the 300 Languages Project," webpage accessed July 27, 2023, https://rosettaproject.org/projects/300-langua ges/about/.
2. Statista, "Languages Most Frequently Used for Web Content as of January 2023, by Share of Websites," accessed July 27, 2023, https:// www.statista.com/statistics/262946/most-common-languages-on-the-internet/.
3. See, for example, the Endangered Languages Project, https://www.end angeredlanguages.com/.
4. Federico Blank, "Most Spoken Languages in the World in 2023," blog post (Lingua Language Center, Broward College, April 23, 2023), https://lingua.edu/the-most-spoken-languages-in-the-world/.
5. Yu Zhang and James Qin, "Universal Speech Model (USM): State-of-the-art speech AI for 100+ languages" (Google blog post in Research,

March 6, 2023), https://ai.googleblog.com/2023/03/universal-speech-model-usm-state-of-art.html.

6. Jane Recker, "A New A.I. Can Help Historians Decipher Damaged Ancient Greek Texts," *Smithsonian Magazine* (March 16, 2022), https://www.smithsonianmag.com/smart-news/a-new-ai-can-help-historians-decipher-damaged-ancient-greek-texts-180979736/.

Myth 10: Social Media Is an Existential Threat to Democracy

That digital technologies are a "threat to democracy" is now the conventional wisdom. Democrats complained about technology abuses in the 2016 election, as Republicans did in 2020 and 2022. But non-technology factors have done much more to undermine America's electoral confidence than anything digital. Perhaps even worse, today's exaggerated electoral accusations have also given new life and power to the full range of dubious Big Tech critiques.

Politicians, pundits, academics, psychologists, and consultants have been trying to understand why people vote the way they do for as long as democratic elections have been held. There are many theories, studies, and exit polls, but few definitive conclusions. Which was most decisive: the economy, a particular issue, the candidate's image, advertising, campaign spending, technology, organizing, voting rules, unforeseen events, the mood of the times, or some other factor? There's usually no way to definitively say, especially when an election is very close.

These fundamental uncertainties have spilled over into the debate about America's declining faith in election integrity. As with voting decisions, there are many possible, yet unquantifiable explanations, making it easy to blame social media or really anything else. Proving a negative is even harder; there's no way to conclusively demonstrate that any one factor had no impact at all. The best we can do is stack up the evidence, weigh the factors, and be skeptical of any claims of 100 percent certainty. Such an analysis strongly suggests that non-technology factors have done much more to undermine electoral trust than social media.

© The Author(s), under exclusive license to Springer Nature Switzerland AG 2024
R. D. Atkinson and D. Moschella, *Technology Fears and Scapegoats*,
https://doi.org/10.1007/978-3-031-52349-6_11

2016 as a Turning Point

Claims that social media is damaging democracy became widespread in 2016, first because of the UK's Brexit referendum in June, and then in November with the election of Donald Trump. Looking back, those two votes were a tipping point in how the technology industry is seen, especially by the left. Not only did both losing sides place much of the blame on social media, but since then, just about every Big Tech critique—privacy, misinformation, polarization, monopoly power, etc.—has been given new life and force. Seemingly overnight, Big Tech CEOs went from the rock stars of Davos to greedy purveyors of dangerous misinformation. The *techlash* had begun.

However, even a cursory review shows that there are many reasons why America's faith in election integrity has declined, some related to technology, most not. The non-technology factors alone are more than enough to give voters of all political leanings cause for concern. Consider the ten sources of distrust below, most of which were underway well before 2016:

1. **Close Elections**. America had extremely close presidential elections in 2000 and 2016, and has had a great many close ones at the state and local level. As we saw in Florida in 2000, given America's byzantine voting processes, no amount of recounts or audits will fully convince the losing side's voters if the difference is just a few hundred votes out of millions. In both 2000 and 2016, it was the Democrats who were upset and distrustful. In 2020, it was the Republicans. But the bottom line is that today's 50/50 electorate places almost unbearable pressures on America's hodgepodge of voting systems.
2. **The Electoral College**. In both 2000 and 2016, the democratic candidate won the popular vote, but lost in the Electoral College, something that hadn't happened since 1888. While one can defend the value of the Electoral College on numerous grounds, many Americans—especially those on the losing side—understandably believe that the "winner" having fewer votes than the "loser" is fundamentally undemocratic. Complaints about the Electoral College were particularly virulent in 2016 and could easily reoccur in 2024 or a future election cycle.
3. **New Voting Processes**. Largely because of the pandemic, the 2020 election rules were radically changed in many states—more mail-in ballots, less signature verification, ballot drop-off boxes, early voting, new machines, and more. These changes, coupled with the long time—sometimes more than a month—needed to count sacks of mail-in votes fueled doubts about ballot custody and other possible abuses. When combined

with close elections, these new practices are a formula for distrust from the losing side. Many countries rely on in-person voting because of similar concerns, but in America most of the Covid-19-driven changes remain in place.

4. **Candidate Complaints**. Al Gore was remarkably gracious about the Supreme Court's 5–4 ruling in *Bush vs Gore*. But in 2016, Hillary Clinton—and many other leading Democrats—deemed Donald Trump's presidency "illegitimate," because of alleged voter suppression, voter rolls purging, Russian hacking, and misinformation.[1] Likewise, Stacey Abrams refused to concede her 2018 Georgia governorship loss because of alleged voter suppression.[2] In 2020, Trump took charges of election illegitimacy to an entirely different level by legally challenging the certified outcome, as did Arizona gubernatorial candidate, Kari Lake, in 2022. When the candidates themselves complain about election integrity, it's not surprising that many of their supporters follow.

5. **DOJ/FBI Influence**. Arguably, the single most decisive moment in the 2016 election was when FBI Director, James Comey, went on TV to reopen the Hillary Clinton email investigation just days before the November election. The fact that the reopening involved then accused, now convicted, sex offender, Anthony Wiener, made for particularly damaging headlines. In 2020/22, Republicans complained about DOJ/FBI because of their now admitted malpractices in the Russia collusion investigation, their role in censoring the Hunter Biden laptop story, and their close involvement in the *Twitter Files and Facebook Papers*. Given the 2023 indictments of President Trump and ongoing investigations into the Biden family, DOJ is playing an even bigger role in 2024.

6. **Media Bias**. Perhaps Russia thought it could help Donald Trump win in 2016 or perhaps it just wanted to sow divisions before Clinton's *inevitable* victory. But it's a certainty that American media overwhelmingly favored Hillary Clinton and Joe Biden, who both received the vast majority of major newspaper endorsements.[3] This continued favoritism leads many on the right to conclude that American voters do not get a balanced view of the issues and candidates, and this contributes to the right's belief that *the system* is tilted against them. The combination of a 50/50 electorate and a perceived 80/20 national media makes both groups distrustful of the other, as is now on full display.

7. **Money**. For decades, Democrats complained that Republicans had such a huge fund-raising and *dark money* advantage that public financing of campaigns was required. Since Democrats raised much more money than Republicans in both the 2016 and 2020 presidential elections, these

calls have largely vanished. Similarly, Republicans strongly objected to Mark Zuckerberg's donation of some $400 million to help cope with the demands that Covid-19 put on 2020 election processes. Although the FEC unanimously ruled that these efforts were legal, there will always be suspicions when outside money is used in this way, especially when the donor is a known supporter of one party.[4]

8. **Out of Touch Elites**. Many media, academic, and other establishment figures viscerally disapproved of the Brexit and Trump results. But instead of acknowledging that voters were expressing their dislike of unnecessary wars, unchecked globalization, outsourced jobs, the 2008 financial crisis, rapidly changing cultural norms, and other societal changes, many claimed that the real problem was that *less educated* voters were being manipulated by misinformation, targeted social media, and Russian bots. It often seemed as if the governing class would rather undermine election integrity than focus on its own failings.

9. **Voter Suppression**. For decades, many voters have been discriminated against because of inadequate polling places, long voting lines, inaccurate voter rolls, bans against felons who have served their time, gerrymandering, and other tactics. In October of 2022, President Biden even warned of a new "Jim Crow 2" era. Given this old and recent history, it's only natural that many people—particularly those from minority communities—might question the official outcomes of very close elections.

10. **Mainstream Misinformation**. Whether we are looking at government or mainstream media's claims about the Hunter Biden laptop, the Steele Dossier, the Wuhan lab Leak theory, the effectiveness of vaccines in preventing the spread of Covid-19, or that the 2020 election was the "safest in history," citizen skepticism of mainstream media is understandably high.[5] Today's decline in electoral trust is inseparable from the loss of societal trust in government, politicians, media, law enforcement, the intelligence community, universities, churches, and other pillars of society. In most of these areas, social media plays a relatively minor role.[6]

These ten dynamics have greatly undermined societal trust in our electoral system, affecting just about every voter to at least some extent. Democrats can point to the *Bush vs Gore* decision, the *undemocratic* nature of the Electoral College, improper intervention by the FBI in 2016, and America's long history of voter suppression. Republicans are troubled by radical changes in voting processes, the biases of the media, Big Tech and the elite, double standards within the judicial system, and the role of Mark Zuckerberg's money.

Both parties know that in an extremely close election, America's ability to count votes with total accuracy is often questionable. Many independent voters are understandably unsettled by all of these factors.

Some of these dynamics cast doubt on the way the overall electoral system is designed and operates; others are more about influencing who turns out to vote and for whom, and still others are about the degree to which election results are accepted. Overall, it's a serious list of problems, most of which show no signs of going away. Taken together, they provide the balance against which any electoral distrust caused by social media must be weighed.

Social Media's Role Revisited

The main Democratic complaints about social media's impact on U.S. elections are that: It was used by the Russians to damage Hillary Clinton's 2016 campaign and help Donald Trump's; Facebook data was improperly used to target 2016 voters; and social media played a central role in the events of January 6. Revisiting these issues shows that social media's importance has been significantly exaggerated, as explained below:

- **Damaging Clinton.** Russian state or associated actors allegedly broke into the computer systems of the Democratic National Committee as well as the personal email of Clinton campaign chief John Podesta. A steady flow of internal DNC and Clinton campaign communications was then released via WikiLeaks. The leaked messages confirmed the already widespread belief that the DNC favored Hillary Clinton over Bernie Sanders in the Democratic primary. As this was mostly an issue within the Democratic Party, it's doubtful how much impact these revelations had in the general election. But regardless, the hacking of the DNC had little to do with Big Tech and social media (unless one sees WikiLeaks as a form of social media).

- **Helping Trump.** Russian aligned actors posted content and used bots on Facebook and Twitter to influence voters and support Donald Trump. The effectiveness of these efforts is a matter of much debate. The Trump and Clinton 2016 campaigns spent $2.4 billion trying to influence voters, some 16,000 times the $150,000 Russia is said to have spent with Facebook.[7] To make the case that Russia was a significant factor, one would have to believe that, on a per dollar basis, its bot and content efforts were dramatically more effective than not just those of the two campaigns, but all the other election influencers as well. While one can't prove the negative that these efforts had no significant effect, there is no evidence, or even a plausible theory, as to why this was the case.

- **Voter Profiling**. The Trump campaign used Facebook data to target specific types of voters. While the effectiveness of extensive voter profiling is also a matter of much debate, there is nothing illegal about this practice. Just about every advertiser and campaign team does it to at least some extent. The problem was that the data was improperly obtained by Cambridge Analytica, by all accounts without Facebook's knowledge or permission. It's a case of Facebook failing in its data protection oversight, not an indictment of social media's effect on democracy. Third-party misuse of data should be a correctable problem, but detailed voter profiling will surely continue.

- **January 6**. Social media is often blamed for the attack on the U.S. Capitol. But this gets the story backwards. The reasons so many people came to Washington are the same as those discussed earlier. It was a close election; there were major changes to election rules; the longer the vote counting took, the more it favored President Biden; people didn't believe what the mainstream media was saying; they distrusted the FBI and the *deep state*, and first and foremost by far, then President Trump kept telling them— in person, on TV, and via social media—that the election was stolen, that he would prove it, and that it was legal to change the certification process. Since Trump supporters are often intensely loyal and have lived through years of often unproven charges against the former president, many believed him. Social media further aggravated and helped organize this already highly motivated crowd, but it was clearly a secondary factor, as it will likely be again in 2024 given the multiple indictments of the former president.

In contrast, Republican complaints about social media in the 2020 and 2022 elections are basically the same as those with traditional media. They see huge bias in terms of both what is covered and how it is covered. The *Twitter files*, similar revelations about Facebook, and the recent decision of Federal Judge Terry Doughty in Missouri have shown that, regardless of their intent or motive, Big Tech blocked, banned, and shadow banned a great deal of content that might have been helpful to Republicans, most notably the Hunter Biden laptop story.[8]

While these were certainly significant events, they say less about social media and then they do about bias and censorship across all media. Pretty much everything that Big Tech banned was also banned or ignored by traditional media as well. More pointedly, when people talk about *social media misinformation,* they are typically referring to false information posted by *users.* But in the 2020/22 elections, the bias and censorship of *providers* was the more powerful misinformation force, even though the term *misinformation* is almost never used in this way.

Conclusion

Looking back, it's debatable which electoral problem should be more alarming, the largely secretive activities of a hostile foreign power, or the largely secretive actions of America's own government and some of its most powerful media firms. But given that throughout its history America has engaged in various forms of election interference countless times all around the world, one can make a strong case for the latter. What happens inside of America's borders will almost certainly prove the biggest electoral trust factor over time.

The intensive focus on Russia's use of social media in 2016 was driven by the surprising—and very close—election of Donald Trump, the wider Russia collusion investigation, and to put it bluntly, the fact that much of the media and Washington establishment despises the former president. In contrast, the Big Tech and media practices that stopped or limited American citizen's use of social media in 2020 and 2022 received enormous coverage in conservative media, but relatively little from anywhere else. These divisions are widening as we head toward 2024.

But whereas the ten non-technology election distrust factors seem baked into America's future, the Big Tech concerns appear much more manageable. All the major social media firms now have dedicated teams to identify and limit foreign influences on their platforms. These companies know that they paid a price for their censorship, and they have strong incentives to avoid such controversies in the future. X wants to do this by supporting free and open political speech, while Meta has hinted that it might reduce its role in politics altogether. The entire tech industry knows it must address new trust concerns such as deep fakes and AI.

But the bottom line is that compared to the non-technology dynamics, social media is a relatively minor factor in America's electoral trust decline. The use of social media by citizens has been less of a concern than its use by foreign actors and the censorship of America's online and offline media providers. Demonstrating that these two problems can be fixed is an essential step toward reversing the *techlash* and restoring the trust of technology consumers, regulators, and society overall. Hopefully, a few years from now the conventional wisdom will be: "Claims that social media is an existential threat to American democracy are largely false." Such claims might even be labeled as *misinformation*.

— DM

Notes

1. Colby Itkowitz, "Hillary Clinton: Trump is an 'illegitimate president'," *The Washington Post* (September 26, 2019), https://www.was hingtonpost.com/politics/hillary-clinton-trump-is-an-illegitimate-pre sident/2019/09/26/29195d5a-e099-11e9-b199-f638bf2c340f_story. html; Sabrina Siddiqui and Richard Luscombe, "In North Carolina and Florida, is the Trump voter suppression plan working?" *The Guardian* (November 3, 2016), https://www.theguardian.com/us-news/2016/ nov/03/donald-trump-voter-suppression-campaign-north-carolina-flo rida.
2. Glenn Kessler, "Did racially motivated voter suppression thwart Stacey Abrams?" *The Washington Post* (October 30, 2019), https://www.was hingtonpost.com/politics/2019/10/30/did-racially-motivated-voter-sup pression-thwart-stacey-abrams/.
3. Reid Wilson, "Final newspaper endorsement count: Clinton 57, Trump 2," *The Hill* (November 6, 2016), https://thehill.com/blogs/ballot-box/ presidential-races/304606-final-newspaper-endorsement-count-clinton- 57-trump-2/.
4. Ben Kamisar, "Federal election officials clear Zuckerberg's 2020 election administration grants," *NBC News* (September 8, 2022), https://www. nbcnews.com/meet-the-press/meetthepressblog/federal-election-offici als-clear-zuckerbergs-2020-election-administrat-rcna46844.
5. David Moschella, "It's Not Just Facebook—'Old Media' Spreads Misinformation, Too," (ITIF Defending Digital commentary, January 10, 2022), https://itif.org/publications/2022/01/10/its-not-just-facebook- old-media-spreads-misinformation-too/.
6. David Moschella, "Digital Innovation Isn't Undermining Societal Trust; It's the Other Way Around," (ITIF Defending Digital commentary, February 1, 2023), https://itif.org/publications/2023/02/01/digital-inn ovation-isnt-undermining-societal-trust-its-the-other-way-around/.
7. Darren Samuelson, "Facebook: Russian-linked accounts bought $150,000 in ads during 2016 race," (Politico, September 6, 2017),

https://www.politico.com/story/2017/09/06/facebook-ads-russia-lin ked-accounts-242401.

8. Josh Gerstein and Kyle Cheney, "Appeals court temporarily blocks order that restricted feds' contact with social media firms," (Politico, July 14, 2023), https://www.politico.com/news/2023/07/14/social-media-injunction-temporary-stay-00106431.

Technology & Big Tech

Myth 11: The Pace of Technology Change Is Accelerating

Comparisons with devices such as radio and television show that the rate of technology adoption is not increasing. Acceleration proponents often fail to acknowledge the differences between device and application adoption rates; the former have always taken much longer than the latter. Overestimating the speed of change leads to exaggerated fears and anxieties, and an anti-innovation mindset.

The misunderstanding isn't surprising. ChatGPT was used by some 100 million people in just its first two months, a rate of acceptance no previous Internet service had come close to matching. It's an impressive accomplishment, and a tribute to the excitement that this new AI platform has triggered. Sign-ups for Meta's Twitter competitor Threads were similarly rapid. But a more nuanced look shows that the implications of this have been greatly exaggerated. Those who claim that the rate of technology change is accelerating are mistaken.

There are at least three valid ways to assess the rate of technology adoption: (1) We can compare the adoption rates for personal computers, smart phones, and tablets to the acceptance of previous devices such as telephones, radios, and televisions; (2) we can look at the length of time between the major digital technology eras—mainframes, minicomputers, PCs, smart phones, Internet, and now AI, or (3) we can look at the adoption of the content and/or services that run on top of those hardware devices and platforms—be they radio broadcasts, television programs, musical recordings, software applications, Internet services, or ChatGPT searches. All three perspectives show that the rate of technology change is not accelerating.

R. D. Atkinson and D. Moschella, *Technology Fears and Scapegoats*, https://doi.org/10.1007/978-3-031-52349-6_12

Device Comparisons

Since radios, TVs, PCs, and smartphones all need to be purchased, determining how long it took for each of these products to be acquired by fifty percent of a nation's households has become a standard way of comparing rates of device adoption. (Using percentages is a much more fair way to make comparisons across eras than comparing the total number of devices in use, as population sizes have increased greatly over time).

Applying this approach to the United States shows that radios were first commercialized in 1922, and reached the fifty percent threshold nine years later. Televisions became broadly available in 1946, and reached the fifty percent level eight years later. In contrast, telephones took some 36 years to be in half of American homes.[1] The relatively slow spread of telephony isn't surprising as wired telephones required vast new national infrastructure, whereas broadcast radio and television did not. This is why the eight/nine-year figure is the standard to which computer device adoption rates should be compared.

Depending on whether one uses the early Apple and Commodore personal computers of the late 1970s, or the IBM PC introduced in 1981, it took either sixteen or twelve years for PCs to reach the 50 percent mark, which occurred around 1993. Smart phones took about twelve years, and eBooks/tablets about nine years.[2] While one can debate what it means to be *first commercialized*, the figures are broadly accurate, and clearly show that PCs and smart phones were not adopted faster than radios and TVs. If anything, the rate was slower.

This pattern is even more pronounced for newer digital devices. Smart watches, smart thermostats, smart doorbells, home blood pressure devices, home robots (such as Roomba), personal fitness devices (like Fitbits), consumer drones, virtual reality headsets, augmented reality glasses, and personal 3D printers have been around for many years, but none are close to reaching the 50% level. Only smart speakers, such as Amazon's Alexa (introduced in 2014), have enjoyed rapid success, but even here the 50 percent threshold has not yet been reached. Once again, compared to the past, there's been an overall device adoption slowdown.

Computing Eras

What about the rate of change just within the computer sector? As with when a product was *first commercialized*, people can debate when the major computing eras began and ended, but by looking at a major early success of each era, a clear pattern emerges. IBM's 1401 mainframe was launched in 1959; Digital Equipment's PDP-11 minicomputer in 1970, the IBM PC in 1981, Netscape's Internet browser in 1993, and the iPhone in 2007. This suggests eras lasting eleven, eleven, twelve, and fourteen years, respectively, supporting the long-standing observation that the IT industry's center of gravity tends to shift every decade or so. The emergence of large language models in 2022 is also in line with this pattern. So overall, the rate of generational technology change is best described as steady.

One could, of course, make a strong case that although the speed of adoption has been remarkably constant, the impact of each generation of computing technology has increased dramatically. There's little doubt that the Internet and smart phones have changed more people's lives than business' use of mainframes and minicomputers, and it seems very likely that AI will continue this pattern. (Personal computers can be seen as the bridge between the corporate and consumer computing eras.) But this is an argument based on the societal impact of each technology generation, not the speed of change.

Applications

Applications is where the fastest technology growth has always taken place. Radio programs such as The Shadow and Amos "n" Andy, television shows such as The Milton Berle Show and I Love Lucy, songs such as Rock Around the Clock and She Loves You were heard or watched at least occasionally by just about every household with a radio or TV. It's widely reported that many stores and restaurants closed when Berle's show was on the air because just about everyone was home watching. Even the Super Bowl doesn't come close to matching that.

The rate of adoption for Facebook, Twitter, or ChatGPT is best compared to these earlier content successes. Like radio and broadcast television, Internet services are mostly free and supported by advertising. Whether one is listening to the radio, watching TV, or surfing the Internet, there is a mix of information and entertainment available, as well as both high- and low-brow content.

The fact that, unlike broadcast media, social media is highly interactive isn't relevant to determining the rate of adoption.

While ChatGPT has been adopted much faster than the major social media, it's easy to see why. Facebook, Twitter, Instagram, WhatsApp broke a lot of new conceptual ground, and had to prove their value to consumers. They also required significant consumer learning and interaction. Perhaps most importantly, these services also had very strong network economics in that they are not particularly valuable unless other people use them. In contrast, most people use ChatGPT like a search engine, which delivers value whether others use it or not. It's much more like Google search, which literally billions of people are already very familiar with. Little consumer learning, behavioral change, or network effects have been required.

Comforting Consistency

None of this is to disparage the rapid acceptance of ChatGPT, but its success is much more due to its fascinating customer experience, obvious potential, and ease of use than any change in the overall rate of technology adoption. AI and large language models are ushering in a new era of computing that will define the next decade or so. It's a pattern we've seen many times before, pretty much every ten or so years. This steady rate of change should be comforting to those who fear that the world is changing too fast. As we have seen with the Internet and smart phones, ten years gives people sufficient time to adjust to new norms and realities.

— DM

Notes

1. Radio, television, and telephone data is drawn from Historical Statistics of the United States, Colonial Times to 1970, U.S. Department of Commerce, 1975.
2. David Moschella and Mike Lawrie, *Seeing Digital: A Visual Guide to the Industries, Organization, and careers of the 2020s*, DXC Technology 2018, p. 49.

Myth 12: Technology Increases Societal Biases

Human decisions are shaped by our values, beliefs, experiences, inclinations, prejudices, and blind spots. These "biases" can easily leak into information system design. But overall and over time, modern technology will lead to more fair and objective societal decision-making, as machines will prove to be less biased than most people. An exaggerated fear of technology bias can easily slow down important forms of societal innovation.

You've probably heard the joke. Two campers see a bear approaching. One starts putting on her sneakers. The other asks: "What are you doing? You can't outrun a bear." The response is obvious: "I don't have to outrun the bear; I just have to outrun you."

So it is with the "objectivity" of information systems. The question is not whether digital services are—or ever can be—completely unbiased. It's whether they can outperform the available human alternatives. Much more often than not, they can and will.

Pervasive Human Biases

The word "bias" is now mostly used as a pejorative term, but biases should be seen along a spectrum of human attitudes spanning our values, beliefs, allegiances, opinions, preferences, interests, stereotypes, prejudices, and misunderstandings. This broader definition shows how deeply biases are built into the human psyche, and why they can never be fully eliminated.

© The Author(s), under exclusive license to Springer Nature
Switzerland AG 2024
R. D. Atkinson and D. Moschella, *Technology Fears and Scapegoats*,
https://doi.org/10.1007/978-3-031-52349-6_13

Some biases—such as taking care of our family and friends first—are generally seen as "good" and to be built upon; others such as racial or gender discrimination are "bad" and in need of remedies. Sometimes there is a clear consensus as to what is good or bad, but often this is a matter of debate.

Additionally, it's all too easy to believe that bad biases are the result of a lack of understanding, and if only people were more informed, society would be much more objective and fair. While lack of knowledge can certainly lead to bias, professional expertise doesn't fare much, if any, better. Whether we are looking at judges, lawyers, professors, scientists, doctors, engineers, architects, writers, journalists, politicians, investors, economists, managers, coaches, consultants, or computer programmers, sharp differences and entrenched opinions are the norm. Deep experience and expertise do not necessarily lead to objective consensus. As behavioral scientists have long noted, subject matter experts tend to:

1. Rely too much on both societal and professional stereotypes.
2. Overvalue their personal experiences, especially recent ones.
3. Overvalue their personal gut feel.
4. Prefer anecdotes that confirm their existing views.
5. Have limited knowledge of statistics and probability.
6. Resist admitting mistakes.
7. Struggle to keep up with the skills and literature in their fields.
8. Burn out and/or make mistakes in demanding work environments.
9. Avoid criticizing, evaluating, and disciplining their peers.
10. Become less open-minded over time.

For decades, we have seen the unfortunate results of these traits in criminal sentencing, student grading, medical diagnoses, hiring and salary negotiations, financial services, editorial coverage, athletic evaluations, political processes, and many other areas. Fortunately, data analytics, expert systems, algorithmic operations, and—most recently—machine learning can establish a software and data foundation upon which better and more consistent decision-making can be built. It's hard to think of any other approach that addresses these long-standing societal challenges more directly.

AI Biases in Perspective

While AI offers many important benefits, the potential risks get most of the media attention.[1] Will AI usher in a surveillance society? Will it eliminate jobs and diminish human worth? Will it increase the divide between the haves and have nots? Will any one nation gain a decisive edge? Will humans still be in control? Compared to these existential questions, the challenge of machine learning bias is both more manageable and a lesser danger. It is less dangerous because AI can mitigate human shortcomings, and it is more manageable because AI bias is often correctable, as businesses and governments have strong incentives to improve their systems over time.

That this bias exists is undeniable. A machine learning system is only as objective as its underlying data set. If this data reflects historical biases, then so will the system. If certain populations are not sufficiently represented statistically, then the system will be weak in those areas. These situations are analogous to the way surveys work. If a survey sample is not representative of the real world, or if the wording of a survey's questions is slanted in some way, these deficiencies will affect the survey's results. Similarly, if a facial recognition system doesn't have enough faces from people of color, it will be less effective in identifying those faces, just as some Asian systems perform worse on non-Asian faces.

The good news is that just as survey professionals strive to design random samples and ask neutral questions, so can AI developers take steps to improve the quality of their underlying data. Systems can, for example, be tested for bias by isolating criteria such as race, gender, location, and other factors. Facial recognition weaknesses can and have been corrected through better data. These and similar techniques will only improve over time, as business practices mature and as the volume of relevant data steadily increases. While eliminating all bias is impossible (and often not desirable), building systems that outrun the average human is a very achievable task.

Related Critiques

Unfortunately, building systems that demonstrably outperform or complement human decision-making is not enough to satisfy many of today's AI critics, as machine learning systems are now disparaged on numerous related fronts. Most of these critiques are not about bias per se. Rather, they reflect an underlying anti-technology, anti-corporate bias. But if citizens are to accept the widespread use of AI, then the machine learning community must do a better job of answering the five questions below:

1. **What Sort of AI Systems Do We Want?** Different societies will need to find their own balance between, for example, the security and convenience benefits of an effective facial recognition system versus the potential risks of mistakes or oppressive visual surveillance.

2. **How Well Do AI Systems Work in the Real World?** As with any innovation, governments and businesses need to evaluate when a system is ready for widespread use. It's a familiar cost/benefit/risk calculation. Some systems have been branded as biased when the real problem is that they just aren't good enough yet.

3. **Should AI Decisions Be Explainable?** While the logic behind data analytics and traditional rule-based algorithms is often transparent, the inner workings of most machine learning systems are not, and won't be for the foreseeable future. Important AI applications, such as medical image diagnoses, are essentially black boxes that need to be evaluated on the quality of their output, not their level of explainability.[2]

4. **What Recourse Should Citizens Have?** Given the lack of explainability, citizen recourse may well be required in sensitive areas such as loan approvals or school acceptances. Sometimes, business and government AI operators will have to be able to do more than just say, "that's what the system says," and be able to match the recourse available in the pre-AI era.

5. **Are the Results of These Systems Socially Acceptable?** An AI application might be based on a representative data set and provide accurate output in the areas it was designed for. But if that output has an adverse effect upon a particular race, class, gender, or other group, the system might still be criticized as biased. We often see this with auto insurance, where premiums are based on a variety of risk factors that sometimes result in different rates for different demographic groups.

Fears of AI bias also reflect the familiar hi-tech double-standard. A single potent example of an AI failure—such as the brief racist rantings of Microsoft's chatbot, Tay, Google's comically woke Gemini, or a deadly accident involving a self-driving Tesla—will get vastly more media coverage than everyday car crashes or human misbehavior. Likewise, organizations such as the Algorithmic Justice League will continue to effectively publicize AI's risks, failures, and injustices. It's important that the AI community be able to respond to concerns such as those in AJL's movie, *Coded Bias*.[3]

Conscious vs. Unconscious Bias

Thus far, the bias we have discussed has been mostly unconscious in nature. Organizations almost never set out to build a system that discriminates by age, gender, race, disability, or any other factor, and most AI developers want to use the best data available. However, as these developers are usually technologists at heart, it's fair to say that they sometimes fail to prioritize this issue—although this is now changing. Similarly, many human biases are also unconscious in nature. We may think that we are being impartial and fair, but our minds are full of stereotypes, preconceptions, self-interests, confirmation biases, and other discriminatory characteristics.

Conscious bias is another thing altogether. Conservatives might have a conscious bias toward systems that treat everyone the same, while liberals are more likely to favor systems that factor in historical inequities. Should college admissions be based mostly on empirical test scores, or should the backgrounds of applicants be given more weight? Should criminal sentencing be uniform, or is adjusting for individual circumstances essential to justice? Similar debates exist in virtually every professional field. As there are no consistently right or wrong answers, changes in policy are often a matter of which conscious biases prevail at any one time or in any one situation.

Conscious bias will be of increasing importance in the design of machine learning systems going forward. Developers will improve the quality of the data they are relying on. But when this data still produces results that society deems "problematic," what should be done? It's not hard to imagine a future where AI developers will be expected to train their systems to produce socially desirable outcomes. In this scenario, AI applications that were originally designed to mitigate "bad" unconscious human biases may soon be expected to entrench "good" conscious ones. Such systems will no longer just have to outrun the bear; they will be the bear, as human and machine decision-making co-evolve, and increasingly become one and the same.

— *DM*

Notes

1. Robert D. Atkinson, "'It's Going to Kill Us!' and Other Myths About the Future of Artificial Intelligence" (ITIF, June 2016), https://itif.org/publications/2016/06/06/its-going-kill-us-and-other-myths-about-fut ure-artificial-intelligence.

2. Joshua New and Daniel Castro, "How Policymakers Can Foster Algorithmic Accountability" (Center for Data Innovation, May 2018), https://datainnovation.org/2018/05/how-policymakers-can-foster-algorithmic-accountability/.

3. Michael McLaughlin and Daniel Castro, "The Critics Were Wrong: NIST Data Shows the Best Facial Recognition Algorithms Are Neither Racist Nor Sexist" (ITIF, January 2020), https://itif.org/publications/2020/01/27/critics-were-wrong-nist-data-shows-best-facial-recognition-algorithms.

Myth 13: Big Tech Faces No Competition

The dominance of today's Big Tech leaders isn't a permanent reality. It briefly appeared that way during the pandemic, but the market power of today's major players is receding in the face of new geopolitical, technological and societal priorities. The case for aggressive antitrust and/or regulatory interventions is diminishing.

Competition in the IT industry has followed a consistent pattern. Every dozen years or so, a new wave of innovation spawns a new generation of market leaders. Whether it was mainframes in the 1950s and 1960s, mini-computers in the 1970s and 1980s, personal computers in the 1980s and 1990s, the Internet in the 1990s and 2000s, smartphones and social media in the 2010s and 2020s, or AI in the coming decade, the dynamic has been the same. Companies beginning with a clean sheet of paper and a focus on the future have bypassed even the most powerful incumbents. The very success of those incumbents made it hard for them to accept that their world was fundamentally changing. Responding in a timely and effective manner often proved even harder.

As we look at the second half of the 2020s and into the 2030s, the digital landscape is shifting once again. During the Covid-19 pandemic, Alphabet, Amazon, Apple, Meta, Microsoft, and Netflix played an essential role in helping us work from home, receive necessary goods and services, keep in touch with friends and family, and stay entertained. For reliably providing these vital societal services, they earned their riches. What would America have done without them?

© The Author(s), under exclusive license to Springer Nature Switzerland AG 2024
R. D. Atkinson and D. Moschella, *Technology Fears and Scapegoats*,
https://doi.org/10.1007/978-3-031-52349-6_14

But going forward, there are many scenarios that could greatly reduce the centrality of today's "Big Tech." Indeed, most of them are obvious to anyone who wants to see them. They can be grouped into three main types of change—shifts in global leadership, shifts in technology, and shifts in societal priorities. Although some of these shifts are more likely than others, someday we will look back and see that the power of today's Big Tech leaders peaked during the pandemic, with the 2020s and 2030s driven by new players and dynamics. Unfortunately, technology's critics too often ignore this ongoing "Schumpeterian" competition and seek to intervene with the heavy hand of antitrust.

Shifts in Global Leadership

Much of the antitrust narrative against Big Tech ignores the fact that these firms power U.S. competitiveness in the global economy. Not since the rise of Japan in the 1980s, has America's global technology leadership been seriously threatened. But today, the challenge from China is greater, especially as Japan was and is a U.S. military ally, while China is America's main geopolitical rival. To cite just a few possible scenarios, during the 2020s and 2030s China could for various reasons seek to disrupt America's leadership by:

- Taking over Taiwan, and limiting Western access to the most advanced semiconductors.
- Shutting down Apple factories, banishing it from China's vast domestic market, or restricting access to appstore applications.
- Limiting Amazon's or Walmart's access to inexpensive Chinese-made goods.
- Adopting alternatives to Alphabet's Android operating system and/or Microsoft's Windows and Office systems.
- Disrupting America's social media and e-commerce companies through services such as TikTok and Shein.
- Manufacturing semiconductors or quantum computers superior to those now based on Intel, Arm, and Nvidia designs, and/or surpassing America's use of AI.
- Successfully marketing its e-commerce, social media, surveillance, drones, 5G, digital currency, and/or other technologies throughout Asia and other parts of the developed and developing worlds.

And that's just a partial list for China.[1] While policymakers have woken up to America's dependence on China, our similar reliance on India is rarely mentioned. But today, just about every large American firm relies heavily on India for its back-office operations delivered through Indian companies (such as Infosys, TCS, Wipro, and HCL), Western companies (such as IBM, Accenture, and DXC which do much of their actual work in India), or through their own India-based operations.

The presence of Indian talent in Silicon Valley and America's elite universities is also pervasive to the point of worrisome dependency, even in advanced semiconductor design. It's only natural that India will leverage its growing influence by expanding up and across the value chain, generating more of its own companies, reshaping the terms of trade, and other strategies.[2] While many in America see India as a natural counterweight to China, this could easily prove to be naive, as China and India have strong incentives to work together in many areas, including hi-tech.

More broadly, Silicon Valley will increasingly have to share the global innovation stage, as advanced technologies are designed and developed in China, India, the UK, South Korea, Japan, Israel, Singapore, Brazil, Europe, Russia, Iran, and elsewhere. Additionally, many countries now prefer to have their own versions of Uber, Amazon, Airbnb, PayPal, etc., and will implement laws and regulations that make globalized services more difficult. The Digital Markets Act in Europe is a good example of new rules aimed directly at limiting the power of the leading U.S. firms.[3] Many more such rules will likely follow as national support for digital sovereignty rises, and faith in globalization declines.

Shifts in Technology

Technology innovation has always been the main source of digital disruption, and even before Open AI and ChatGPT, there was a clear shift underway. The key technology drivers of recent years—smartphones, Internet services, e-commerce, and streaming media offerings—are all maturing, which is why the Big Tech players have increasingly turned on each other. Amazon and Apple are now taking on Netflix in streaming entertainment. Amazon, Microsoft, and Alphabet are fighting it out in cloud, and Apple and Alphabet continue to push each other in smartphones.

Open AI's ChatGPT and other AI efforts introduce potentially powerful new players and raise the stakes of these developments, as serious threats to both Google search and the major cloud architectures emerge. Similarly, the open standard RISC-V architecture has the potential to disrupt the way semiconductors are designed, potentially breaking up the dominance of Western companies such as Intel, Arm and Nvidia, which rely on proprietary designs. Then there is the extraordinary rise of TikTok in the social media space. Taken together, the core of the Internet's technological ecosystem is being challenged, potentially repeating the disruptions of the past.

Meanwhile, electric vehicles, robotics, autonomous systems, smart grids, space applications, satellites, clean energy, drones, indoor farming, and other capabilities are still in their early stages. But taken together, they highlight the rise of the physical world. That Elon Musk—maker of cars and rockets—is now the world's richest person—and could buy Twitter on a whim—seems symbolic of this emerging technological shift.

Less certain is the so-called Web 3.0 movement, an envisioned decentralized Internet grounded in cryptocurrencies, blockchains, Non-Fungible Tokens (NFTs), and other peer-to-peer (P2P) services. This approach is basically the opposite of today's centralized cloud-based model, where the major Big Tech companies are powerful gatekeepers for e-commerce, app stores, digital advertising, customer profiling, and other applications. In a Web 3.0 world, there would be few such gatekeepers, with power and wealth migrating back to product providers and content creators.

Of course, many cryptocurrencies and NFTs collapsed in 2022. But the wild price swings of Bitcoin, Ethereum, and countless others tend to obscure the real value that digital currencies can provide in hedging against inflation, simplifying financial transfers, reducing the need for currency conversions, and similar automation. Despite the failure of many cryptos, the two most important ones—Bitcoin and Ethereum—seem to have more than weathered the storm; taken together, they were worth over $1.8 trillion as of March 2024, more than Meta, and about the same as Amazon.

More speculatively, technologists have long theorized that peer-to-peer (P2P) architectures will be used in many areas beyond digital currencies. They imagine a future where there are Facebook-like services without a Facebook-like intermediary or X-like messaging without X (see Mastodon.social). Ditto for Uber without Uber, Spotify without Spotify, Airbnb without Airbnb, telecom networks without telecom providers (via P2P mesh architectures), and even Amazon retail without Amazon. For the latter, imagine a search engine that finds the best price and connects consumers, manufacturers, and delivery services, eliminating the need for giant Amazon-like warehouses. While most P2P systems have been slow to catch on and face many implementation challenges, today's cloud gatekeepers will remain tempting targets for many years to come.

In short, there are multiple scenarios for technology-driven Big Tech disruption, especially—AI, RISC-V, blockchains, P2P systems, and the automation of the physical world. It's the type of pattern shift the tech industry has seen many times before.

Shifts in Societal Priorities

Perhaps self-driving cars, robots, blockchains, and new architectures won't ever catch on and perhaps Big Tech will either fend off or successfully coexist with an increasingly powerful China and India. But even if both of these scenarios occur, developments in the wider global economy will still tend to significantly reduce the power of Big Tech. The internet boom has been mostly driven by consumers, with Alphabet, Amazon, Apple, Meta, Microsoft, and Netflix all having their roots in consumer products and services.

But the markets of the 2020s and 2030s will be shaped by more industrialized forces—supply chain resiliency, clean energy availability and affordability, potential shortages of food, raw materials and minerals, the risks of climate change, sustainable products and packaging, infrastructure modernization, worker shortages, increasing automation, reducing inequalities, aging populations, human migrations, and ongoing and potential conflicts. These challenges can make consumer services and digital advertising seem trivial in comparison, and in this sense, the future might be less about digital disruptions and more about a major shift in economic focus.

Moreover, the major Big Tech players have mostly avoided these difficult societal issues thus far, and when they have engaged in areas such as health care, transportation, and education, the results have generally been disappointing. Looking ahead, we should expect that companies which effectively address the most important societal challenges will be the leaders of the future, just as Big Tech and Big Pharma were during the pandemic. (On the other hand, if Big Tech companies help address these new challenges too, they will have earned their riches once again.) President Xi has been clear about the need for China to shift from a consumer economy to a more broad-based and resilient "common prosperity" society, and while America won't follow China's overall approach, it's a message that many U.S. policymakers have also embraced.

From Offense to Defense

None of the above is meant to minimize the importance of Big Tech or predict any sort of imminent demise. Far from it. History clearly shows that industries and companies can recede in economic centrality, and still be very large and successful entities. For example, Microsoft and Intel both missed the mobility and dot-com booms, yet both are still rich and powerful firms, although Intel has faced serious competitive challenges in the last few years. There is still plenty of life left in e-commerce, smartphones, search, cloud computing, and social media—both in the United States and around the world—and today's Big Tech players show few signs of dangerous complacency.

But the geopolitical, technological, and social priority shifts of the 2020s and 2030s will make it increasingly difficult for Big Tech to maintain the global dominance it has enjoyed in recent years particularly as China gets stronger. American policymakers should expect that over the longer term these developments will address many of their current fears of unchecked market power.[4] They should also recognize that major antitrust interventions have often been launched after an apparent monopoly company had already passed the peak of its power, and that these interventions can create more harm than good. Given their long run of astonishing success, it's easy to overlook the fact that Big Tech is vulnerable. But eventually, the great disruptors of every era have had to shift from offense to defense. Given that there are now multiple paths to fundamental industry change, odds are that this history will repeat itself.

— DM

Notes

1. David Moschella and Robert Atkinson, "Competing With China: A Strategic Framework" (ITIF, August 2020), https://itif.org/publications/2020/08/31/competing-china-strategic-framework.
2. David Moschella and Robert Atkinson, "India Is an Essential Counterweight to China—and the Next Great U.S. Dependency" (ITIF, April 2021), https://itif.org/publications/2021/04/12/india-essential-counterweight-china-and-next-great-us-dependency.
3. Aurelien Portuese, "The Digital Markets Act: European Precautionary Antitrust" (ITIF, May 2021), https://itif.org/publications/2021/05/24/digital-markets-act-european-precautionary-antitrust.
4. David Moschella, "Theory Aside, Antitrust Advocates Should Keep Their 'Big Tech' Ambitions Narrow" (ITIF, March 2022), https://itif.org/publications/2022/03/07/theory-aside-antitrust-advocates-should-keep-big-tech-ambitions-narrow.

Myth 14: Silicon Valley Doesn't Value Diversity

The white male stereotype of the hi-tech industry is badly out of date, and Silicon Valley's overall diversity record is much better than typically described. As in just about every professional field, a strong flow of talent from leading universities remains the key to overcoming long-standing gender, racial and ethnic workplace imbalances.

One of the longest-running charges against the technology industry is that it lacks sufficient diversity. But whereas most of the other societal complaints about Big Tech are specific to the digital world, the need for diversity cuts across many industry sectors. Just about every large organization now says it: wants a racially balanced workforce; welcomes the advances of working women; supports the LGBTQ community; enables increased workplace accessibility; treats older and younger employees even-handedly; and seeks to rid itself of all forms of religious discrimination.

These six diversity challenges have been particularly prominent in the professions—medicine, law, architecture, engineering, accounting, investing, journalism, academia, government, and other fields that require specialized education and/or training. By comparing the dynamics within these sectors to that of the information technology profession, we can develop an objective analysis of the state of diversity within the IT industry today. We will see that three areas—race, gender, and age—receive most of the criticism, often excessively. In contrast, the digital world's acceptance of differing gender dynamics, support for the disabled, and religious tolerance are all above average, and thus go largely unmentioned.

© The Author(s), under exclusive license to Springer Nature
Switzerland AG 2024
R. D. Atkinson and D. Moschella, *Technology Fears and Scapegoats*,
https://doi.org/10.1007/978-3-031-52349-6_15

Outdated Racial Views

It's easy to see where the idea that the digital field is too "pale and male" came from. The 1960s, 1970s, and 1980s were led almost exclusively by white men—Thomas Watson Sr. and Jr., Gene Amdahl, Seymour Cray, Ross Perot, Gordon Moore, Andy Grove, Ken Olsen, and others (with An Wang a notable exception). But most of these gentlemen could walk down the street and go unrecognized. The faces that fully entrenched the white male stereotype emerged in the 1990s and early 2000s—especially Steve Jobs, Bill Gates, Michael Dell, Jeff Bezos, Mark Zuckerberg, Larry Ellison, Larry Page, Sergey Brin, and Elon Musk.

But during the twenty-first century the face of the industry has changed. Today, the CEOs of Microsoft, IBM, Alphabet, Adobe, SanDisk, Micron, and NetApp are all of Indian heritage. The next level of management in Silicon Valley is even more India-intensive, especially the important chief technology officer role. Similarly, two of the world's most important semi-conductor companies were founded by Taiwanese-Americans. Morris Chang spent 25 years at Texas Instruments before founding Taiwan Semiconductor Manufacturing Corp. (TSMC), now the world's largest chip manufacturer. Jensen Huang moved to America from Taiwan when he was nine years old. After graduating from Stanford and working in Silicon Valley, he co-founded Nvidia, now the world's most valuable chip firm by market capitalization. Then there is Eric Yuan—born in China and now a U.S. citizen—who founded Zoom after many years working at Webex and Cisco.

The importance of Indian and Asian technology professionals is even greater when the IT industry is viewed from a global perspective. Chinese, Korean, Taiwanese, Japanese, and Indian firms now rival the U.S.-based tech giants in many areas. Most of the computers, smartphones, and networking equipment we use are made in Asia, just as India does much of the back-office IT work that keeps large U.S. companies operating 24*7. The heavy presence of Asian and Indian students and professors at America's most elite STEM universities is also striking, to the point of worrisome dependence. This global ecosystem of Asian and Indian students, teachers, entrepreneurs, executives, investors, mentors, and manufacturers gets stronger every year.

Given all of this, the claim that the twenty-first-century IT industry is dominated by white males is not just wrong; it's becoming absurd. So why does this outdated stereotype persist? Basically, it's a way of saying that the number of African-Americans and Hispanic-Americans in the technology industry is much lower than their share of the overall population, without having to make the obviously offensive statement that there are "too many

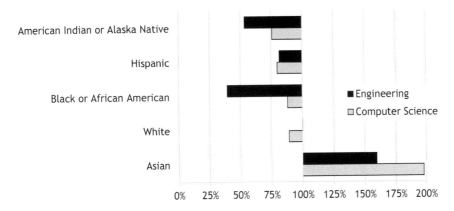

Fig. 1 Academic concentration ratios by race and ethnicity (share of STEM degrees divided by share of all degrees, 2017)[2]

Asians." Harvard University also tried to avoid saying this in its now lost affirmative action case.[1]

But as Fig. 1 shows, Asians are the only racial group that has a higher share of STEM degrees than their share of total U.S. degrees. Indeed, the key message of this chart is that, other than Asians (which here includes India), every race is under-represented in tech, including Whites. This reality is most visible at America's leading universities. For example, a 2020 Stanford study showed that the share of white students in the school's Computer Sciences program was just 34 percent, with "South and East Asia" over 50 percent.[3] Black and Hispanic populations are also under-represented, but in proportions similar to those in medicine, architecture, and other sciences.[4]

In short, the biggest racial story in the twenty-first-century technology industry is not White dominance; it's the dramatic rise of India and East Asia in virtually every STEM-based field. Importantly, there is little doubt about how this remarkable progress has been achieved. It wasn't through quotas, targets, outreach programs, or any form of preferential treatment. It was done through rigorous schools, hard study, intense merit-based competition, and national governments that recognize that a strong STEM-trained workforce is a high societal priority. Taken together, these efforts have overcome the deep prejudices that many Asian and Indian Americans have often faced.

But Why Still Male?

The modern feminist movement emerged during the 1960s, and in the ensuing decades the economic progress of women has been unlike anything seen in human history. Whether we are looking at science, medicine, law, accounting, architecture, academia, or journalism, the pattern has been the same. All of these fields were once almost entirely male, with women actively discouraged from even considering such careers. When women weren't being barred outright, they were discriminated against, marginalized, underpaid, denied promotions, expected to perform secretarial functions, and often sexually harassed. From Wall Street to academia to the courtrooms and the major media, there are countless horror stories in every field and from every decade.

While these problems have not gone away, the progress has been extraordinary. In U.S. graduate schools today, women outnumber men in medicine, law, journalism, teaching, and accounting. The gains in government and politics are also obvious for all to see. As the gender balance within a profession becomes more equal, the bad behavior of the past becomes less tolerable and harder to cover up. Over time, the students of today become the leaders of tomorrow, and supporting networks naturally grow. Eventually, businesses and institutions learn to accept the obvious: that many of their customers—especially female customers—strongly prefer female doctors, lawyers, teachers, and financial advisers. Looking ahead, this still-rising wave of female talent is transforming many professions to the point where men may soon become a distinct minority.

These changes have clearly altered the face of society. But for our purposes the key question is how this extraordinary progress has been achieved. As with race, the advancement of women in the professions hasn't been primarily led by government programs and affirmative action policies, and it certainly hasn't been led by a suddenly enlightened male population. Once again, it was achieved via education, skills, credentials, hard work, ambition, and the perseverance needed to overcome entrenched barriers and stereotypes. In this sense, the gains of Indian and Asian professionals and the progress of women are similar in terms of both what they had to overcome and how they did it.

But within the computer industry, the story is still different, with male computer scientists and engineers outnumbering females by roughly 4:1.[5] Why is this? There are two main theories, one at an educational level and one at an industry level.

From an educational perspective, there is the so-called pipeline theory—the belief that the share of women in high-tech leadership positions will over time tend to mirror the share of women in advanced STEM programs at leading universities. The evidence here is compelling. According to the National Science Foundation, in 2018 women accounted for just 22 percent of doctorates, 32 percent of master's degrees, and 20 percent of bachelor's degrees in computer science. The numbers are similarly low for engineering, math, and statistics. In contrast, NSF reports that, "In biological sciences, women received over 60 percent of bachelor's and master's degrees, and over half of the doctoral degrees. Similarly, in the biopharma industry women STEM workers outnumber male ones, while in agricultural sciences, women earned over half of the bachelor's and master's degrees and 47.5 percent of doctorates."[6]

Despite this revealing data, many people bristle at the pipeline argument because they believe it justifies inaction or lets companies off the hook. But even if you accept the pipeline reality, this begs the question of why so many women choose to study STEM fields other than IT. Some people suggest that women tend to find the heads-down, screen-oriented nature of many hi-tech activities less appealing than other forms of professional work that involve more human interaction. Others emphasize the lack of mentors, role models, and supporting networks, as well as gender-based cultural expectations and similar stereotypes. The debate continues.

At an industry level, the tech sector is often accused of being less welcoming to women than other professional fields. But as noted above, strong resistance has been a shameful part of every industry's history. If anything, the tech industry should be more welcoming as it tends to have younger workers, less steeped in the patriarchies of the past. Supporters of the *tech is less welcoming theory* sometimes counter with the stereotype that tech people are more socially awkward and thus are less comfortable working with women. Maybe.

But the number of organizations, initiatives, sponsorships, and awards supporting women in IT has never been higher. Consider also the excitement that built up around Elizabeth Holmes and Theranos, which demonstrated that the world was keen—it turned out too keen—to celebrate someone who many thought might be the first female Steve Jobs. Most importantly, it's not as if the demand for female STEM talent is not there; many companies would like to hire more women in these roles and have active efforts to do so. But given the relatively small talent pool, the competition can be fierce.

Although the root causes of the relatively low participation rate of women in many STEM fields are not fully understood and agreed upon, the lack of a strong and steady talent pipeline remains. This means that the low representation of women in IT starts well before anyone is actually employed in the technology industry. If the total population of women within computer science and engineering departments starts to rival men at America's leading universities, greater professional equality will almost surely follow. It always has.

Predictable Ageism

Although not as high profile a topic as racial and gender discrimination, Silicon Valley is also often accused of age discrimination, and the media is full of stories of people using Botox, dying their hair, and hiding their age on their LinkedIn profiles to appear more youthful. Although the data is sketchy, by most accounts the average tech worker is five to seven years younger than the average non-tech worker.[7] But is it really surprising that older industries such as banking, insurance, manufacturing, and agriculture would tend to have older workers? Of course not.

The most iconic personal computer companies were created by very young men. Bill Gates was 19, Steve Jobs 21, and Michael Dell 18 when they founded Microsoft, Apple, and Dell. Building giant companies at such a young age had never happened in any industry, even in hi-tech. For example, Ken Olsen was 31 when he founded Digital Equipment Corporation, as was An Wang when he started Wang Laboratories. Ross Perot was 32 when he founded Electronic Data Systems, as was Larry Ellison when he started Oracle. Gordon Moore was 39 and Robert Noyce 41 when they founded Intel. These ages are much more like those of the famous founders of other industry sectors such as oil, electricity, aerospace, and television.

The success of exceptionally young entrepreneurs has continued into the cloud computing and social media era. Mark Zuckerberg was 19 when he started Facebook, as was Vitaly Buterin (born in Russia) when he founded Ethereum. Daniel Ek (who is Swedish) was 23 when he founded Spotify; Larry Page and Russia-born Sergei Brin were 25 when they founded Google. Kevin Systrom was 27 when he founded Instagram, as was Brian Cheskey when he founded Airbnb. Jack Dorsey founded Twitter when he was 29. Travis Kalanick was 32 when he founded Uber.

It was entirely predictable that these young men would surround themselves with relatively younger workers, for reasons of both skills and culture. Managers naturally hire people from the networks they have, and many young executives are understandably not fully comfortable supervising people who are their parents' or grandparents' age. And let's face it, many older managers also choose to hire younger, cheaper workers. But over time, ages and hiring practices tend to revert to the norm. At the time of this writing,

Tim Cook is 63; Jeff Bezos is 60; Satya Nadella is 56; and Sundar Pichai is 51. Increasingly, Big Tech will have an age profile not that different from other industry sectors, as the current crop of IT-savvy workers inevitably ages.

Areas of Tech Industry Leadership

Amidst all the race, gender, and age criticism, the diversity achievements of the digital world go largely unmentioned. This is unfortunate, as the IT industry deserves high marks in at least three areas. First, the tech industry has long exhibited strong support for the LGBTQ community. Given that the technology industry is centered in urban areas such as San Francisco and Boston, that its workers are relatively young, and its politics relatively liberal, it's probably not a coincidence that in 2014 Apple's Tim Cook became the first CEO of a major U.S. corporation to be openly gay, an event that, happily, was both celebrated and seen as no big deal.

Similarly, has any industry done more to improve workplace accessibility? Technology companies build devices and machines that help the visual and hearing impaired; they create jobs that don't require high levels of physical strength and mobility; they have synthesized speech and enabled voice commands, and increasingly they are able to translate human thought into physical world actions to help the truly immobile. In addition to these tremendous quality-of-life improvements, these innovations have made it much easier for the disabled to effectively work across an ever-wider share of the overall economy. Further accessibility advances are a virtual certainty.

Lastly, it's easy to forget the terrible religious discrimination that characterized many professions during the twentieth century, with subtle and not-at-all-subtle prejudices against Jews, Muslims, Catholics, Hindus, and pretty much anyone else that was not of the traditional Protestant stock. Today's digital world is a largely secular one, with relatively little interest in the religious divides of the past. If anything, the technology industry needs to improve its tolerance of the deeply devout, as well as those who are socially and politically conservative.

Still Work to Do

None of the above is meant to suggest that everything is fine, and that nothing needs to be done. Clearly, efforts to draw more students from the African-American and Hispanic communities should continue, and the digital world will benefit if it attracts and retains more women in many STEM fields. In both of these areas, the technology industry should recognize that as long as today's imbalances persist, they can result in negative feedback loops. The fewer minorities that are hired, the weaker their networks and the more that stereotypes take hold. The fewer women, the more likely it is that bad behavior will proliferate, driving more women out of the field. The fewer older workers, the more uncomfortable those workers will be. The fewer minority-owned businesses, the fewer mentors and ties to the venture capital community. These cycles can become entrenched, and thus need to be addressed.

Fortunately, many such efforts are now underway. Today, despite the recent Diversity, Equity, and Inclusion (DEI) backlash, just about every major tech company has significant diversity initiatives; they also monitor their progress in this area much more systematically than they have in the past, with many making public commitments, including targets, grants, scholarships, internships, fellowships, and leadership programs. There are equally important efforts outside of the vendor community. Organizations such as Black Girls Who Code, TechLatino, and the many nonprofits promoting IT to women, many of which are funded at least in part by tech companies, demonstrate the sincere and widespread wish to create a more representative digital world.

Although such initiatives are not new, and there is no guarantee that they will succeed, the scale of today's effort provides further evidence that a broad indictment of the technology industry is not justified. The extraordinary success of Indians and Asians shows that information technology is far from a Whites-only business. The relatively low presence of African-Americans and Hispanics in the IT industry closely resembles the situation in other STEM-based fields. The patterns in law, medicine, accounting, journalism, and other professions show that equality for women starts with the talent pipeline from leading universities, but this pipeline is still weak in computer science and engineering. The younger-than-average digital workforce is entirely understandable and will move closer to the norm over time. The technology industry's strengths in supporting the LGBTQ community, increasing accessibility, and largely eliminating traditional forms of religious discrimination should be applauded. While greater diversity within hi-tech remains a societal goal and ongoing industry challenge, critics of the digital world are significantly overstating their case.

— *DM*

Notes

1. Lawrence Hurley, "Supreme Court strikes down college affirmative action programs," *NBC News* (June 29, 2023), https://www.nbcnews.com/politics/supreme-court/supreme-court-strikes-affirmative-action-programs-harvard-unc-rcna66770.
2. Authors' calculations using data from the National Science Board, "Bachelor's degrees awarded, by citizenship, field, race, and ethnicity: 2000–17," Table S2-7 in *Science & Engineering Indicators 2020*, NSB-2019–7, September 4, 2019, https://ncses.nsf.gov/pubs/nsb20197/.
3. Sophie Andrews and Lucia Morris, "Diversity in CS: Race and gender among CS majors in 2015 vs 2020," *The Stanford Daily* (August 8, 2020), https://stanforddaily.com/2020/08/08/how-has-diversity-within-stanfords-cs-department-changed-over-the-past-5-years/.
4. Jasmine Weiss, et al., "Medical Students' Demographic Characteristics and Their Perceptions of Faculty Role Modeling of Respect for Diversity," *JAMA Netw Open*, vol. 4(6) (2021), e2112795. https://doi.org/10.1001/jamanetworkopen.2021.12795.
5. National Science Board, "Bachelor's degrees awarded, by citizenship, field, race, and ethnicity: 2000–17," Table S2-7 in *Science & Engineering Indicators 2020*, NSB-2019–7, September 4, 2019, https://ncses.nsf.gov/pubs/nsb20197/.
6. UC Berkely School of Information, "Changing the Curve: Women in Computing," (Berkley School of Information, July 2021), https://ischoolonline.berkeley.edu/blog/women-computing-computer-science/.
7. Matt Asay, "Is tech getting older or less ageist? The answer is complicated," (TechRepublic, April 7, 2022), https://www.techrepublic.com/article/is-tech-getting-older-or-less-ageist-the-answer-is-complicated/.

Myth 15: Facial Recognition Is Inherently Biased

In today's digital economy, few technologies have generated as much opposition as facial recognition. Critics have labeled the technology as inherently sexist and racist—claims that the media have repeatedly amplified. Activists have called for, and in some cases achieved, complete bans on the technology. Yet the actual evidence tells a very different story. Independent testing shows that facial recognition technology can be highly accurate, including across different races and genders, while providing many benefits to individuals and society.

Facial recognition technology—which compares images of faces to determine their similarity—didn't really exist until the 2010s. Today's systems typically perform two types of functions: The first is "verification," or one-to-one matching, which is simply comparing two facial images to determine whether they are the same. It's an automated version of what security guards do when they check people's IDs to make sure they look the same as the cardholders' faces.

The second type of facial recognition system is "identification," or one-to-many matching. With identification, the technology searches a database of images to find potential matches with an initial image of someone's face. It's an automated version of what a witness to a crime does when they look through binders of mugshots to see if they recognize a perpetrator.

Both applications use algorithms that detect unique features, such as the distance between people's eyes, to create a mathematical model of the similarity between faces. Two facial images can then be considered a possible match if their similarity scores in the mathematical model meet or exceed a

© The Author(s), under exclusive license to Springer Nature
Switzerland AG 2024
R. D. Atkinson and D. Moschella, *Technology Fears and Scapegoats*,
https://doi.org/10.1007/978-3-031-52349-6_16

minimum acceptable threshold set by the system's operator. A facial recognition system's false-positive and false-negative rates are common ways to measure its accuracy, while other metrics, such as how fast the system can perform a search, also affect its performance.

Misused Data

As part of their campaign to delegitimize facial recognition, opponents argue that the systems are too inaccurate. In addition, they say that such systems are biased against women and people with darker skin, so they are effectively "sexist" and "racist." In these cases, critics have presented evidence that does not withstand serious scrutiny. Yet the media has repeated these claims, spreading the narrative that facial recognition systems are fundamentally flawed. In large part due to this misinformation, policymakers in a number of cities, including San Francisco, Boston, and Portland (OR), have banned government use of the technology.[1]

Privacy and civil liberties groups have been some of the most strident opponents of facial recognition technology. For example, prominent advocacy groups, including the American Civil Liberties Union (ACLU), Electronic Frontier Foundation (EFF), and Electronic Privacy Information Center (EPIC), sent a joint letter to President Biden asking him to sign an executive order banning the federal government's use of the technology.[2]

But they and other anti-technology activists repeatedly get their facts wrong. The ACLU served up a prime example of the overheated and inaccurate rhetoric that comes from opponents when it wrote soon after the Biden administration took office that facial recognition has "a disturbing record of racial bias and inaccuracy that endangers people of color and other marginalized groups" and, as evidence, they pointed to a study that it claimed, "found alarming racial and gender disparities in commercial face recognition systems."[3]

In fact, the study in question was evaluating facial analysis systems designed to determine a person's gender from a photo—it was not evaluating facial recognition systems. They may sound similar, but they are as different as apple trees and apple sauce: Facial analysis systems predict features such as age, gender, or emotion, whereas facial recognition systems determine whether images match.[4] Unfortunately, activist opponents of facial recognition and the media continue to ignore this important distinction. Even respected think tanks get this easy-to-understand difference wrong. The Wilson Center, a DC-based think tank funded by Congress, wrote in the summer of 2020 that, "the 2018 Gender Shades study evaluated the performance of different facial recognition algorithms."[5] (No, it actually evaluated the performance of facial analysis systems).

Another erroneous tactic used by groups that oppose facial recognition is to ignore the confidence levels returned by matching algorithms. Facial recognition algorithms generally do not return a binary true or false on whether two images match. Instead, they return a confidence score, such as a 90 percent confidence in a match. Opponents of facial recognition have artificially inflated claims of inaccurate systems by using low confidence thresholds. Indeed, the ACLU did exactly this when it wrote an article arguing that Amazon's facial recognition system falsely matched 28 members of Congress to a database of mugshots. However, the ACLU later admitted that it had used a low confidence threshold of 80 percent, despite recommendations from the vendor that law enforcement uses a 99 percent confidence threshold. At the correct threshold, the false positives disappeared.[6] But the damage was done, with people thinking that facial recognition systems are flawed.

The Evidence Tells a Different Story

In response to concerns about the potential bias of facial recognition technology, the U.S. Department of Commerce's National Institute of Standards and Technology (NIST) launched in 2019 an independent, third-party assessment of the technology's accuracy across different demographics. NIST already had a long history of testing the accuracy of facial recognition algorithms, so these tests expanded on its prior work.

NIST examined the false-positive and false-negative rates of over 200 facial recognition algorithms.[7] Two key findings emerged. First, the most accurate identification algorithms had "undetectable" differences between demographic groups. This means that the facial recognition algorithms had similar levels of false positives and false negatives regardless of race and gender.

Second, the most accurate verification algorithms had low false positives and false negatives across most demographic groups. For example, 17 of the highest-performing verification algorithms had similar levels of accuracy for black females and white males: false-negative rates of 0.49 percent or less for black females (equivalent to an error rate of less than 1 in 200) and 0.85 percent or less for white males (equivalent to an error rate of less than 1.7 in 200).[8] NIST's findings definitively refute opponents' narrative that facial recognition technology is biased and strongly suggest that it is the opponents and their sympathizers in the media who are biased—against technology.

Indeed, media coverage of NIST's study completely twisted its findings. The *Washington Post* showed it was wedded to the facial-recognition-is-bad narrative by running an unequivocally dour headline: "Federal study confirms racial bias of many facial-recognition systems, casts doubt on their expanding use."[9] Instead of saying the federal study found that these systems are biased, more accurate coverage would have distinguished the best-performing algorithms' results from those of the worst-performing algorithms, which would have led readers and policymakers to the obvious conclusion that any uses of these systems, whether by government or the private sector, should use only NIST-approved systems.

The *Post's* story went on to reveal the reporter's sloppiness by incorrectly stating that "The [new] federal report confirms previous studies from researchers who found similarly staggering error rates"—again citing the study on facial analysis, not facial recognition. Whether mistakes of that sort stem from laziness or a deeply ingrained bias against technology, the result has been that advocacy groups' accusation that the technology is "racist" has stuck.[10]

The Cost to Society

Moving forward, attempts to ban or restrict applications of facial recognition technology will come at a substantial cost to society. For example, facial recognition can make security screening at airports and border crossings faster and more accurate. Likewise, law enforcement can use facial recognition technology to help identify victims, suspects, and witnesses, as well as locate missing children. In more extreme cases, facial recognition has proved to be essential for rapid response in the case of a terrorist attack or active-shooter situation, such as the Boston Marathon bombing or the Capital Gazette shooting in Annapolis, Maryland. Then there are the minor conveniences of making it easier to enter your office or gym, use an ATM machine, or log onto your PC or smartphone. Perhaps most importantly, facial recognition and analysis systems can also help in determining online user ages and thus protect children.

Critics worry that more widespread use of facial recognition will lead to wrongful arrests or harassment. Indeed, there have been a few such cases. However, in each instance, the cause has always been poor police work or company misuse. Indeed, vendors of facial recognition systems have repeatedly stressed to potential law enforcement that these systems are only meant as investigative tools. Facial recognition systems can automate what would normally be a tediously slow process of trying to identify individuals. But a match should never be used as conclusive evidence for arresting somebody. Unfortunately, critics often conflate poor policing practices with the value of the technology.

It is also important to note that facial recognition technology is often used to replace an existing human process. For example, facial recognition technology might replace a border control agent or the work of a police detective looking through mugshots. In so doing, the technology would likely *reduce* bias, since multiple studies have found that humans are particularly prone to their own biases in identifying faces across different races.[11] For example, Asians are typically more accurate at identifying faces of other Asians, but less accurate at identifying faces of non-Asians.

As society grapples with the ethical implications of facial recognition technology, there are concrete steps that stakeholders can take to shape its future trajectory. Developers can and should continue to improve the accuracy of their facial recognition systems across demographics by refining their algorithms and testing across diverse datasets. In parallel, governments should continue to provide independent testing and establish minimum standards for the accuracy of any facial recognition systems that it deploys. Organizations must use these systems carefully. But to claim that facial recognition is an inherently "racist" technology is not only factually wrong; it's stubbornly biased.

— *RA*

Notes

1. Taylor Hatmaker, "Portland passes expansive city ban on facial recognition tech," *TechCrunch* (September 9, 2020), https://techcrunch.com/2020/09/09/facial-recognition-ban-portland-oregon/.
2. "Coalition Letter to President Biden on Use of Facial Recognition Technology," *ACLU* (February 16, 2021), https://www.aclu.org/documents/coalition-letter-president-biden-use-facial-recognition-technology.
3. Kate Ruane, "Biden Must Halt Face Recognition Technology to Advance Racial Equity," *ACLU* (February 17, 2021), https://www.aclu.org/news/privacy-technology/biden-must-halt-face-recognition-technology-to-advance-racial-equity.

4. Daniel Castro, "Note to Press: Facial Analysis Is Not Facial Recognition," (ITIF, January 27, 2019), https://itif.org/publications/2019/01/27/note-press-facial-analysis-not-facial-recognition/.

5. Anne Bowser, "Why Facial Recognition is Not Enough," (Wilson center, August 2020) https://www.wilsoncenter.org/blog-post/why-banning-facial-recognition-not-enough.

6. Daniel Castro, "Banning Police Use of Facial Recognition Would Undercut Public Safety," (ITIF, July 30, 2018), https://itif.org/publications/2018/07/30/banning-police-use-facial-recognition-would-undercut-public-safety/.

7. Patrick Grother, Mei Ngan, and Kayee Hanaoka, "Face Recognition Vendor Test (FRVT): Part 3: Demographic Effects," *NIST* (December 2019), https://nvlpubs.nist.gov/nistpubs/ir/2019/NIST.IR.8280.pdf.

8. Michael McLaughlin and Daniel Castro, "The Critics Were Wrong: NIST Data Shows the Best Facial Recognition Algorithms Are Neither Racist Nor Sexist," (ITIF, January 27, 2020), https://itif.org/publications/2020/01/27/critics-were-wrong-nist-data-shows-best-facial-recognition-algorithms/.

9. Drew Harwell, "Federal study confirms racial bias of many facial recognition systems: Casts doubt on their expanding use," *The Washington Post* (December 2019), https://www.washingtonpost.com/technology/2019/12/19/federal-study-confirms-racial-bias-many-facial-recognition-systems-casts-doubt-their-expanding-use/.

10. "Racial bias in facial recognition algorithms," (Amnesty International, March 2023), https://www.amnesty.ca/surveillance/racial-bias-in-facial-recognition-algorithms/.

11. Joseph Robinson, et al., "Face Recognition: Too Bias, or Not Too Bias?" (CVPR, 2020), https://openaccess.thecvf.com/content_CVPRW_2020/papers/w1/Robinson_Face_Recognition_Too_Bias_or_Not_Too_Bias_CVPRW_2020_paper.pdf.

Myth 16: Big Tech Should Be Arbiters of "The Truth"

Since in many important areas, there is no consistently reliable source of truth, neither consumers nor policymakers should want Big Tech firms to enforce official claims of what is true or false. The events of recent years have shown that such efforts are often mistaken, and reduce trust more than increase it. Technology companies need to be humble about their ability to identify "misinformation," and much more skeptical of both inside and outside information arbiters.

Since business use of the Internet became widespread in the 1990s, computer security experts have talked about the need for *Zero Trust* architectures. The main idea is that in today's mobile world the traditional notion of a secure corporate *firewall* is no longer viable. Whether you are a senior executive deep inside company headquarters or a contractor sitting in a Starbucks in a foreign country, the network access process should be essentially the same. Trusting no one hasn't entirely solved the network trust challenge, but it has surely helped.

Today, it often feels like we are living in a *Zero Trust* society. America's traditional distrust of politicians and news organizations has worsened. It's also been joined by rising doubts about the police, the FBI/CIA/NSA, the judicial system, corporations, schools, churches, the scientific establishment, the military, and now AI.[1] It's unfortunate that Americans have become so suspicious in so many areas. But as it has with network security, a *Zero Trust* approach can be a foundation for significant improvement over time.

Big Tech will be central to any such approach. We are constantly told that online services are to blame for dangerous misinformation. If only tech firms

© The Author(s), under exclusive license to Springer Nature
Switzerland AG 2024
R. D. Atkinson and D. Moschella, *Technology Fears and Scapegoats*,
https://doi.org/10.1007/978-3-031-52349-6_17

were more responsible, the truth would emerge, and societal trust would improve. But this mostly just sets up the technology industry as a convenient scapegoat. In the most important areas, there is often no reliable source of truth, which is why promoting the "true" and banning the "false" is often an impossible task. Instead, consumers and policymakers should want technology platforms, content moderators, and algorithms to enable open debates about politically divisive issues. More speech won't entirely solve the societal trust problem, but it will help.

Flawed Arbiters

As Meta CEO, Mark Zuckerberg, has acknowledged, Big Tech's enforcement of various *official truths* that eventually turned out to be false has undermined trust in both the leading tech companies and society overall.[2] In addition to their own content moderators, four other parts of what is sometimes referred to as the *Censorship Industrial Complex* have sought to determine what is deemed misinformation, disinformation, and so-called mal-information. All four entities have serious shortcomings as described below:

- **Government.** Whether it was the claims that Russia blew up its own Nord Stream pipeline, that the Covid-19 lab leak scenario is a racist conspiracy theory, that the Hunter Biden laptop was Russian disinformation, that the withdrawal from Afghanistan was "an extraordinary success," or that China's spy balloon was "more embarrassing than intentional," a great many Americans simply don't believe what Washington says.[3] Politicians have always engaged in mis-, dis-, and mal-information (sometimes they pretty much have to), but insisting that governments are a non-debatable *source of truth* is textbook Orwell.
- **Mainstream Media.** Given that U.S. media trust is at an all-time low, how can these organizations possibly serve as accepted arbiters of truth? *The New York Times, the Washington Post,* and similar news organizations used to be instinctively skeptical of the military, the FBI/CIA/NSA, and other government agencies. Today, it often seems that they are part of the same organization (Cable TV is now like a second home for many former intelligence officials).[4] By working so closely with this national security and media nexus, Meta, Alphabet, and Twitter (now X) aligned themselves much more with official authorities than an open information ecosystem should.

- **The Scientific Community.** During the chaos of the pandemic, many mistakes were made. That's to be expected. The problem was the censoring and demonizing of any critics, even though questioning, learning, and change have always been the essence of science. Similarly, the constantly repeated mantras of "the science is settled," "follow the science," and even "the science" are not helpful. Like military generals, scientists shouldn't make final policy decisions because they are ill-equipped to weigh the economic and societal trade-offs. Should we listen to "the science"? Certainly. Should we always follow it? Certainly not. Likewise, is there a single major field of science that is "settled"? Changing views are especially important in medicine whose history has often been about reversing the terrible misunderstandings and malpractices of the past.

- **Self-Appointed Guardians.** The names are hard to keep straight: Newsguard; the Stanford Virality Project; the Digital Trust Project; Project Origin: Securing Trust in Media; the Digital Trust and Safety Partnership; the Disinformation Governance Board (disbanded); the Global Disinformation Index (GDI); and many other groups and organizations all say they want to improve digital trust. But they are mostly a mix of traditional institutions and media convinced that new media is the problem. They also tend to be reflections of partisan groupthink. For example, all of GDI's most trusted sources are left leaning; all of its least trusted are more on the right.[5]

It's not that these groups can't be trusted; it's that they all have their own agendas and can't be trusted to be right all of the time. Questioning, skepticism, and debate are still essential for the free flow of accurate information and ideas, and ultimately for sustained societal trust. Whether we are looking at government agencies, the major media, the scientific community, or supposedly neutral third parties, organizations—like humans—are often reluctant to admit mistakes and can be hostile to their critics. They are also inclined to prioritize their own power and position. They should never be above questioning.

Pressured or Inclined?

Theories vary as to why the tech sector aligned itself so closely with the *official truth* movement during Covid-19. Although many company actions were surely well-intentioned, there also seem to be less noble motivations. When President Biden accused social media firms of "killing people" by spreading "misinformation" that led to vaccine hesitancy, it was hard for companies not to seriously respond, especially given the potential threat of changes to Section 230.[6] Others point to the liberal leanings of much of the Big Tech community, and see the embrace of censorship as a prime example of Trump Derangement Syndrome (dislike of the former president and his supporters is so intense that people do things they ordinarily wouldn't). Lastly, if you hire or seek the services of an army of content moderators, don't be surprised when they seek to exercise their power.

All of these factors probably played a role. But the bottom line is that enormous censorship pressures were put on Big Tech, which largely succumbed. Of course, tech firms are legally free to ban just about any content they want (despite recent efforts to legislate otherwise). But the public now knows that quite a few claims that were labeled as "false" and broadly censored—the myocardial effects of Covid-19, the lab accident theory, the dubious efficacy of vaccinating infants, children, and healthy young adults, the Hunter Biden laptop—have all turned out to be either true or quite possibly true. [7] How these serious errors will affect the perceptions of tech firms and other *truth-tellers* in the overall marketplace remains to be seen. But the Bud Light, Target, and Disney controversies show the potential risk of sudden losses of public support.

Hopefully, the pandemic will prove to be a one-off crisis that led to uniquely extreme measures. However, there are many other topics where official truths are now often asserted. These include: election integrity, climate change, school curricula, judicial fairness, crime, immigration, systemic racism, changing gender norms, pronoun usage, and the Ukraine War. In these and other areas, the tech sector has every reason to be skeptical whenever anyone insists that they know the truth, and it's up to Big Tech to enforce it. Whether *Missouri vs Biden* is upheld will be an important test of whether it is even legal for the federal government to pressure private organizations to abridge otherwise perfectly legal speech, although distinguishing between government pressures and mere suggestions is inherently difficult to determine and enforce.[8]

Hunger for Debate

Elon Musk's purchase of Twitter is, of course, a potential game-changer in terms of how free speech decisions and truth determinations are made. Despite all the initial chaos, Musk's against-all-odds business successes—PayPal, Tesla/SolarCity, SpaceX/Starlink and others—and his extraordinary energy and personal determination make him a hard man to bet against, and projects such as the open-source fact-checking Community Notes show real promise. Musk clearly believes that there is a need—and a potentially big market—for live, in-depth debates with connected audiences, as opposed to the predictable sound bites that characterize most television broadcasts. On the other hand, Musk himself has been credibly accused of blocking speech that he doesn't like, and if that continues, it could easily undermine his efforts.[9] But the now widespread antipathy to Musk shows how much resistance support for open speech currently faces.

Two relatively minor events suggest that there is a hunger for more open and direct debate. On June 13, 2023, Sean Hannity used his entire one-hour Fox News show to debate California Governor, Gavin Newsom. In theory, there should be nothing newsworthy about this, except that such debates almost never happen within today's highly partisan media. Fox viewers, who rarely hear a good word about Newsom, got to see an articulate and person-able leader more than capable of responding to his critics. Most Newsom supporters would never watch Sean Hannity, but if they saw this show, they would have seen a conservative TV personality trying hard to have a civil discussion with a liberal government official. Although both men often talked over each other, it made for pretty good television. On November 30, 2023, Hannity moderated a debate between Newsome and Ron DeSantis which was even more combative but also widely watched.

Looking back, there were remarkably few high-profile televised debates about the best way to manage Covid-19, an extraordinary development given the many uncertainties and high stakes involved. For example, the Great Barrington Declaration should have been much more openly debated, instead of being almost completely suppressed. After its launch in October 2020, thousands of scientists and healthcare professionals endorsed the view that America's approach to Covid-19 should be more like Sweden's: isolate the elderly and vulnerable; keep schools and businesses open; and trust citizens to live their lives responsibly.

As the pandemic has (hopefully) receded and the effects of lockdowns on children and the economy become more obvious, there is now some—but still not much—debate about whether this approach would have been better for America or not. Respectfully presenting the Declaration's views while also explaining why the U.S.—and most of the international community—were taking a much more restrictive approach would have led to greater societal trust than the banning and smearing that took place.

Political Speech Is Different

To be clear, none of the above says anything about how social media firms should or shouldn't manage other speech-related challenges such as online decency, violent imagery, bullying, hate speech, and use by children. While these are obviously important issues, they are not central to the societal trust and political polarization debates. The Great Barrington and other censorship examples often involved formidable people who rarely, if ever, relied on hateful or extreme language and threats. In this sense, purely political speech seems a more manageable challenge than other free speech domains which often come with many gray areas and difficult judgment and constitutional calls.

Understanding the need for a more skeptical and objective stance in political areas should be easy for Big Tech. As this book shows, the technology industry is routinely accused by governments, the media, and third-party organizations of being greedy, destroying privacy, discriminating by race and gender, manipulating consumers, monopolizing markets, and many other sins. These charges are, at a minimum, nuanced and worthy of in-depth debate. Often they are much more wrong than right. Yet many of these accusations are now close to being the conventional wisdom. Imagine if the belief that the technology industry was doing more harm than good was deemed an *official truth* that should no longer be openly questioned. Would Big Tech feel obliged to enforce bans on defending itself?

— *DM*

Notes

1. David Moschella. "Digital Innovation Isn't Undermining Societal Trust; It's the Other Way Around," (ITIF Defending Digital Series, no. 14, February 1, 2023), https://itif.org/publications/2023/02/01/digital-inn ovation-isnt-undermining-societal-trust-its-the-other-way-around/.
2. Gabriel Hays, "Zuckerberg Says 'Establishment' Asked Facebook to Censor COVID Misinfo That Ended Up True: 'Undermines Trust'," *Fox News* (June 9, 2023), https://www.foxnews.com/media/zuckerberg-says-establishment-asked-facebook-censor-covid-misinfo-ended-true-undermines-trust.
3. President Joe Biden, "Biden Calls Afghanistan Withdrawal an 'Extraordinary Success' as He Defends Evacuation Mission," (YouTube, August 31, 2021), https://www.youtube.com/watch?v=LzLh2puvsQA;

Julia Shapero, "Biden on Chinese Spy Balloon: 'It Was More Embarrassing Than it Was Intentional'," *The Hill* (June 17, 2023), https://thehill.com/homenews/administration/4055470-biden-on-chinese-spy-balloon-embarrassing/.

4. Jack Shafer, "The Spies Who Came in to the TV Studio," (Politico, February 6, 2018), https://www.politico.com/magazine/story/2018/02/06/john-brennan-james-claper-michael-hayden-former-cia-media-216943/.

5. Henry A Brechter, "Misinformation Watch: 'Disinformation Risk Assessment' Lacks Transparency, Shows Bias Against the Right," (AllSides, February 20, 2023), https://www.allsides.com/blog/global-disinformation-risk-assessment-shows-media-bias-against-right.

6. Zolan Kanno-Youngs and Cecilia Kang, "'They're Killing People': Biden Denounces Social Media for Virus Disinformation," *The New York Times* (July 16, 2021), https://www.nytimes.com/2021/07/16/us/politics/biden-facebook-social-media-covid.html.

7. Carma Hassan and Helen Regan, "WHO Experts Revise Covid-19 Vaccine Advice, Say Healthy Kids and Teens Low Risk," (CNN Health, March 29, 2023), https://www.cnn.com/2023/03/29/health/who-updates-covid-vaccine-recommendations-intl-hnk/index.html.

8. Jenin Young, "America's Censorship Regime Goes on Trial," (Tablet Mag, April 10, 2023), https://www.tabletmag.com/sections/arts-letters/articles/americas-censorship-regime-goes-on-trial-missouri-biden.

9. Katherine Tangalakis-Lippert, "Despite Calling Himself a 'Free Speech Absolutist,' Elon Musk Has a History of Retaliation Against Employees and Critics," (Insider, March 26, 2022), https://www.businessinsider.com/free-speech-absolutist-elon-musk-censors-employees-critics-2022-3.

Myth 17: Digital Technology Is Increasingly Disruptive

While artificial intelligence has great potential, predictions of ever-increasing digital disruption thus far have proven to be false. Looking ahead, the most significant societal shifts won't be driven by digital technology; they will stem from the more pressing demands of the physical world.

The impressive capabilities and unprecedented growth of ChatGPT have released the hype all over again. Technology is about to disrupt white-collar jobs, customer support, education, writing, and even mighty Google itself. Maybe. But before getting too excited, it's worth noting that we've heard these predictions before only to see that, while individual companies rise and fall, dramatic industry shifts are relatively rare.

Even the most affected sectors tend to carry on. Telephone companies, book publishers, news organizations, advertising agencies, record labels, and retail stores are all still here. Airbnb didn't destroy the hotel business; taxis still roam the streets; and banks haven't been bypassed. Businesses and industries are not stupid; they can learn and adjust. Innovations tend to be more additive than zero-sum.

As amazing as ChatGPT and large language models are, their overall economic impact remains uncertain. Consider that the leap from paper documents to instantaneous Internet searches changed information access at least as much as the jump from Google to today's ChatGPT, and yet online search engines have had relatively little effect on the fundamental workings of health care, finance, education, government, and other information-intensive businesses.

© The Author(s), under exclusive license to Springer Nature Switzerland AG 2024
R. D. Atkinson and D. Moschella, *Technology Fears and Scapegoats*,
https://doi.org/10.1007/978-3-031-52349-6_18

AI's potential to supplant Google is arguably a more likely scenario, but even in that case there is reason for caution. ChatGPT can produce remarkably well-written answers to an extraordinary range of questions; it's often a great starting point for many types of learning. But because its answers are sometimes wrong, out of date, or bland, its use is problematic in areas where verifiable accuracy, explicit sources, current information, and differing opinions are important. From an information industry perspective, content providers are particularly concerned that large language models often use their information without acknowledgment, let alone links or compensation.[1] Lastly, Google, Microsoft, Baidu, and others are developing their own generative capabilities, and these will likely complement, rather than replace, their existing search engine offerings.

Looking ahead, search engine competition should increase substantially, weakening the case for antitrust intervention.[2] Indeed, the long pattern of U.S. antitrust cases being launched at the very moment the market leader's power has begun to recede risks being repeated. ChatGPT-type offerings will surely help people who don't write well and greatly increase the productivity of those who do. Their potential in creating content, developing software, translating languages, creating images, and many other tasks is hard to overestimate. But just as Google search has greatly increased the capabilities of countless individuals without making them obsolete, generative AI is much more of a powerful new tool than a radical economic and employment shift, at least for now.

Definitional Divides

We tend to overestimate the extent of industry and employment change because the term "disruption" has two very different meanings. A typical dictionary definition is "the action of preventing something, especially a system, process, or event, from continuing as usual or as expected."[3] In this everyday English language sense, digital technology and the Internet have been highly disruptive as many industries, organizations, and individuals have had to significantly transform the way they work. Using this definition, ChatGPT and its successors will also prove disruptive in many areas.

But within business schools, the technology industry, and many policy-making circles, the phrase "disruptive innovation" has a much more specific meaning. It is shorthand for a process of creative destruction where one or more new players deploy a radically different technology or business model to obsolete—or seriously diminish—the leaders in a particular market. This definition was famously articulated by the late Clayton Christensen in his seminal 1997 book, *The Innovator's Dilemma.*[4]

Christensen made the important distinction between disruptive versus sustaining innovation. They can be equally potent, but the former undermines established market leaders, while the latter supports them. Christensen-style disruptive change has occurred repeatedly within the IT industry, most famously in the 1980s and 1990s when personal computers and local area networks replaced the once formidable minicomputer industry. Similar disruptions have also occurred outside of the IT sector, but less frequently—with bookstore chains, film-based cameras, and CD/DVD stores among the most iconic examples. If ChatGPT were to seriously damage Google, that would be yet another example of disruption within the IT sector, but disrupting non-IT sectors remains a much higher and less likely bar.

So, depending on whether one uses the dictionary or Christensen definition, industry disruptions are either very common or relatively rare. These two entirely different usages explain why there has always been a lot of talk about industry disruption even though, in the Christensen sense, disruption has actually been in a lull in recent years, as blockchains, the Internet of things, self-driving cars, expert systems, etc., have not come close to supplanting existing market systems and leaders. Few economic terms are used so loosely and confusingly, and much of today's ChatGPT disruption talk reflects the fact that both meanings are so well entrenched.

The gap between these two definitions will be especially important over the coming years. If we use the dictionary meaning, Western societies will face massive disruptions during the 2020s—moving away from fossil fuels, electrifying transportation, developing more sustainable products and services, reducing dependencies on China, coping with climate change, potential military conflicts, and more. Virtually all of these challenges are taking place within the physical world, and thus digital technologies are likely to play a secondary role.

But whether these physical world shifts will be disruptive in the Christensen sense remains to be seen. Thus far, incumbent market leaders have responded to changes in the automobile, energy, agricultural, and other markets. However, it's still early in the game, and as Tesla and the Chinese EV-maker BYD have shown, long-term leadership by new Western firms or those from China, India, or elsewhere is entirely possible. One thing is clear: Given that both disruption definitions continue to be widely used, confusion about the extent of industry change won't go away anytime soon. We should all use the term "disruption" more carefully, but we almost certainly won't.

— *DM*

Notes

1. Mary Rasenberger, "How Will Authorship Be Defined in an AI Future?" (The Authors Guild, October 4, 2022), https://authorsguild.org/res ource/how-will-authorship-be-defined-in-an-ai-future/.
2. David Moschella, "Theory Aside, Antitrust Advocates Should Keep Their 'Big Tech' Ambitions Narrow" (ITIF, March 2022), https://itif. org/publications/2022/03/07/theory-aside-antitrust-advocates-should-keep-big-tech-ambitions-narrow/.
3. Cambridge Dictionary, "disruption," accessed online February 28, 2023, https://dictionary.cambridge.org/us/dictionary/english/disrup tion.
4. Clayton Christensen, *The Innovator's Dilemma: When New Technologies Cause Great Firms to Fail* (Cambridge, Massachusetts: Harvard Business School Press, 1997), https://www.amazon.com/Innovators-Dil emma-1st-first/dp/B0076ZFPKW.

Myth 18: Strong Privacy Regulations Spur Digital Adoption

It is often claimed that stronger privacy regulations increase consumer trust in digital technologies, and this increase leads to more technology adoption. However, the evidence shows that the relationship between privacy regulation and consumer trust is not linear, as more regulation doesn't necessarily lead to more trust. Instead, policymakers should aim for regulations that balance privacy protections with the benefits of lower costs and more innovation.

Regulation is a balancing act between limiting potential harm and minimizing detrimental economic impacts. Strict regulation can impose higher compliance costs that create an economic drag, whereas weak regulation may not effectively protect consumers. The EU came down on the stricter side of this balancing act in 2016 when it passed its General Data Protection Regulation (GDPR). Since then, many other jurisdictions around the world have considered or adopted strong, comprehensive privacy regulations of their own, often using GDPR as inspiration.[1]

The arguments for a more targeted approach to privacy regulation point out the higher cost of the GDPR-style approach. The difference between strict and targeted privacy regulation can amount to hundreds of billions of dollars in compliance costs as well as lower productivity and innovation. For example, companies in Europe reported spending an average of $1.3 million on GDPR compliance in the first year after the law passed and were expected to spend an additional $1.8 million in 2018 when the law became enforceable.[2] If a GDPR-style law passed in the United States, ITIF has estimated it could cost the economy $122 billion per year, whereas a more targeted law would cost only $6 billion per year, 95 percent less.[3]

© The Author(s), under exclusive license to Springer Nature
Switzerland AG 2024
R. D. Atkinson and D. Moschella, *Technology Fears and Scapegoats*,
https://doi.org/10.1007/978-3-031-52349-6_19

But supporters of tough privacy regulation respond to criticisms about cost and innovation by claiming that stricter privacy regulation, as well as strong AI regulation, will increase digital adoption by increasing consumer trust in digital technologies and platforms. If consumers know technology is strongly regulated, the logic goes, then they will have more trust in technology and will feel safer using it. If stronger privacy regulation increases adoption, then the economy would benefit.[4] In this way proponents can claim a win–win: strong privacy and strong digital adoption. The fact that this spin lets policymakers and advocates off the hook for any negative effects from tough privacy rules is why it's so popular, trotted out at most forums and meetings on the topic.

Why Does This Matter and Where Did It Come From?

The arguments policymakers use to justify regulation affect the form the regulation takes, which in turn has far-reaching consequences for consumers, businesses, and the economy. By definition, regulation imposes costs on businesses, forcing them to divert resources away from innovation, pass costs onto consumers, or a combination of the two.[5] Less innovation translates to less productivity and economic growth.[6] Targeted privacy regulation that addresses concrete harms would still impose some costs on businesses, but seeks to limit the negative impacts.

The GDPR went above this commonsense baseline, and it was able to do that in part because restoring consumer trust in online services was a major selling point. "Our digital future can only be built on trust," said Andrus Ansip, then-European Commission Vice President for the Digital Single Market, months before the GDPR went into effect in 2018. "Everyone's privacy has to be protected."[7] Many in America share this sentiment. In 2021, leadership of the Senate Committee on Commerce, Science, and Transportation and the House Committee on Energy and Commerce wrote in a letter to President Biden, "Absent much-needed federal data privacy legislation, we risk losing consumers' trust and confidence in the internet marketplace."[8]

If it was in fact true that consumer trust linearly improves with the stringency of privacy regulation, and if that increased trust translated into increased adoption, then the EU would have much more justification for GDPR's strict privacy approach.[9] But the evidence doesn't not support either claim.

Why Is This a Myth?

Before examining the evidence on how privacy regulation affects consumer trust and digital adoption, it is necessary to know how much consumers currently trust digital technologies. It is easy to assume that trust in technology is low, given the ongoing backlash against Big Tech companies and technology in general.[10] The narratives consumers see in the media and hear from government are often pessimistic, overstating the potential harms while glossing over the many benefits.

However, studies of consumer trust in technology do not support these narratives. For example, Edelman surveyed 32,000 consumers in 28 countries in 2023 and found that 75 percent of respondents trusted the technology sector. This number was higher than for any other sector, including education, food and beverage, health care, hospitality, manufacturing, telecommunications, airlines, entertainment, retail, consumer packaged goods, professional services, energy, fashion, and financial services. Notably, however, social media was included as a separate sector. Only 44 percent of respondents trusted social media, lower than any other sector.[11]

In another study, Fleishman-Hillard surveyed adults in seven countries in North America, Europe, and Asia in 2020, and found that 72 percent of respondents trusted in technology companies either "somewhat" or "a great deal."[12] Finally, a 2022 Ipsos survey of nearly 15,000 Internet users in 20 countries found that 63 percent of respondents said they trust the Internet.[13]

These numbers suggest there is not a crisis of consumer trust in digital technologies and platforms, outside of social media. However, the longer-term trend shows that consumer trust in digital technologies and platforms is in decline.[14] So, if there was evidence supporting the argument that strict regulation builds trust, then there might be grounds for it. But there is no such evidence.

Rules vs Trust

If stronger privacy regulation increased consumer trust, then consumer trust would be higher in countries with more regulation. But ITIF analyzed available data on consumer trust in the Internet in 2018 and found that countries with heavy or robust Internet regulation were no more likely than those with limited or moderate regulation to have high levels of trust. In fact, three countries with limited regulation—Indonesia, India, and Pakistan—all had very high levels of trust, close to 90 percent. Japan had the lowest level (57 percent) and China had the highest (91 percent), despite both countries having robust regulation.[15]

Particularly relevant to the U.S. privacy debate are comparisons between consumer trust in EU member states, where the GDPR is in effect, and the United States, which has no comprehensive federal data privacy law. Interestingly, trust levels turn out to be largely the same.[16] The 2020 Fleishman-Hillard study produced similar results from country to country: 67 percent of U.S. respondents trusted technology companies, compared to 65 percent in Germany, 67 percent in Italy, and 63 percent in the UK (which is no longer an EU member state but maintains its implementation of the GDPR).[17]

Differences in consumer trust between countries could be the result of other factors unrelated to regulation, such as cultural differences. But if stronger privacy regulation increases consumer trust, then at the very least consumer trust should be higher in a country after it enacts a strong privacy regulation than before the regulation was in place. To test that proposition, we can turn to measurements of consumer trust in the EU before and after the GDPR went into effect. Six months into GDPR enforcement, European consumers' trust in the Internet was at its lowest level in a decade.[18]

Trust vs Adoption

Nor does existing evidence support the second-order claim that privacy regulation increases digital adoption. In a 2022 survey of American households that do not use the Internet, the National Telecommunications and Information Administration (NTIA) found that the majority, 58 percent, did not use the Internet because they had no interest, and another 18 percent cited affordability as their main concern. Only 2 percent cited privacy and security concerns, meaning that for 98 percent of respondents, stronger privacy regulation is unlikely to convince people to start using the Internet at home.[19]

Comparing Internet usage statistics between countries also reveals the lack of a relationship between strong privacy regulation and Internet adoption. For example, among EU member states, Internet use ranges from 75 to 95 percent of the population. The United States, with 92 percent, is at the higher end of this range.[20] As the NTIA survey illustrates, there are many factors that influence Internet use, but improving access and affordability would have a greater impact than privacy regulation.

That said, while most consumers do not avoid the Internet wholesale because of privacy concerns, some avoid certain online behaviors. In a 2019

Ipsos survey of over 25,000 Internet users in 25 countries, 40 percent of respondents avoided certain Internet sites, 32 percent avoided certain Web applications, 15 percent engaged in fewer financial transactions because of privacy concerns, 12 percent made fewer online purchases, and 11 percent closed a social media account.[21] This indicates the need for some baseline level of privacy and security protections for consumers.

But too much privacy regulation could have the opposite effect that policymakers intend by decreasing adoption. As previously mentioned, more regulation increases the cost of doing business, and some of these costs get passed onto consumers. Since survey data on American households that do not use the Internet shows affordability far outranks privacy as a barrier to adoption, the higher costs that come from regulation could increase the number of consumers who choose not to use certain digital technologies and platforms, especially social media platforms, search engines, and other online services that consumers are used to accessing for free.

Data on consumers' willingness to pay for more data privacy supports this conclusion. In a 2019 survey of over 3,000 U.S. adult Internet users, the Center for Data Innovation found that only 27 percent of respondents wanted online services to collect less of their data if it meant having to pay a monthly subscription fee.[22]

So Where Are We?

Policymakers frequently parrot the argument that stronger digital regulations, including on privacy and AI, will increase consumer trust and digital adoption as a rationale for strict privacy regulations. As seen with GDPR, these initiatives often fail to increase trust but succeed at hindering innovation, as evidence in the decline in venture funding and deals for European start-ups in the year following the GDPR's enactment.[23] This is because their argument is based on myths, not facts.

There is no compelling evidence to prove a relationship between stronger privacy regulation and consumer trust/digital adoption. In fact, there is evidence that consumer trust in technology is not as low as it is often portrayed, that the relationship between privacy regulation and consumer trust is not linear, and that there are many other factors that more strongly influence the adoption and use of digital technologies and platforms.

Rather than following in the EU's footsteps, the United States should pass targeted, comprehensive federal privacy legislation that improves the business environment by preempting a patchwork of state laws, addresses concrete privacy harms by distinguishing between sensitive and nonsensitive personal data, and discourages meritless lawsuits. This reasonable baseline would assuage consumers' most relevant privacy concerns while saving businesses and the economy billions per year.

— *RA*

Notes

1. Jonathan Keane, "From California to Brazil: Europe's privacy laws have created a recipe for the world," (CNBC, April 8, 2021), https://www.cnbc.com/2021/04/08/from-california-to-brazil-gdpr-has-created-recipe-for-the-world.html.
2. IAPP and Ernst & Young, "Annual Governance Report 2018," (IAPP and Ernst & Young, 2018), https://iapp.org/resources/article/iapp-ey-annual-governance-report-2018/.
3. Ashley Johnson and Daniel Castro, "Maintaining a Light-Touch Approach to Data Protection in the United States," (ITIF, August 2022), https://www2.itif.org/2022-light-touch-data-protection.pdf.
4. Thomas Niebel, "ICT and Economic Growth—Comparing Developing, Emerging and Developed Countries," (Centre for European Economic Research, December 2014), https://madoc.bib.uni-mannheim.de/37488/1/dp14117.pdf.
5. Dustin Chambers, Courtney A. Collins, and Alan Krause, "How do federal regulations affect consumer prices? An analysis of the regressive effects of regulation," (Public Choice, 180 2019), https://eprints.whiterose.ac.uk/122980/1/Regulation_PC_wp.pdf.
6. Michael Greenstone and Adam Looney, "A Dozen Economic Facts About Innovation," (The Hamilton Project, August 2011), https://www.brookings.edu/wp-content/uploads/2016/06/08_innovation_greenstone_looney.pdf.
7. Christian Wigand and Melanie Voin, "Commission publishes guidance on upcoming new data protection rules," (European Commission, January 24, 2016), https://ec.europa.eu/commission/presscorner/detail/en/IP_18_386.
8. Roger F. Wicker et al., "Committee Leaders Urge President to Prioritize Data Privacy Legislation," (U.S. Senate Committee on Commerce, Science, and Transportation, July 16, 2021), https://www.commerce.senate.gov/2021/7/committee-leaders-urge-president-to-prioritize-data-privacy-legislation.

9. Eline Chivot and Daniel Castro, "What the Evidence Shows About the Impact of the GDPR After One Year," (Center for Data Innovation, June 2019), http://www2.datainnovation.org/2019-gdpr-one-year.pdf.

10. Robert D. Atkinson et al., "A Policymaker's Guide to the 'Techlash'—What It Is and Why It's a Threat to Growth and Progress," (ITIF, October 2019), https://www2.itif.org/2019-policymakers-guide-techlash.pdf.

11. Tonia E. Ries et al., "2023 Edelman Global Trust Barometer: Global Report," (January 2023), https://edl.mn/3X0QXQE.

12. Sophie Scott, "Techlash 2020: Why the technology sector needs to lean in now on consumer expectations," (Fleishman-Hillard, September 2020), https://fleishmanhillard.com/wp-content/uploads/2021/03/Techlash-2020-Why-the-Technology-Sector-Needs-to-Lean-in-Now-on-Consumer-Expectations.pdf.

13. Ipsos, The New Institute, and the Social Sciences and Humanities Research Council of Canada, "Trust in the Internet," (Ipsos, November 2022), https://www.ipsos.com/sites/default/files/ct/news/documents/2022-11/Trust%20in%20the%20Internet%2C%20Nov%202022.pdf.

14. Ibid.

15. Alan McQuinn and Daniel Castro, "Why Stronger Privacy Regulations Do Not Spur Increased Internet Use," (ITIF, July 2018), https://www2.itif.org/2018-trust-privacy.pdf.

16. Ibid.

17. Scott, "Why the technology sector needs to lean in now on consumer expectations," (Techlash, 2020), https://fleishmanhillard.com/wp-content/uploads/2021/03/Techlash-2020-Why-the-Technology-Sector-Needs-to-Lean-in-Now-on-Consumer-Expectations.pdf.

18. Daniel Castro and Eline Chivot, "The GDPR Was Supposed to Boost Consumer Trust. Has It Succeeded?" (European Views, June 6, 2019), https://www.european-views.com/2019/06/the-gdpr-was-supposed-to-boost-consumer-trust-has-it-succeeded/.

19. National Telecommunications and Information Administration, "Digital Nation Data Explorer," (October 5, 2022), https://ntia.gov/other-publication/2022/digital-nation-data-explorer#sel=privSecMainReason&demo=&pc=prop&disp=chart.

20. "Individuals using the Internet (% of population)," World Bank, accessed July 27, 2023, https://data.worldbank.org/indicator/IT.NET.USER.ZS?view=map.

21. Ipsos et al., "CIGI-Ipsos Global Survey: Internet Security & Trust 2019 Part I & II: Internet Security, Online Privacy & Trust," (Ipsos, 2019), https://www.cigionline.org/sites/default/files/documents/ 2019%20CIGI-Ipsos%20Global%20Survey%20-%20Part%201% 20%26%202%20Internet%20Security%2C%20Online%20Priv acy%20%26%20Trust.pdf.

22. Daniel Castro and Michael McLaughlin, "Few Americans Willing to Pay for Privacy," (Center for Data Innovation, January 16, 2019), https://datainnovation.org/2019/01/survey-few-americans-wil ling-to-pay-for-privacy/.

23. Eline Chivot and Daniel Castro, "What the Evidence Shows About the Impact of the GDPR After One Year," (ITIF, June 2019), https://itif.org/publications/2019/06/17/what-evidence-shows-about-impact-gdpr-after-one-year/.

Myth 19: Big Tech Practices "Data Imperialism" in Emerging Markets

> *If one accepts the premise that data is the "new oil," then it follows that cross-border data flows are simply pipelines for "digital imperialism" or "digital colonialization" from the "global north," chiefly U.S. tech firms, which operate like the digital descendants of the Dutch East India Company. But the reality is the opposite. Digital users in low-income nations benefit from free online services, and tech firms providing those services generate much less revenue than they do from high-income nations. Big Tech operations in less developed nations are not digital imperialism; they're much more like digital aid.*

As the digital economy has grown—and as it has become clear that the major digital players are large U.S. firms—progressives and advocates for developing nations have spun a narrative in which data is "the new oil" and cross-border data flows are an extractive, zero-sum process that benefits rich tech firms over impoverished users in low-income nations. Academics Nick Couldry and Ulises Mejías have articulated this vision of oppressive digital development, writing that:

> if historical colonialism annexed territories, their resources, and the bodies that worked on them, data colonialism's power grab is both simpler and deeper: the capture and control of human life itself through appropriating the data that can be extracted from it for profit.[1]

Framing it as "data imperialism" leads to demands for change. Parminder Jeet Singh, executive director of IT for Change, an Indian NGO in special consultative status with the UN, has stated that American and European efforts to focus on issues like global privacy or trade simply give "globally

R. D. Atkinson and D. Moschella, *Technology Fears and Scapegoats*, https://doi.org/10.1007/978-3-031-52349-6_20

dominant digital interests time and cover to entrench their business models and economic domination globally. It would soon also convert to social, political and cultural domination." For Singh, and others, the ideal policy is "that communities own their data, and national data is a sovereign asset which should be employed for a country's own development."[2]

In this view, users don't get any value from engaging online nor do they have agency to decide what to do online, including whether or not to share their data, or with whom. However, while it is true that the value added to the global economy from data is large, the analogy of colonial extraction is nonsensical. The Internet's ability to connect people, firms, and governments around the world with cloud, search, and other large-scale digital services—at little or no cost to users—is not a plot by the evil "North" to oppress the victims in the "South." It is an innovation that benefits all nations at all levels of development.

In opposing laws and trade deals that enable data flows and digital trade, critics want countries, especially developing ones, to have "policy space" to enact rules in the "public interest"—both of which are code for protectionist tariff and non-tariff barriers to discriminate against foreign tech firms and support local ones, and/or coercive pressures on tech firms to donate money to local causes. While large countries such as India and Brazil might—like China—be able to support their own large data-driven firms, most nations will not.

Mutual Benefits

When U.S. tech companies move data out of a country, they are not exploiting it in a zero-sum interaction—it is win–win for both consumers and producers. Countless people and organizations share data daily via both free and paid services. Users provide information about themselves in exchange for a free service such as email, search, or maps. Meanwhile, firms receive information about the user for advertising or other uses.

The sharing of data—far from being a one-way transaction—is a fundamentally different exchange of value than other economic transactions. Data is non-rivalrous, meaning many different firms can collect, share, and use the same data. When consumers exchange data to access a website, they still have the same data after the transaction as before. This contrasts with oil where if you have a barrel of oil, then I don't.

Those who believe in the data-colonialism myth also ignore the fact that the global Internet creates a huge consumer surplus—the difference between the consumers' willingness to pay for a service and the amount that they actually pay. Researchers have used willingness-to-accept estimates to show that the median U.S. consumer in 2016 valued online search at $14,760 per year and valued the rest of the Internet at $10,937 per year.[3] The reality is that few people would actually pay that much, but it does suggest that the consumer surplus from Internet services is quite large.

To put this surplus in perspective, spending on digital advertising in the United States totaled roughly $240 billion in 2022—some 62 times more than in India, where the figure was around $3.9 billion.[45] On a per capita basis, U.S. ad spending was 293 times greater than in India. Virtually all the value from Google searches, YouTube videos, X tweets, Facebook posts, and more comes from selling ad placement to companies that want to get their messages in front of customers. But despite these vast differences in value, the price and quality of these services is pretty much the same all around the world. Indian users get the same Facebook and Google experience as American users. Yet they contribute far less to support these companies. As such, the digital "North" is actually subsidizing the South.

Data Needs to Flow

Cross-border data flows and digital trade involve large and small firms in every sector of the economy in countries all around the world. From mining and retail to finance and manufacturing, firms that have operations, suppliers, or customers in more than one country rely on data flows. Businesses need data to engage with customers, discern market demand, adapt products and services, operate production systems, manage global workforces, monitor supply chains, support products in the field, and countless other tasks.

There is probably not a single company with operations, suppliers, and customers in more than one nation that does not rely on moving data across international borders. Moreover, no international trade can take place without collecting and sending certain data—such as names, addresses, and billing information—across borders. Opponents of data flows and digital trade seek an economic model where local firms are protected from foreign competition, but this protection would also cut them off from the use of global digital tools, essentially forcing them to remain small players in their home markets.

Likewise, opponents portray digital activity as if the Internet is ungovernable and that a country's laws somehow don't apply online. Academic Julie Cohen sees parallels between the legal justification of "terra nullius," or "no man's land," which countries used to justify colonialism, and the view that data is simply "out there" for firms collect and use, assuming that country laws don't apply online the same way they do offline.[6] But that isn't true. Governments often enact data privacy, cybersecurity, and other laws and regulations to govern the nature of these interactions.

Some 137 countries have enacted laws governing the collection, use, sharing, and protection of personal information.[7] For example, Google, Facebook, etc., must comply with Indian privacy law for the data they collect in India, even if they process that data outside of India.

Maximizing Value

Like other economic inputs—from labor to intellectual property—the value added by data comes when it is used and combined in new and innovative ways. In and of itself, data is not valuable. Nor does forcing firms to store data in a local data center create value. Without the right infrastructure, skills, and regulatory environment, the data is not going to be useful. It sometimes seems that many proponents of the data-colonialism myth prefer to attack U.S. and other foreign tech firms instead of focusing on how they can improve their own digital economies—through infrastructure, digital skills, and a conducive regulatory environment.[8]

Policymakers need to help local residents and firms play bigger roles in the digital economy, not by closing off their markets, but by helping people and firms connect. As new technologies and methods make it easier to collect, store, analyze, and share data, using it to create value has become increasingly important to economic growth, competitiveness, scientific discovery, and social progress. Fears of "data colonialism" or "data imperialism" tend to be proxies for broad opposition to capitalism and global trade. Policymakers should ignore most of these attacks as they distract from the more important task of helping everyone get the most from today's data technologies.

— *RA*

Notes

1. Anri van der Spuy, "Colonising ourselves? An introduction to data colonialism," (LSE, March 2020), https://blogs.lse.ac.uk/medialse/2020/03/19/colonising-ourselves-an-introduction-to-data-colonialism/

2. Parminder Jeet Singh, "Why owning their national data is important for developing countries," (IT for Change, March 2019), https://itforc hange.net/why_owning_their_national_data_is_impt.

3. Erik Brynjolfsson, Avinash Collis, and Felix Eggers, "Using massive online choice experiments to measure changes in well-being," (PNAS, March 2019), https://www.pnas.org/doi/10.1073/pnas.1815663116.

4. "Indian Digital Marketing Market Share, Size, Growth, Analysis: By Type: Email Marketing, Search Engine Optimization (SEO), Blogging and Podcasting, Social Media Marketing, Influencer Marketing, Digital OOH Media, Affiliate Marketing, Others; By End Use; Regional Analysis; Market Dynamics: SWOT Analysis; Competitive Landscape; 2023–2028" Expert Market Research, 2023, https://www.expertmarket research.com/reports/indian-digital-marketing-market

5. "Digital Advertsiing—United States," (Statista, 2023), https://www.sta tista.com/outlook/dmo/digital-advertising/united-states.

6. Julie Cohen, "The Biopolitical Public Domain: the Legal Construction of the Surveillance Economy," *Philosophy & Technology*, vol. 31 (2018), 213–233, https://link.springer.com/article/10.1007/s13 347-017-0258-2; Anja Kovacs and Nayantara Ranganathan, "Data sovereignty, of whom? Limits and suitability of sovereignty frameworks for data in India," (Data Governance Network, November 2020), https://cdn.internetdemocracy.in/idp/assets/downloads/policy/policy-brief-data-sovereignty-of-whom-limits-and-suitability-of-sovere ignty-frameworks-for-data-in-india/Anja-Kovacs-and-Nayantara-Ran ganathan-Policy-brief-Data-sovereignty-for-whom.pdf

7. "Data Protection and Privacy Legislation Worldwide," United Nations Conference on Trade and Development, https://unctad.org/page/data-protection-and-privacy-legislation-worldwide

8. Nigel Cory, "The False Appeal of Data Nationalism: Why the Value of Data Comes From How It's Used, Not Where It's Stored," (ITIF, April 2019), https://itif.org/publications/2019/04/01/false-appeal-data-nationalism-why-value-data-comes-how-its-used-not-where/

Myth 20: Big Data Systems Can't Protect Individual Privacy

Many privacy advocates claim that personal data cannot be used safely in Big Data systems because, despite efforts to make it anonymous, data can be easily re-identified to a specific individual. But modern de-identification methods can result in a very low risk of re-identification, enabling safe, data-driven societal innovation in a wide range of private and public sector fields. The West turns against the use of Big Data analytics at its peril.

We live in a "dumb" world, not a smart one. Sure, we know certain things. But imagine if we knew vastly more; things like the main characteristics of people who get cancer, why some kids do well in school and others don't, and why particular government policies work and others do not. Those and vastly more insights are now possible because of the digital economy and "big data" analysis. But none of the potential benefits will fully emerge if policymakers and the public buy into the myth that the data needed for such analysis can always be linked back to particular individuals and therefore constitutes a major invasion of privacy.

We have privacy regulations to protect consumers from harm, but it is impossible to escape the fact that these protections come with both compliance costs for businesses and broader economic costs as a result of decreased productivity and innovation. So, it's best for regulations to strike a balance between consumer protection and societal value.

One such compromise is exempting de-identified data—data that does not link back to a named individual—from the stronger levels of data protection applied to sensitive personal data. For example, a person's medical records

© The Author(s), under exclusive license to Springer Nature
Switzerland AG 2024
R. D. Atkinson and D. Moschella, *Technology Fears and Scapegoats*,
https://doi.org/10.1007/978-3-031-52349-6_21

could be aggregated and analyzed with millions of other records, but de-identified if their name and specific address is stripped off, with characteristics like gender, year of birth, and state of residence still included.

Forms of de-identified data include anonymized data, in which identifiers that would link the data to an individual are erased or encrypted; pseudonymized data, which replaces identifiers with pseudonyms, and aggregated data, which data holders collect from multiple individuals and combine into one shared dataset. These are all ways to protect individual privacy while still retaining access to the data for analysis.

However, many privacy advocates argue that de-identification doesn't work. They fear that such data can be easily re-identified, linking back to the individuals it came from. If this is true, then society shouldn't aggregate large data files of potentially sensitive information, even if the learning that would result from the data analysis could be enormous, because people's privacy would be violated.

If de-identification is not sufficient to protect individuals' privacy, then policymakers should instead pass other privacy measures—such as opt-in consent, data minimization, and purpose specification requirements—to reduce access to data, limit data sharing, and constrain its use. On the other hand, if de-identification is effective and the risk of re-identification is low, then large amounts of data can be safely analyzed. Society could "have its cake and eat it too." It's a critical issue.

Where Did This Come From?

The idea that de-identified data can be easily re-identified emerged from studies that suggested full or partial re-identification could be possible under certain circumstances. These studies pointed out the risk of "de-identifying" data when a system removes information that directly identifies an individual but fails to remove other characteristics that, on their own or taken together, can link back to that individual.

For example, a 2019 study by researchers from the United Kingdom and Belgium found that 99.98 percent of Americans could be correctly re-identified in any dataset containing 15 demographic attributes. But this is not really saying much. If you list someone's address, gender, age, and birth-date there is a 100 percent chance of correctly identifying them. The real issue is whether a particular data set has enough attributes to have a more than minimal chance of identification.

Such studies, and reporting that overstates the risk of re-identification, have led to the myth that re-identification is easy or even inevitable. Many cite a pithy claim by law professor Paul Ohm, who wrote in 2010 that, "Data can either be useful or perfectly anonymous but never both." Some internet services that use privacy as a selling point also reference this view, including the search engine DuckDuckGo, which wrote in its "Privacy Mythbusting" series that, "The only truly anonymized data is no data."

The myth of easy re-identification has even reached the White House. The Obama administration in its 2014 report on big data stated:

"When data is initially linked to an individual or device, some privacy-protective technology seeks to remove this linkage, or "de-identify" personally identifiable information—but equally effective techniques exist to pull the pieces back together through "re-identification.""

More recently, President Biden mentioned re-identification in his 2022 "Executive Order on Ensuring Robust Consideration of Evolving National Security Risks by the Committee on Foreign Investment in the United States," which states that "advances in technology, combined with access to large data sets, increasingly enable the re-identification or de-anonymization of what once was unidentifiable data."[1]

Why Is This a Myth?

Despite widespread concern fueled by privacy advocates and the media, existing evidence does not support broad, sweeping statements about the ease of re-identification. Moreover, dismissing de-identification as an effective privacy measure has far-reaching consequences for how policymakers regulate privacy and the effects such regulation will have on the economy and society.

It is true that effectively de-identifying data is more complex than simply removing direct identifiers. An individual's name, Social Security Number, or credit card information are all direct identifiers that easily link to that individual. However, a number of other identifiers, called indirect identifiers, can also link to an individual when enough of them are present. For example, data that does not include any direct identifiers of an individual but includes their gender, zip code, and date of birth may still include enough information to link to that individual with a high degree of probability.

It is also true that some forms of data such as mobility data are unique enough to determine which data likely belongs to a specific individual. But this *data trail* on its own is not enough to re-identify the individual. An adversary would need another form of personal data—such as an individual's home address and name, work address, and other frequently visited locations—to match the mobility data trail to the individual. Contrary to privacy advocates' warnings, this identifying information typically is not easy to find. Even the researchers behind the 2013 study on mobility data trails did not go through the process of fully re-identifying the data trails they found, instead only suggesting that it theoretically could be possible.

Neither the existence of indirect identifiers nor the uniqueness of certain forms of data validates the conclusion that re-identifying de-identified data is easy or inevitable, nor does research into how full or partial re-identification could be possible under certain circumstances. Rather, this research informs the best practices for safely de-identifying data by identifying potential weaknesses and other challenges.

Best Practices

One such challenge is whether the data in question is unique, as is the case with mobility data. Highly unique forms of data pose a greater privacy challenge than less unique forms. Fortunately, there are many forms of data that fit this less unique profile—such as gender, age range, education level, and even many health conditions. These pose a very low risk of re-identification.

Data holders can further reduce the risk of re-identification by obfuscating or abstracting unique data. Obfuscation involves replacing real sensitive data with convincing fake data, whereas abstraction involves replacing detailed data with less detailed data, such as replacing an individual's zip code with their home county or just their year of birth. In cases where a highly unique form of data cannot be de-identified without sacrificing data quality, data holders can take additional privacy precautions, such as restricting who can access the data and under what circumstances.

There are cases where it may be easier than it normally would be to re-identify a unique data trail, such as when it belongs to a high-profile individual. This was the case in 1996 when former Massachusetts Governor Bill Weld's hospital medical records were re-identified from publicly available data about voters in Cambridge. However, the technique used to re-identify Weld would not work for the average individual who is not a public figure because most people do not have a story written about them in their local newspaper when they enter the hospital. Furthermore, this case took place before the Health Insurance Portability and Accountability Act (HIPAA) Privacy Rule went into effect in 2002, establishing a national standard for protecting individuals' medical records in the United States. De-identification methods have improved significantly since the 1990s.

In some cases, studies that privacy advocates have cited as evidence that de-identification doesn't work actually show it is effective. For example, a pair of researchers from the University of Texas in 2008 re-identified a few Netflix users in an anonymous dataset of movie ratings by comparing the ratings to the users' public movie ratings on the Internet Movie Database (IMDb). The study also revealed that Netflix had not properly de-identified its users—and yet the researchers were only able to re-identify two users out of the nearly 500,000 whose reviews were included in the dataset.[2]

Policy Implications

It is important for policymakers to understand the reality of de-identification when crafting and enforcing privacy regulations or when supporting the creation of large data sets for analytic purposes. De-identification seeks to strike a balance between protecting individuals' privacy and getting the most out of data collection and analysis. Privacy advocates who spread the myth that re-identifying de-identified data is easy suggest alternatives that fail to strike a similar balance. These include requirements such as opt-in consent, data minimization, and purpose specification, all of which would significantly limit the promise of data innovation.

For example, opt-in consent requirements result in fewer users sharing their data because most users select the default option of not giving consent. Data minimization requires data holders to collect no more data than is necessary to meet specific needs. Finally, purpose specification requires data holders to disclose to users the purposes for which they are collecting data and not use it for any other reason. These are all important limiting factors.

So Where Are We?

In the face of the compelling societal need for data, de-identification is an important tool to ensure innovation while protecting individual privacy. While it is impossible to guarantee that even the best de-identification will work 100 percent of the time, effective de-identification minimizes privacy risks. Current research does not support the conclusion that re-identification is easy or inevitable. Instead, it shows that data holders can continuously

improve their methods of de-identification. The existence of indirect identifiers, the uniqueness of certain forms of data, and the theoretical ability to
link de-identified datasets to datasets that include identifying information are
hurdles to overcome, but not hard limits. De-identification is also not a one-
size-fits-all solution. Different de-identification methods result in different
outcomes, some with a lower risk than others.

The myth that de-identified data can be easily re-identified is unlikely to
disappear from public debate and discussion. Experts must remain vigilant in
denying this myth when and where it arises, and policymakers should avoid
legislating from a position of exaggerated risk, overblown fear, and the misin-
terpretation of industry research. De-identifying data isn't always easy, but in
a wide range of applications it will prove essential and well worth the effort.
—RA

Notes

1. "Executive Order on Ensuring Robust Consideration of Evolving
   National Security Risks by the Committee on Foreign Investment in
   the United States," The White House, September 2022, https://www.
   whitehouse.gov/briefing-room/presidential-actions/2022/09/15/execut
   ive-order-on-ensuring-robust-consideration-of-evolving-national-sec
   urity-risks-by-the-committee-on-foreign-investment-in-the-united-sta
   tes/.
2. Arvind Narayanan and Vitaly Shmatikov, "Robust De-anonymization of
   Large Datasets (How to Break Anonymity of the Netflix Prize Dataset),"
   2008 IEEE Symposium on Security and Privacy (2008), 111–125,
   https://arxiv.org/pdf/cs/0610105.pdf.

Jobs & The Economy

Myth 21: Data Is the New Oil

> The war in Ukraine and the return of persistent inflation have made it clear that energy is still much more important to people's lives than digital data. Given the challenges of climate change, this is unlikely to change during the 2020s.

If only people didn't need to worry about heating their homes, buying food, getting to work, and the overall cost of living. If only modern nations didn't rely on fragile energy supply chains and messy things like plastics, fertilizers, batteries, cement, steel, and internal combustion engines. If only governments didn't feel the need to compete for resources, and worry about their self-sufficiency, resiliency, and economic security. If only we could end pollution, and the climate would just stay the same. Imagine.

We could then live in a world defined more by our mental than our physical needs. We could prioritize having information at our fingertips, personalizing our health care and education, enjoying virtual and augmented realities, exploring the wonders and possibilities of artificial intelligence, and addressing technology's various downsides. We could then say with confidence that data is indeed the new oil, and that the digital economy has superseded the dirty demands of the industrial world.

Maybe someday. But today we can't plausibly say such things. Although AI and large language models show us what a data-driven world might someday look like, the physical world is still pre-eminent, and from food to batteries to military equipment and inflation, it dominates the political agenda. Perhaps the most we can say today is that energy is the new oil. But whether this energy comes from fossil fuels, renewables, or nuclear power, it's uniquely

© The Author(s), under exclusive license to Springer Nature Switzerland AG 2024
R. D. Atkinson and D. Moschella, *Technology Fears and Scapegoats*,
https://doi.org/10.1007/978-3-031-52349-6_22

vital to the modern world. Data doesn't come close in necessity. One can imagine a world where reliable, clean, storable, and inexpensive power is taken as a given, but Putin's horrible war and the growing power of Saudi Arabia, Iran, and other oil states have shown us that this goal won't be achieved anytime soon.

Tempting Similarities

It's easy to see why the data is the new oil meme once spread so widely. The phrase goes back to at least 2006 and is widely credited to the British mathematician and entrepreneur, Clive Humby. It accurately reflects the enthusiasm of the developing Internet economy. Then and now, the parallels are numerous, most prominently the Rockefeller-like wealth and Standard Oil-like market shares within many tech sectors. There is also the general-purpose nature of both oil and information; each provides foundational capabilities for new and existing businesses alike. Then there are the less direct but aesthetically uncanny similarities. Both oil and data need to be extracted and refined. Both can also have negative externalities. Just as fossil fuels can affect the climate and the air we breathe without us necessarily knowing it, data exhaust might potentially harm individuals and society in indirect ways.

As economic analogies go, these are very strong. There are, of course, significant differences, especially the fact that data is non-rivalrous and can be copied perfectly and infinitely at essentially zero marginal cost. But the data is the new oil analogy would be just fine if it were not for the fact that energy/oil is still so much more important. As long as this is the case, data can't be the new oil. As the saying goes, to be the king, you have to beat the king, and the energy king is still standing, arguably as tall as ever.

How might this change? There are two scenarios—one appealing and one not. If the world shifts to energy sources that are clean, abundant, and inexpensive, energy will no longer reign over the global economy, and information technology will very likely take its place. But successfully making such a transition will require a breakthrough in either large-scale power generation or storage, and neither capability is currently in sight. Wind and solar still can't answer the basic question of how a nation meets its 24-hour energy needs when the sun doesn't shine and the wind doesn't blow.

The more troubling, and in the short term more probable, scenario is that the growing tensions between America, China, and Taiwan seriously disrupt the global flow of semiconductors and related technologies. The resulting shortages, rising prices, and stagflation might well resemble the major oil shocks and embargoes of the past. No one wants data to be the new oil in this sense of scarcity and geopolitical conflict, but in light of recent U.S./China technology export restrictions, the possibility is no longer just theoretical.

The New Space Race

The geopolitical tension scenario above suggests that *semiconductors are the new oil* might be the more accurate phrase because chips, even more than data, underlie so much of the global economy, and are more vulnerable to supply-side disruptions. Semiconductors also have strong parallels with oil—essential and diverse applications, supplier dependencies, trade deficits, wealth, power, embargoes, and more. Once again, there are important differences, especially the fact that the same oil companies and countries have been selling basically the same fossil fuel products for many decades. In contrast, the global information technology industry is now intensely competitive. In this sense, it's much more like the space race.

Like the space race, computer design, manufacturing, and usage are important tests of national will, capability, competitiveness, prestige, and even societal model. No one says this about fossil fuels, given that so much of the global supply comes from the Mideast, Russia, Venezuela, and other places that aren't seen as nations to be emulated. When America bested the former Soviet Union in the race to the moon, it said a lot about the merits of two fundamentally different economic systems. If China becomes the world leader in advanced technologies, many will draw a similar conclusion.

Limits to Analogies

Whether one believes that data is the new oil or semiconductors are the new space race, analogies help us see patterns and make sense of complex situations. The data/oil analogy forces us to ask what is really driving the global economy, and this helps us see that data has yet to reach the dominant stage, even as its importance to the economy and quality of life increases. The semiconductor/space race parallel suggests an ongoing nation state competition whose outcome, while not yet clear, could determine global technology leadership for many years to come. However, while analogies can help us frame the past and present, they don't help us predict the future, as history doesn't always repeat itself. Information technologies might power a post-fossil fuel AI-driven economy. But they could also result in OPEC-like shortages, trade wars, and geopolitical tensions. Today's analogies suggest two very different futures: one hopeful, and the other best avoided.

—*DM*

Myth 22: Productivity Gains No Longer Benefit U.S. Workers

It's now conventional wisdom that labor productivity gains no longer benefit U.S. workers in the form of higher wages. If this is true, then economic policy should focus on redistributing wealth, not fostering it. But applying proper analytical methods shows that this claim is false; workers have always benefited from increased productivity, and they continue to today. Governments should make maximizing productivity a central economic policy goal.

Throughout U.S. history, Americans have mostly supported productivity innovations, even when they lead to some worker displacement, because they have understood that productivity increases result in higher wages and living standards. Unfortunately, in recent years a dangerous myth has emerged that productivity and wage growth are now decoupled. Productivity gains are now portrayed by many as a tool for greedy corporations to jack up their profits at the expense of workers. Rather than pursuing tech-led productivity, the dominant narrative now favors redistribution and the protection of existing jobs.

A case in point is a recent analysis by American Compass, a conservative think tank with a focus on "workers, communities, and the national interest," which asserted with a persuasive-looking chart that: "Productivity, Profit, and GDP Have Risen in Lockstep Since the 1960s, While Wages Stagnated."[1] The left is no different. The Economic Policy Institute has written that there has been a "gap between the growth of productivity and that of a typical worker's pay."[2]

Even the political center has jumped on the bandwagon. The Brookings Institution has written that "wages have stagnated in recent decades for typical workers"[3] while the Institute for New Economic Thinking has warned that "the trend toward wage stagnation seems to be particularly strong."[4] Financial Times writer Rana Foroohar agrees, writing that "If tech is driving the 'productivity bandwagon', it's time to hit the brakes" because workers are only being hurt. MIT professors and technology skeptics Daron Acemoglu and Simon Johnson write that "Automation and productivity have multiplied corporate profits."[5]

But as unsettling as these narratives sound, repeating something that is not true does not make it so, and this narrative is simply not true.

Why Does It Matter, and Where Did It Come From?

The emergence of this new "productivity doesn't benefit workers" narrative matters because a range of government policies—from tax policy to science policy to business regulation—affect productivity growth for good or ill. And if the assumption is that the benefits from productivity gains are no longer widely shared, then support for economic growth and technological progress will wither and be replaced by a focus on redistribution and preserving the status quo. Why seek more productivity growth if 90 percent of Americans will see no benefit?

If this myth has a single origin, it is the widely cited work of economists Thomas Piketty and Emanuel Suez, who purported to show in 2014 that U.S. median real income growth declined by 8 percent between 1979 and 2014, a period when labor productivity more than doubled.[6] If this was true, then people would be justified in turning their backs on productivity. But it was not true, as Piketty and Suez themselves recognized several years later.

Why Is This a Myth?

As liberal labor economist Stephen Rose noted in a study for the Urban Institute, the original Piketty and Saez study suffers from a number of serious methodological problems, including looking at individual tax filers rather than households and not including the value of rapidly growing employer-sponsored health insurance.[7]

It turns out that measuring the growth of real incomes, wages, and output per hour (e.g., productivity) is fraught with difficulties and therefore full of often biased assumptions. As Rose notes, different studies get different answers because they use different definitions of income, different price deflators, and different units of analysis. However, there is an internationally agreed upon methodology to measure income growth known as the Canberra method, and while no U.S. study has exactly met this standard, some have come close.[8]

When Rose adjusts for differences using the Canberra method, he estimates that real median income grew 43 percent from 1979 to 2014. The Congressional Budget Office has estimated it was even higher, 51 percent.[9] According to the Atlanta Federal Reserve Bank wage growth tracker, the lower half of the wage distribution saw gains of 3.8 percent per year from 2000 to 2022 compared to 3.5 percent for the top half. And median wage growth grew 1 percent faster for non-whites than for whites.

Even Piketty and Saez (working with Zucman), using a more appropriate methodology, found in 2017 that median income grew by 33 percent, instead of declining by 8 percent.[10] To be sure, this does not mean that income inequality did not grow, too—it did—but 33–51 percent growth in worker incomes is a far cry from an 8 percent decline. However, few people cite the new Piketty work; after all it doesn't support the narrative anymore. Best to stick with the 8 percent decline story.

Into the Data Weeds

Other analysts have come to similar more positive conclusions. Much of this discussion gets into the technical weeds. But that is where the truth lies. Those who have an interest in advancing the myth that productivity and profits grew, and wages did not will tend to gravitate to methods that support this view. At a basic level, they do so by undercounting wage growth and overcounting output (productivity) growth.

First, many studies measure only wage growth, not total compensation growth, which includes healthcare and retirement benefits. As the Federal Reserve Bank of St. Louis has cautioned, "economists long have noted that focusing on average hourly earnings [AHE] rather than total compensation yields an inaccurate picture of labor compensation due to the omission from AHE of employer-provided benefits."[11] Such non-wage compensation has risen as a share of total compensation from around 14 percent in the 1970s to around 19 percent today.[12] Notably, the American Compass does not include non-wage compensation.

Second, studies such as the one from American Compass also include only non-supervisory workers. But there are millions of middle-wage supervisory workers in America and an accurate assessment of wage growth should include them.

Third, the main way redistributionists undercount wage growth is through the price deflator they choose. All monetary measures over time must be adjusted to account for inflation. American Enterprise Institute economist Michael Strain has rightly noted that when comparing wage growth to output growth, the same deflator should be used (the output price index). However, those looking to paint a picture of wages not keeping up with productivity use the consumer price index for wages and the output price index for output.[13] When the same deflator is used for wages and output (producer prices), the divergence shrinks significantly.

Fourth, it matters how productivity is measured. Everyone agrees that productivity is the amount of goods and services produced in the economy (output) for every unit of labor. But not everyone agrees on how to measure this. The studies raising alarms about wage and productivity divergence use gross output because it exaggerates productivity growth. As Strain has written:

> Gross output includes capital depreciation, while net output does not. Since depreciation is not a source of income, net output is the better measure to use when investigating the link between worker compensation and productivity.[14]

When using only wages for production and non-supervisory workers, plus different deflators, plus gross output, American Compass has concluded that wages grew just 1 percent from 1973 to 2012 while productivity grew by 140 percent. Using the appropriate measures, Strain found wages increased 63 percent and productivity increased around 76 percent. To be sure, it would have been better if wages had grown 76 percent, but a 13-percentage point divergence is hardly proof that productivity no longer benefits workers.

Finally, over the last two decades official government statistics have significantly overstated productivity because of how they measure the output of the computer sector. Measurement of output from the computers and electronics industry (NAICS 334) is a particularly tough problem.[15] "Moore's law" has meant that computers get more powerful every year. But when a company makes a computer (or cell phone or other device with a chip in it) that is twice as fast as the one it made two years ago, the Bureau of Economic Analysis (BEA) counts it as if they produced two computers. This is why, according to BEA, the computer and electronics sector increased its real (inflation-adjusted) U.S. output over 5.17 times from 2000 to 2010.

Compare this with electrical equipment, which saw a decline in real output of 12 percent.[16]

It defies logic that the U.S. computer and electronics sector was producing 5.17 times more in the United States, especially as employment in the sector declined by 43 percent, and according to the U.S. Census Bureau the number of units of consumer electronic products shipped from U.S. factories actually fell by 70 percent.[17] When controlling for this huge overstatement of output growth, it appears that manufacturing productivity grew just 32 percent, not the reported 72 percent.

This means that measured output and GDP were about 25 percent less than often claimed.[18] When this is factored in, there is now no divergence between wage and productivity growth using Strain's analysis. Let us say that again: When using the right methods and controlling for statistical mismeasurement, there has been no divergence between productivity growth and wage growth. To the extent that real wage growth has been slow, it's because productivity growth was slow.

Finally, if productivity was growing more than wages, one would expect to see profits growing dramatically. Where else would all this increased output go. And that is what American Compass claims: a whopping 200 percent profit increase. Yet according to BEA, domestic corporate profits were about the same in the late 2010s as they were in the 1970s.[19] This is much more in line with the reality that wages and productivity have more or less kept pace than with the myth that wages are stagnant and profits are going through the roof.

So Where Are We?

One might hope that the prevailing narrative about productivity and wages would reflect the updates that Piketty and Saez have issued and the numerous other studies showing that the median worker still benefits from productivity growth. As John Maynard Keynes once famously stated, "when the facts change, I change my mind." But it would appear we are not all Keynesians today. David Leonhardt, a *New York Times* economic columnist, referencing the 2014 Piketty study, not his revised one, wrote in 2019 that before the 1970s workers enjoyed consistently rising wages, but "profits have soared at the expense of worker pay. The wealth of the median family today is lower than two decades ago."[20] Leonhardt is not an outlier. Despite solid evidence to the contrary, many people have simply made up their minds that productivity doesn't benefit most Americans, and they have turned to redistribution as the only valid economic policy goal.

Why did this pessimistic view become the dominant narrative? One reason is that it seemed to comport with people's selective experiences. For example, college and housing have become less affordable for most workers. But computers, appliances, food, clothing, and many other items have gotten more affordable (with price increases lower than the CPi).[21] However, it's often easier to focus on the more expensive items instead of the cheaper ones.

A second reason is that this narrative is fodder for a growing anti-corporate movement that wants to transform American society into something different: government-managed industries, heavily regulated corporations, and many more small, individually owned businesses. If you can advance the narrative that productivity, especially from large companies, no longer helps the average worker, then there is little to lose from such changes.

Finally, this endlessly repeated myth leads naturally to a policy of redistribution, something an increasingly liberal Democratic Party seeks above all else. If productivity isn't helping average working American households who are struggling with college and housing costs, that opens the door to a social democratic system like the Scandinavian nations had in the 1970s and 1980s, before they rejected it for failing to produce sufficient growth.

The reality is if we want higher-wage growth, then we need faster productivity growth, which has been too low over the last 15 years. That doesn't mean we shouldn't also take other steps, especially increasing the federal minimum wage (which will have the added benefit of spurring more automation of low-wage jobs), reducing the financialization of the economy, and raising taxes on wealthy individuals.[22] But at the end of the day, redistribution is a one-time transfer that will never get bigger. Productivity growth is exponential. As such, it is still the American workers' friend.

—RA

Notes

1. *Rebuilding American Capitalism* (American Compass, June 2023), https://americancompass.org/rebuilding-american-capitalism/responsive-politics/the-american-condition/, 9.
2. Lawrence Mishel, Elise Gould, and Josh Bivens, "Wage Stagnation in Nine Charts" (Economic Policy Institute, January 2015), https://www.epi.org/publication/charting-wage-stagnation/.

3. Jay Shambaugh and Ryan Nunn, "Revitalizing Wage Growth: Policies to Get American Workers a Raise" (Brookings Institute, February 2018), https://www.brookings.edu/articles/revitalizing-wage-growth-policies-to-get-american-workers-a-raise/.

4. Claudia Fontanari and Antonella Palumbo, "Wage Stagnation and Productivity: Challenging the Conventional Analysis" (Institute for New Economic Thinking, July 2022), https://www.ineteconomics.org/perspectives/blog/wage-stagnation-and-productivity-a-fresh-analysis.

5. Daron Acemoglu and Simon Johnson, *Power and Progress: Our 1000-Year Struggle Over Technology & Prosperity* (MIT Press, May 2023), https://shapingwork.mit.edu/power-and-progress/.

6. Stephen Rose, "Sensational, But Wrong: How Piketty & Co. Overstate Inequality in America" (Information Technology and Innovation Foundation, March 2018), https://itif.org/publications/2018/03/05/sensational-wrong-how-piketty-co-overstate-inequality-america/.

7. Stephen Rose, "How Different Studies Measure Income Inequality" (Urban Institute, December 2018), https://www.urban.org/research/publication/how-different-studies-measure-income-inequality.

8. Ibid.

9. Ibid., 3.

10. Ibid.

11. Richard Anderson, "How Well Do wages Follow Productivity Growth?" (St Louis Federal Reserve, Economic Synopses, 2007 Number 7), https://files.stlouisfed.org/files/htdocs/publications/es/07/ES0707.pdf.

12. Michael R. Strain, "The Link Between Wages and Productivity Is Strong" (Aspen Institute *Expanding Economic Opportunity for More Americans*, February 2019), https://www.aei.org/research-products/report/the-link-between-wages-and-productivity-is-strong/, 172.

13. Ibid., 175.

14. Ibid., 173.

15. Susan Houseman, Timothy Bartik, and Timothy Sturgeon, "Measuring Manufacturing: How the Computer and Semiconductor Industries Affect the Numbers and Perceptions" (W.E. Upjohn Institute for Employment Research, January 2014), https://research.upjohn.org/cgi/viewcontent.cgi?article=1226&context=up_workingpapers.

16. Robert Atkinson, "Productivity Growth Still Benefits American Workers; Saying It Doesn't Reduces Support for Technological Innovation" (ITIF, June 2023), https://itif.org/publications/2023/06/27/productivity-growth-still-benefits-american-workers-saying-it-doesnt-reduces-support-for-technology-led-growth/.

17. Robert Atkinson, Luke Stewart, Scott Andes, and Stephen Ezell, "Worse Than the Great Depression: What the Experts Are Missing About American Manufacturing Decline" (ITIF, March 2012), https://itif.org/publications/2012/03/19/worse-great-depression-what-experts-are-missing-about-american-manufacturing/.

18. Ibid.

19. Joe Kennedy, "Monopoly Myths: Is Concentration Leading to Higher Profits?" (ITIF, March 2020), https://itif.org/publications/2020/05/18/monopoly-myths-concentration-leading-higher-profits/.

20. David Leonhardt, "A CEO Who's Scared for America," *New York Times* (March 2019), https://www.nytimes.com/2019/03/31/opinion/peter-georgescu-capitalism.html.

21. "Consumer Price Index," *US Bureau of Labor and Statistics*, https://www.bls.gov/cpi/#:~:text=In%20July%2C%20the%20Consumer%20Price,over%20the%20year%20(NSA).

22. Robert Atkinson, "The Pro-Growth Minimum Wage" (ITIF, June 2018), https://itif.org/publications/2018/06/12/pro-growth-minimum-wage/.

Myth 23: Corporate Profits Are at an All-Time High

In their quest to shrink the role of large corporations in the United States, anticorporate activists claim that corporate profits are an all-time highs. But a closer look shows that this is a myth; profits aren't inexorably increasing. The current antitrust system is sufficient, especially as many proposed changes would do more harm than good.

A growing number of advocates, pundits, and policymakers in recent years have argued that corporate profits are too high and contributing to a variety of social ills, including reduced capital investment, higher prices, and a decrease in the share of national income going to workers.[1] These advocates typically associate corporate growth and profitability with monopolistic abuse stemming from insufficient competition, so to remedy the situation they recommend stronger antitrust enforcement. Some even recommend breaking up large companies just because they are big. For many, the underlying desire is to return America to a small business ideal championed in the early twentieth century by the late U.S. Supreme Court Justice Louis Brandeis.[2]

Why Does This Matter and Where Did It Come From?

The "soaring profits" narrative serves as an impetus to generate public and political pressure to shrink large corporations by enacting stricter antitrust measures or allocating more resources for antitrust enforcement agencies. After all, if profits are soaring, this means that something is out of whack in the U.S. economy, and reducing the size and power of corporations is a sensible solution.

This myth emerged in the 2010s as a core argument of the New Brandeis movement, which sees large corporations as inherently problematic and seeks to "reinvigorate American antitrust laws."[3] To listen to champions and sympathizers of the so-called neo-Brandeisian movement, it would seem there is little debate that corporate profits have risen substantially. Former Clinton administration Labor Secretary Robert Reich wrote that recent changes in the economy have "resulted in higher corporate profits, higher returns for shareholders, and higher pay for top corporate executives and Wall Street bankers—and lower pay and higher prices for most other Americans."[4] Economist Thomas Philippon argues that, "Over the past two decades … profits have outpaced economic growth, and the after-tax profit share has increased to around 10 percent [of GDP]."[5] Channeling this thinking, the Biden White House has declared, "there is evidence that market concentration, as well as profits and markups, are rising across industries."[6]

Indeed, this myth has now become mainstream. Center-left economist Larry Summers concluded in 2017 that "we live in an economy where a few firms can get for themselves massive amounts of profits and persist in their dominant position for years and years."[7] *New York Times* columnist Paul Krugman wrote in 2016 that "profits are at near-record highs."[8] That same year, *The Economist* wrote that, among S&P 500 firms, domestic profits (excluding foreign earnings) were at near-record levels relative to GDP.[9]

Why This Is a Myth?

Most claims that profits are rising tend to focus on trends since the 1980s, but while it is true that corporate profits have trended upward since then as a share of GDP, it is also an oversimplification.

The first mistake many make is lumping together foreign and domestic profits. But to assess the state of domestic competition, one should consider only domestic profits. If profits are higher due to limited domestic competition, this is where it should show up. However, if corporate profits are high due to overseas sales, then the increases should be welcome, especially if U.S. firms are creating new markets or taking market share from foreign competitors. American companies, workers, and shareholders all benefit from that. At the end of the day, any purported lack of competition in overseas markets is a problem for foreign antitrust regulators, not American ones.

In addition, according to the U.S. Bureau of Economic Analysis (BEA) an accurate measure of profits includes adjusting for changes in both the value of inventory and the correct measure of capital consumption. Doing so gives a more accurate picture of corporate profits from an ongoing business.

Importantly, looking at after-tax profits, which Thomas Philippon did, does not control for changes in tax policy, such as the recent reduction in U.S. corporate tax rates in response to foreign governments' twenty years of corporate tax cuts to boost the global competitiveness of their economies. When looking only at pre-tax domestic profits, there is less of an increase. According to data from the BEA, pre-tax total profits as a percentage of GDP rose by 1.4 percentage points, from 12.1 percent in 1997 to 13.5 percent in 2019.[10] Domestic profits increased from 5.8 percent to 7.2 percent. Domestic profits also declined between 2014 and 2019, suggesting the recent increase in profits may be correcting itself.

Second, when we enlarge the timeframe, we find that domestic profits are now significantly lower as a share of GDP than in the 1950s and 1960s, a period of very aggressive antitrust enforcement.[11] During that time, U.S. competition authorities were highly skeptical of mergers that allowed acquirers to gain any increase in market share. For instance, in 1962, the Supreme Court upheld the government's challenge of a merger that would have given the combined entity roughly 5 percent of shoe manufacturing and 10 percent of the retail shoe sales.[12] Four years later, it upheld the government's challenge to a merger of two grocery chains in Los Angeles whose combined market share would have been 7.5 percent.[13] So, pundits are mistaken when they claim that "lax antitrust" is to blame for higher profits.[14]

To be fair, it is likely that some of the decline in domestic profits has been due to corporate profit shifting to lower-tax nations. But certainly not all of it. By 2017, around 44 percent of U.S. S&P 500 companies' profits came from abroad.[15] Moreover, overall profits (domestic and foreign) have been the same or slightly lower compared to the earlier period.[16]

Third, excluding the finance sector further dampens the increase. It is appropriate to do so because profit growth in finance resulted mainly from increased value added (overall industry growth) and new practices (interest differentials and noninterest income).[17] Since this increase in profits is mostly unrelated to concentration and had much more to do with the financialization of the U.S. economy, excluding the sector provides clearer estimates of the existence of excess industry concentration. Adjusted domestic nonfinancial profits increased by only 0.8 percentage points in three decades, from 4.5 percent of GDP in 1990 to 5.3 percent in 2019. This marginal uptick is nowhere near a national crisis.[18]

And there is good reason to believe that even this increase is an overestimate. Specifically, as more business capital is taking the form of intangible assets, such as software, brands, intellectual property, and research, and if this capital is undervalued because of its intangible nature, then measured profits should be rising because costs (including depreciation) are underestimated, not because companies are abusing market power.[19]

Finally, the impact of the slight increase in corporate profits on worker income from the 1970s to the present is actually quite small. If domestic, nonfinancial profits increased at the same rate as worker compensation from 1973 (a year of below-average corporate profits) to 2022 (a year of slightly above-average corporate profits), and the profit reduction went to worker compensation, the latter would increase just 1.7 percent.[20]

Flawed International Comparisons

To reduce corporate profits, some have called for U.S. antitrust to emulate European competition policy by adopting the mantra that "big is bad," systematically opposing mergers, and breaking up big companies.[21] These economists allege that, thanks to its stricter antitrust laws, Europe does not suffer from the same "soaring profits" crisis as the United States.

But when we take a closer look at both regions, we find that profit rates in the United States and Western Europe have been converging over the past decade.[22] According to publicly available datasets from NYU professor Aswath Damodaran, as of 2022, profit rates were within 1 percentage point of each other in both regions.[23] Such a small difference could result from various factors other than market power, including the share of higher-risk, higher-reward industries. But if the United States truly had a significant monopoly problem, as Philippon claims, we would expect significantly higher profit rates in the United States than in Western Europe. But such a claim has no basis.[24]

So Where Are We?

The myth of rising profits has been gaining traction in recent years. It has inspired a new wave of political activism, including the American Economic Liberties Project's May 2023 "Antimonopoly Summit," centered around rising market power, with addresses by FTC Chair Lina Khan, Senator Amy Klobuchar (D-MN), and Transportation Secretary Pete Buttigieg.[25]

Many analysts have also blamed the 2021–2023 inflation surge on corporate profiteering when, in reality, it was driven by supply and demand shocks (e.g., Covid-19 supply chains, Russia's invasion of Ukraine, and a massive federal fiscal stimulus).[26] Headlines decrying the rise in "corporate profits" have become commonplace in major journals like the *New York Times* and *Washington Post*.[27]

The resulting calls to action have led to the appointments of Lina Khan and Jonathan Kanter to the FTC and DOJ. They have both proposed sweeping reforms of antitrust, including merger-guideline reform, jeopardizing America's appeal to high-value-adding industries.[28] Kahn in particular has begun an anti-corporate quest to break up big, successful technology companies like Amazon, Apple, and Google, and to stop mergers involving firms like Meta and Microsoft. President Biden's widely publicized 2021 Executive Order on Promoting Competition in the American Economy aimed to "address the recurrent problem of price gouging."[29] The effect of these changes has been muted, thanks in large part to judicial defeats, and an unwillingness of Congress to fix what is not broken in U.S. antitrust laws.[30] The danger, though, is that such an overhaul is possible in a future if this myth is left unchecked.

Many things can and should be done to help boost incomes of working Americans, including a higher minimum wage and a national productivity policy, but breaking up companies in the hope it will lower profits and by extension prices, while also boosting wages, is fantasy that will only slow economic growth. If the neo-Brandeisians get their way, aggressive antitrust interventions will tend to deprive Americans of low-cost, mass-produced goods as well as stable high-paying jobs.[31] Rather than helping Americans, it will erode their living standards, and put the firms that employ them at greater competitive risk.

—RA

Notes

1. Paul Krugman, "Robber Baron Recessions," *The New York Times* (April 18, 2016), https://www.nytimes.com/2016/04/18/opinion/rob ber-baron-recessions.html; Thomas Philippon, *The Great Reversal: How America Gave Up on Free Markets* (Belkamp Press, 2019).

2. Matt Stoller, *Goliath: The 100-Year War Between Monopoly Power and Democracy* (Simon & Schuster, October 2019); Tim Wu, *The Curse of*

Bigness: Antitrust in the New Gilded Age (Columbia Global Reports, 2018).

3. "Senator Klobuchar Introduces Sweeping Bill to Promote Competition and Improve Antitrust Enforcement," United States Senator Amy Klobuchar Working for the People of Minnesota (February 2021), https://www.klobuchar.senate.gov/public/index.cfm/2021/2/senator-klobuchar-introduces-sweeping-bill-to-promote-competition-and-improve-antitrust-enforcement.

4. Robert Reich, "Why We Must End Upward Pre-Distributions to the Rich," *blog post*, robertreich.org (September 27, 2015), http://robertreich.org/post/129996780230.

5. Thomas Philippon, *The Great Reversal: How America Gave Up on Free Markets* (Harvard University Press, June 2017), 54.

6. Heather Bourshey and Helen Knudsen, "The Importance of Competition for the American Economy," *The White House* (July 2021), https://www.whitehouse.gov/cea/written-materials/2021/07/09/the-importance-of-competition-for-the-american-economy/.

7. Larry Summers, "America Has a Monopoly Problem—and It's Huge," *The Nation* (October 23, 2017), https://www.thenation.com/article/archive/america-has-a-monopoly-problem-and-its-huge/.

8. Paul Krugman, "Monopoly Capitalism is Killing US Economy," *The Irish Times* (April 19, 2016), https://www.irishtimes.com/business/economy/paul-krugman-monopoly-capitalism-is-killing-us-economy-1.2615956.

9. "Too Much of a Good Thing," *The Economist* (March 26, 2016), https://www.economist.com/briefing/2016/03/26/too-much-of-a-good-thing.

10. Bureau of Economic Analysis, National Income and Product Accounts, Table 616, Corporate Profits by Industry. Reported Figures are Adjusted with the GDP Price Deflator, https://apps.bea.gov/iTable/iTable.cfm?reqid=19&step=3&isuri=1&nipa_table_list=53&categories=survey.

11. Ibid.

12. Brown Shoe Co, Inc. v. United States, 370 U.S. 294 (1962).

13. United States v. Von's Grocery Co., 384 U.S. 270 (1966).

14. Marshall Steinbaum et al., "Powerless: How Lax Antitrust and Concentrated Market Power Rig the Economy Against American Workers, Consumers, and Communities" (Roosevelt Institute, March 2018), https://rooseveltinstitute.org/publications/powerless-lax-antitrust-concentrated-market-power-rig-economy-workers-consumers-communities/.

15. Adam Shell, "What's driving America's profits? Overseas demand," *USA Today* (May 3, 2017), https://www.usatoday.com/story/money/markets/2017/05/03/wall-street-earnings/101168864/.

16. Joe Kennedy, "Monopoly Myths: Is Concentration Leading to Higher Profits?" (ITIF, May 2020), https://itif.org/publications/2020/05/18/monopoly-myths-concentration-leading-higher-profits/.

17. Costas Lapavitsas and Ivan Mendieta-Muñoz, "Explaining the Historic Rise in Financial Profits in the US. Economy" (Working Paper, 2017), https://ideas.repec.org/p/soa/wpaper/205.html.

18. "Table 6.16D Corporate Profits by Industry," National Data, National Income and Product Accounts, *Bureau of Economic Analysis*, https://apps.bea.gov/iTable/?reqid=19&step=3&isuri=1&1921=survey&1903=239.

19. Hadi Houalla and Aurelien Portuese, "The Great Revealing: Taking Competition in America and Europe Seriously" (ITIF, May 2023), https://itif.org/publications/2023/05/15/the-great-revealing-taking-competition-in-america-and-europe-seriously/.

20. U.S. Bureau of Economic Analysis, Corporate Profits (June 2023), https://www.bea.gov/data/income-saving/corporate-profits.

21. Thomas Philippon, *The Great Reversal: How America Gave Up on Free Markets* (Harvard University Press, June 2017).

22. Hadi Houalla and Aurelien Portuese, "The Great Revealing: Taking Competition in America and Europe Seriously" (ITIF, May 2023), https://itif.org/publications/2023/05/15/the-great-revealing-taking-competition-in-america-and-europe-seriously/.

23. Aswath Damodaran, "Musings on Markets: Effective Tax Rate by Industry" (Aswath Damodaran, January 2017), https://aswathdamodaran.blogspot.com/2017/01/january-2017-data-update-5-taxing-year.html.

24. Hadi Houalla and Aurelien Portuese, "The Great Revealing: Taking Competition in America and Europe Seriously" (ITIF, May 2023), https://itif.org/publications/2023/05/15/the-great-revealing-taking-competition-in-america-and-europe-seriously/.

25. "2023 Antimonopoly Summit" (American Economic Liberties Project, May 2023), https://www.economicliberties.us/event/2023-anti-monopoly-summit/.

26. Ira Kalish and Michael Wolf, "Global Surge in Inflation" (Deloitte Insights, February 2022), https://www2.deloitte.com/xe/en/insights/economy/is-the-global-surge-in-inflation-here-to-stay.html.

27. Chris Bryant and Andrea Felsted, "We've All Been Way Too Accepting of Inflation," *Washington Post* (April 11, 2023), https://www.washingtonpost.com/business/2023/04/11/inflation-consumers-are-too-passive-about-high-prices-for-cars-flights-hotels/3e2d4800-d820-11ed-aebd-3fd2ac4c460a_story.html; Peter Coy, "Are Large Corporate Profit Margins Causing Inflation?," *The New York Times* (June 22, 2022), https://www.nytimes.com/2022/06/22/opinion/inflation-corporate-profits.html.

28. "Proposed Merger Guidelines Would Be a Radical Shift in U.S. Antitrust Policy if Enacted, Says ITIF" (ITIF, July 2023), https://itif.org/publications/2023/07/19/proposed-merger-guidelines-would-be-a-radical-shift-in-us-antitrust-policy/.

29. President Joe Biden, "Executive Order on Promoting Competition in the American Economy," *The White House* (July 9, 2021), https://www.whitehouse.gov/briefing-room/presidential-actions/2021/07/09/executive-order-on-promoting-competition-in-the-american-economy/.

30. Julie Carlson, "The Meteoric Rise (and Fall) of Lina Khan" (ITIF, June 2022), https://itif.org/publications/2022/06/27/the-meteoric-rise-and-fall-of-lina-khan/.

31. Hadi Houalla, "Concentrated Markets are More Productive" (ITIF, May 2023), https://itif.org/publications/2023/05/10/concentrated-markets-are-more-productive/.

Myth 24: Technology Is Wiping Out the Middle Class

We constantly hear that the American middle class is shrinking, and that technology, particularly automation, is to blame. When this is the prevailing narrative, generating support for robust technology-based productivity becomes much more difficult. The reality is that the share of Americans in the middle class has declined, but mostly because of the expansion of the upper-middle class, the movement of manufacturing jobs offshore, increases in low-skilled immigration, and the rise of single-adult households, not automation.

Much of America's traditional identity is based on the idea of a healthy middle class and the belief that anyone can succeed if they work hard enough. While other nations might have a small elite class that inherits its status, and large masses of poor people with limited opportunities, America has always been different. Growth, as John F. Kennedy famously said, lifts all boats, and all Americans are presumed equal.

But many now reject this view because they no longer believe in the meritocratic ideal of the American Dream, and instead demand that government do much more to promote equality. "National conservatives" like Oren Cass of *American Compass* push the view that the middle class has eroded, as do many on the left. Radicals push it even more.

In an article in the socialist magazine *Jacobin*, Goran Therborn wrote that "The middle classes of the Global North are losing their privileged status in the face of automation, casualization, and downward social mobility. Socialists must find ways to mobilize these hard-pressed middle-class layers in a struggle against today's financialized capitalism."[1] He went on to claim that: "The task is to convince the middle class—or substantial parts of it—of the

© The Author(s), under exclusive license to Springer Nature Switzerland AG 2024
R. D. Atkinson and D. Moschella, *Technology Fears and Scapegoats*,
https://doi.org/10.1007/978-3-031-52349-6_25

advantages of equality and human solidarity over neo-pharaonic privileges and rewards for capital and its children."[2]

The core of these critiques is not just that the middle class has been decimated and the rich have taken its wealth, it's that technology is largely to blame. Perhaps the most prominent advocate of this is MIT economist Daron Acemoglu, who argues that the growth in income inequality is due to automation impacting lower-wage jobs more than higher-wage ones, leading to excess lower-wage workers, which in turn lowers wages even further.[3] Acemoglu and Pascua Restrepo have written that automation technologies "reduce overall labor demand because they are displacing workers from the tasks they were previously performing" and that this reduced demand reduces wages.[4] Keynesian economist Robert Skidelsky agrees:

> How long will it take those headed for redundancy to up-skill sufficiently to complement the ever-improving machines? And, pending their up-skilling, won't they swell the competition for lousy jobs?... without collective action to control the pace and type of innovation, a new serfdom beckons.[5]

But these notions are wrong. First, while middle-class jobs have declined, the trends haven't been what most people think. As labor economist Stephen Rose has noted:

> The Pew Research Center and the OECD define middle income as including those with incomes that are between 75 to 200% of median income. From 1971 and 2015, they found that the middle had shrunk by 11 percentage points—61 to 50%. This shrinkage implies a negative outcome but was driven mostly by movement out of the middle class into the high income group (up 7 points), rather than movement out of the middle class into the low income group (up 4 points).[6]

In other words, most of the people being pushed out of the middle class have risen into the upper-middle class. In his analysis of U.S. Census data, Rose identifies five income groups: Poor and Near-Poor (PNP), Lower Middle Class (LMC), Core Middle Class (CMC), Upper Middle Class (UMC), and Rich. The Core Middle Class had an income of between 250 and 499 percent of poverty ($50,000 to $99,999, in 2014 dollars).[7] Census data show that all five income classes saw real income growth from 1979 to 2019, with each ascending step having a slightly higher percentage gain. Rose finds that indeed, the core middle class has declined as a share of all households, from 39 percent in 1979 to 31 percent in 2019. But over the same period the upper-middle class, making between $100,000 and $349,999 in 2014 dollars, increased much more, from 13 to 37 percent of households.

When examining U.S. Census data, American Enterprise Institute economist Mark Perry found similar results, writing:

> Over the last half-century, the share of US households earning incomes of $100,000 or more (in 2020 dollars) has more than tripled. ... At the same time, the share of middle-income households earning $35,000 to $100,000 (in 2020 dollars) has decreased over time, from more than half of US households in 1967 (53.9%) to only 40.3% in 2020. Likewise, the share of low-income households earning $35,000 or less (in 2020 dollars) has decreased from more than one-third of households in 1967 (35.2%) to only slightly more than one in four US households last year (26.2%).[8]

Using an occupation-based definition of class, a study by the European Commission found similar results, with the U.S. upper-middle-class and middle-class households growing 11.6 and 6.1 percent between 1979 and 2019, while the low-skilled working class and skilled working class declining by 8.7 and 9 percent.[9] The Commission concluded:

> There has been no middle-class squeeze over the last decades, neither in terms of employment nor income. In the 1980s and early 1990s, the middle and upper-middle class were still outnumbered by the skilled and low-skilled working class in the six large Western countries that we studied. Yet over the last four decades, the relative sizes shifted as job opportunities expanded for managers, professionals and technicians, while they declined for laborers, assemblers, craft workers and clerks. The ranks of the (upper-) middle class swelled by 10 to 20 percentage points, while those of the working class decreased to the same extent.[10]

The reality is that technological change and automation have boosted labor productivity and created a larger economy, which is why a Congressional Budget Office study found real income gains of more than 50 percent in recent decades.[11] All income groupings got richer, although unfortunately more of the gains (70 percent) went to the upper-middle class and the rich. In absolute terms, the size of the poor, the lower middle class, and the core middle class has shrunk.

Immigration and Household Shifts

There is another reason why the *automation shrank the middle-class* narrative is wrong. If automation eliminated more middle-skill, middle-wage jobs, then the demand for lower-skill jobs should have increased. In fact, it has not materially changed. Jobs requiring a college degree increased from 22 percent of all jobs in 1998 to 24.5 percent in 2022. Jobs requiring only short-term or moderate-term on-the-job training remained constant at 53 percent.[12] This, despite the loss of millions of non-college manufacturing jobs to China, Mexico, and other offshore locations.

Low-skilled immigration has also been a major factor. The number of foreign-born Americans with less than a college degree rose from 9 million in the mid-1970s to 37 million in 2018, a huge boost in less-skilled workers.[13] Of course, many Hispanic immigrants have a college degree, but roughly 80 percent do not, and the number of Hispanic-led households increased 93 percent from 2000 to 2022, compared to an increase of 5 percent of non-Hispanic white-alone households.[14] The latter households earned 29 percent more than the former.[15] This huge increase in relatively low-skill immigration has clearly increased the number of lower-income households.

A less discussed reason for the decline of the middle class is the decline of two-adult households. In 1980, over 75 percent of U.S. households were headed by two adults. But by 2020, it was only about 60 percent. As the Federal Reserve Bank of Cleveland observed:

> On average, individuals are less likely to live with a cohabitating partner in 2018 than they were in 1980. Households headed by two adults tend to have a higher household income and often benefit from shared living expenses and division of household responsibilities. Therefore, the rising share of households having only one adult may have reduced median income growth even within the demographic middle class.[16]

When the Cleveland Fed controlled for this factor, it found that households headed by two persons saw real median income gains from around $67,000 in 1980 to $85,000 in 2017. Clearly the rise of single-adult households tends to increase the need for work such as cleaning, fast food, child care, and other relatively low-paid work that used to be done more within households. This means that much of today's inequality problem is not an economic issue; it's a social one.

Winners Take More

Finally, if automation is the main driver of inequality, then why did inequality actually decline during the 1950s and 1960s when automation-based productivity was at its peak, then grow after 1981, when productivity increased at less than half the earlier rate? The reality, as the left-wing Economic Policy Institute has found, is that inequality did not increase as a result of jobs in middle-wage occupations being eliminated by productivity gains.[17]

Rather, much of the increase in inequality was *within* occupations, with some individuals making winner-take-all incomes within the same occupation. For example, in 1980, basketball star Julius Erving earned about $4 million a year in salary (in 2022 dollars). In 2022, Lebron James earned $47 million. Lebron did not make 12 times more than Dr. J because of automation. Such inequality is not caused by robots, it is caused by the 0.1 percenters gaining an increasing share of national and industry income, a pattern now seen in many economic sectors.[18] Automation didn't create and can't solve the 0.1 percent problem—unless robots somehow put more hedge fund managers out of work!

—RA

Notes

1. Goran Therbron, "The Left Must Appeal to a Middle Class Squeezed by Capitalism" (Jacobin, March 2021), https://jacobin.com/2021/03/middle-class-decline-capitalism-1-percent.
2. Ibid.
3. Daron Acemoglu and Pascual Restrepo, "Tasks, Automation, and the Rise in US Wage Inequality," NBER Working Paper 28920 (June 2021), https://doi.org/10.3386/w28920.
4. Daron Acemoglu and Pascual Restrepo, "The Wrong Kind of AI" (Technology, Academics, Policy, December 21, 2018), http://www.techpolicy.com/Blog/December-2018/The-Wrong-Kind-of-AI.aspx.
5. Robert Skidelsky, "The AI Road to Serfdom?" (*Project Syndicate*, February 21, 2019), https://www.project-syndicate.org/commentary/automation-may-not-boost-worker-income-by-robert-skidelsky-2019-02.
6. Stephen Rose, "Not Your Father's Middle Class" (The Liberal Patriot, July 2023), https://www.liberalpatriot.com/p/not-your-fathers-middle-class.

7. Ibid.

8. Mark Perry, "Animated Chart of the Day: America's Middle-class is Disappearing... but It's Because They're Moving Up, NOT Down!" (AEI, September 2021), https://www.aei.org/carpe-diem/animated-chart-of-the-day-americas-middle-class-is-disappearing-but-its-bec ause-theyre-moving-up-not-down-2/.

9. "The Myth of the Middle Class Squeeze: Employment and Income by Class in Six Western Countries," 19802020, JRC Working Papers Series on Social Classes in the Digital Age (July 2023), https://joint-res earch-centre.ec.europa.eu/system/files/2023-04/JRC131515_Myth_ of_middle_class_squeeze.pdf.

10. Ibid.

11. "The Distribution of Household Income, 2016" (Congressional Budget Office, July 2019), https://www.cbo.gov/system/files/2019-07/ 55413-CBO-distribution-of-household-income-2016.pdf.

12. Michael Handel, "Dynamics of Occupational Change: Implications for the Occupational Requirements Survey" (Bureau of Labor Statistics, July 2016), https://www.bls.gov/ors/research/sample-design/ pdf/dynamics-occupational-change-2016.pdf. And calculations from Table 1.7 Occupational projections, 2022–2032, and worker characteristics, 2022, https://www.bls.gov/emp/tables/fastest-declining-occ upations.htm; and table 5.2, https://www.bls.gov/emp/documenta tion/education-training-system.htm.

13. Abby Budiman, "Facts of US immigrants, 2018" (Pew Research Center, August 2020), https://www.pewresearch.org/hispanic/2020/ 08/20/facts-on-u-s-immigrants/.

14. "Census Bureau Releases New Educational Attainment Data" (United States Census Bureau, February 2023), https://www.census.gov/new sroom/press-releases/2023/educational-attainment-data.html.

15. Gloria Guzman and Melissa Kollar, "Income in the United States: 2022: Table A-2. Households by Total Money Income, Race, and Hispanic Origin of Householder: 1967 to 2022" (United States Census Bureau, September 2023), https://www.census.gov/data/tables/ 2023/demo/income-poverty/p60-279.html.

16. Emily Dohram and Bruce Fallick, "Is the Middle Class Worse Off Than It Used to Be?" (Federal Reserve Bank of Cleveland, Economic Commentary, March 2020), https://www.clevelandfed.org/en/public ations/economic-commentary/2020/ec-202003-is-middle-class-worse-off.

17. Josh Bivens and Lawrence Mishel, *Understanding the Historic Divergence Between Productivity and a Typical Worker's Pay: Why It Matters and Why It's Real* (Economic Policy Institute, September 2, 2015), https://www.epi.org/publication/understanding-the-historic-diverg ence-between-productivity-and-a-typical-workers-pay-why-it-matters- and-why-its-real/.

18. Ibid.

Myth 25: AI Will Lead to the End of Work

Artificial intelligence is so powerful that it can do virtually anything, including replacing most peoples' jobs. Or at least that's what many pundits and experts would have us believe. But by stoking unfounded fears about massive unemployment, they are pushing policymakers and companies to slow the spread of technologies the West desperately needs to sustain competitiveness and raise productivity and wages.

Despite U.S. labor productivity growth and unemployment rates both being near all-time lows, the prevailing narrative now is that technology, especially artificial intelligence (AI), will destroy work. A much-ballyhooed 2013 study by Oxford University researchers Carl Benedikt Frey and Michael Osborne set the tone when it trumpeted the jarring conclusion that 47 percent of U.S. employment was at risk of job loss from new technology.[1]

Indeed, it is almost impossible to read an article on technology and job loss without seeing this study quoted. A typical headline screamed, "Is AI Coming for Your Job? 65% of Workers Are Worried."[2] (Presumably the other 35 percent didn't listen to the news telling them they should be worried.) Silicon Valley gadfly Vivek Wadhwa became an even more full-throated Luddite when he predicted in 2017 that 80–90 percent of jobs will be eliminated by 2030.[3] We are about half-way there as we write this, and his prediction looks to be a bit extreme.

Nonetheless, even a leading technologist like Elon Musk has speculated that all jobs will eventually be eliminated: "AI will make jobs kind of pointless. Probably the last job that will remain will be writing AI software, and then eventually the AI will just write its own software."[4] Even AI "thinks"

© The Author(s), under exclusive license to Springer Nature
Switzerland AG 2024
R. D. Atkinson and D. Moschella, *Technology Fears and Scapegoats*,
https://doi.org/10.1007/978-3-031-52349-6_26

it will kill jobs. When one study asked ChatGPT to list the downsides for workers, it wrote: "Job Losses: One of the potential downsides of AI is that it could lead to increased unemployment as machines begin to replace human workers in a variety of industries."[5]

Of course, the ChatGPT wasn't actually thinking; it was simply regurgitating articles scraped from the Internet, and most articles addressing the issue had this bias. Seemingly everyone agrees that AI and related technologies will cause massive unemployment. To many, the only solution will be putting the lumpenproletariat on the dole (i.e., universal basic income).

Fueling Resistance

The problem with this fear mongering—besides the fact that it is not true—is that it fuels the flames of opposition to technological progress. Indeed, a host of commentators have called for slowing the pace of technological change. Former British Labor Party Leader Jeremy Corbin, Microsoft founder Bill Gates, Senator Bernie Sanders, New York Times columnist Eduardo Porter, and San Francisco City Supervisor Jane Kim have called for taxes on robots. Former New York mayor and presidential candidate Bill DeBlasio has even called for a Federal Automation and Worker Protection Agency from which companies would be required to get a permit in order to automate. A *Vox* article in March 2023 was titled "The case for slowing down AI."[6] Indeed, Musk and other techno-luminaries seekers signed a statement in 2023 calling for a 6-month moratorium on AI research.[7] Even scholars at MIT, a place that used to stand for technological innovation, have issued calls for a robot tax.[8] It's as if a collective panic has swept over a large share of the knowledge class elites.

Such fears are greatly vastly exaggerated. First, AI is not magic, and there are a vast array of things it cannot do. Modern-day Luddites get caught up in the hype of new technologies and overstate their impact. Many assume that we are heading to a transformative "fourth industrial revolution" the likes of which the world has never seen. Economists Berg, Buffie, and Zanna reflect this view writing in a *Forbes*, "The premise of this paper is that we are in the midst of a technological inflection point, a new 'machine age' in which artificial intelligence and robots are rapidly developing the capacity to do the cognitive as well as physical work of large fractions of the labor force."[9]

Alas, that does not seem to be the case. Yes, AI program Dall-E can generate cool pictures, but it can't create a robot that lays carpet.[10] Yes, ChatGPT helped me write a toast for my son's wedding, but it can't take care of people in a hospital. Human work is incredibly complex, and there are a vast arrays of tasks AI and robots simply cannot do: build a road, fight a fire, repair plumbing, be a fashion model, install a hot tub, be a steward on an airline, run a school, harvest crops, and so much more. This is why past predictions of tech-based job losses have always fallen on their face.

Impact on Specific Jobs

Let's revisit Osborne and Frey's dystopian forecast. They scored more than 600 specific occupations—from healthcare workers, to carpet installers, to telemarketers—on a scale from 1 to 100. The higher the score, the greater the chance that computers and software will automate the job. That's how they came up with their "47 percent of jobs will be destroyed" estimate. But as of 2023 the U.S. economy has added 16 million jobs since 2013, with the unemployment rate averaging just 3.6 percent in 2022, and was still around that level as we write this, hardly a sign of job loss? Maybe the robots were striking for higher pay?

In fact, the occupation Osborne and Frey told us had the highest risk of going the way of the buggy-whip manufacturer—insurance underwriters—actually saw employment grow 16.4 percent from 2013 to the end of 2021. In contrast, the occupation least likely to be automated—recreational therapists—saw a job decline of 8.9 percent. Overall, there was a modest negative correlation between the predicted risk of job loss from computerization and actual job loss but it was quite modest at 0.26. In other words, occupations that had a higher-risk score in Osborne and Frey's analysis were only slightly more likely to see job loss, suggesting that computerization (or now "AIization") is not the corrosive job killer that they suggest.

The reason is simple: Machine learning and even large language models are just software. Better than anything we have had before, to be sure. But there are limits to what they can do. But that doesn't stop many from crying wolf. As MIT professor and CEO of Rethink Robotics, Rodney Brooks observed, "Misled by suitcase words, people are making category errors in fungibility of capabilities—category errors comparable to seeing the rise of more efficient internal combustion engines and jumping to the conclusion that warp drives are just around the corner."[11] Beam me up, Scotty.

There's No Lump of Labor

Job loss predictions always seem to assume that there is only so much work to do. But this is obviously a false reading of the process of technological change as it fails to include second-order effects whereby the savings from increased productivity are recycled into the economy in the form of increased demand that in turn creates other jobs.

Consider an insurance firm that can use AI to handle many customer service functions now performed by humans. Let's imagine that the technology is so good that the firm can do the same amount of work with 50 percent less labor. Some workers might take on new tasks but others might be laid off or lost through attrition. Either way, the company's insurance services now costs less to provide. If customers can spend less on insurance they can spend more on other things, like vacations, eating out at restaurants, or getting a gym membership.

This is why most scholarly studies find no net negative effect on employment—and some have even found a positive relationship, with increases in productivity leading to more jobs. An OECD study summed it up, "Historically, the income-generating effects of new technologies have proved more powerful than the labor-displacing effects: technological progress has been accompanied not only by higher output and productivity, but also by higher overall employment."[12] In addition, America's most productive years have been followed by years of lowest unemployment. The McKinsey Global Institute looked at annual employment and productivity change from 1929 to 2009 and found that increases in productivity were correlated with increases—not declines—in employment growth.[13]

Moreover, the idea that technology will lead to fewer jobs is simply not borne out by the evidence. For hundreds of years technology has eliminated jobs (e.g., buggy-whip makers), but it has also created new jobs (e.g., automobile mechanics) and boosted living standards, which have resulted in more demand for workers doing needed tasks (building houses, educating people, selling goods, etc.).

Since 1900, U.S. productivity has increased by around sevenfold: In other words, the average worker in 2023 produces more in an hour than the average worker in 1900 produced in almost a full day. But the unemployment rate today is no higher than back then. Indeed, from 1850 to 2023, employment grew at same rate as the labor force. That's because all those farmers, elevator operators, bowling pin setters, horse stable workers, and others found jobs doing other things. That's not to say that we can't have occasional periods of excess unemployment when the economy is in a recession, but the long-term pattern shows no decline in employment whatsoever.

Infinite Unmet Needs

But what if we run out of things to want to buy? Once again, we can relax. Human needs are far from being satisfied. Ask the average American household today if they would have any problem spending extra money if their incomes increased, and you can pretty much guarantee that most, except for a few simple-living hippies, would say, "No problem; show me the money." People would go on more vacations, go to more concerts, afford better health care, eat out more, eat healthier more expensive foods, send their kids to college, save more for retirement, and pay higher taxes to help beautify our cities and towns, lower class sizes in schools, provide universal health care, and buy more expensive, cleaner energy.[14] Because our needs are so vast, it is farfetched to believe that technology, even AI, will meet all of our wants and needs.

None of this is to say the United States shouldn't do more to prepare workers, especially lower-skilled workers, for transitions into new jobs and occupations. It is a problem that our K-12 schools and universities significantly underperform in their job of ensuring students have the skills they need to thrive, and both employers and the federal government have cut funding for worker training. Moreover, for workers who do get laid off because of technology, the U.S. unemployment insurance system is often too parsimonious, depending on what state you are in. But those are relatively manageable problems that policymakers can solve—given political will and creativity.

One solution we should all reject is universal basic income (UBI). A UBI would only increase unemployment rates, while making the already-massive national debt even worse. Moreover, if the payments are high enough to provide real income security, the program would boost the unemployment rate as many workers would simply take the money instead of focusing on finding job opportunities. And the longer people stay unemployed, the higher the risk that their skills will atrophy.[15] It's the wrong path forward.

Another *solution* that should be rejected is limiting AI to only complementing workers, not replacing them. It has become a common refrain among AI ethicists that using AI to replace a worker is bad. As Princeton professor Janet Vertesi has written: "Replacement raises red flags for AI ethics."[16] This is why for a number of years the National Science Foundation only supported research on robotics that would not replace workers. Would these skeptics have thought that Brunswick bowling pin setters or automatic elevators were unethical because they replaced workers? AI developers should stick to computer science, not economics.

The most important step governments should take to respond to AI and automation is to promote more of it, especially given the steep fall in U.S. productivity growth. After all, why should society choose less efficient ways of producing goods and services if there are more efficient ones available? It would be like rejecting rural delivery drones to remote areas because package delivery jobs would be lost. We need a national technology-based productivity strategy to speed up automation throughout the entire economy, including an investment tax credit on new machinery and equipment.

Finally, it's time to take a deep breath and stop panicking about artificial intelligence and what it portends for jobs. No, AI will not destroy more jobs than it creates. No, the pace of technological and societal change isn't accelerating. Yes, AI and related technologies might boost the rate of labor productivity by a percentage point or two a year, and gradually help boost incomes for all workers. As has happened with pretty much every major technological advance, the economic benefits will greatly outweigh the downsides.

—RA

Notes

1. Carl Benedikt Frey and Michael Osborne, "The Future of Employment: How Susceptible Are Jobs to Computerization" (Oxford Martin Programme on the Impact of Future Technology's "Machines and Employment" workshop, 2013), https://www.oxfordmartin.ox.ac.uk/downloads/academic/The_Future_of_Employment.pdf.
2. Brenden Rearick, "Is AI Coming for Your Job? 65% of Workers Are Worried" (Money, June 2023), https://money.com/ai-job-loss-worker-concerns/.
3. Rob Lever, "Tech World Debate on Robots and Jobs Heats Up" (Phys.org, March 2017), https://phys.org/news/2017-03-tech-world-debate-robots-jobs.html.
4. Abrar Al-Heeti, "Elon Musk Says AI Will Make Jobs Irrelevant" (CNET, August 2019), https://www.cnet.com/science/elon-musk-says-ai-will-make-jobs-irrelevant/.

5. "The Impact of Artificial Intelligence on the Future Work-forces in the European Union and the United States of America" (An economic study prepared in response to the US-EU Trade and Technology Council Inaugural Joint Statement, December 2022), https://www.whitehouse.gov/wp-content/uploads/2022/12/TTC-EC-CEA-AI-Report-12052022-1.pdf, 16.
6. Sigal Samuel, "The Case for Slowing Down AL" (Vox, March 2023), https://www.vox.com/the-highlight/23621198/artificial-intelligence-chatgpt-openai-existential-risk-china-ai-safety-technology.
7. Chris Westfall, "Elon Musk and Other Tech Leaders Call for Slow-down on AI Developments," *Forbes* (March 2023), https://www.forbes.com/sites/chriswestfall/2023/03/29/elon-musk-and-other-tech-leaders-call-for-slowdown-on-ai-development.
8. Peter Dizikes, "Should We Tax Robots?" *MIT News*, December 2022, https://news.mit.edu/2022/robot-tax-income-inequality-1221; https://techcrunch.com/2023/09/02/should-the-us-implement-a-robot-tax/.
9. Carl Benedikt Frey and Michael A Osborne, "The Future of Employment: How Susceptible Are Jobs to Computerisation?" (Oxford University, September 2013), http://wwwoxfordmartin.ox.ac.uk/downloads/academic/The_Future_of_Employment.pdf.
10. OpenAI, "DALL-E: Creating Images from Text," https://openai.com/research/dall-e.
11. Rodney A Brooks, "2015: What Do You Think About Machines That Think?" (Edge, 2015), https://www.edge.org/response-detail/26057.
12. "The OECD Jobs Study: Facts Analysis, Strategies (1994)" (OECD), https://www.oecd.org/els/emp/1941679.pdf, 261.
13. "Jobs Lost, Job Gained: Workforce Transitions in a Time of Automation" (McKinsey Global Institute, December 2017), https://www.mckinsey.com/~/media/BAB489A30B724BECB5DEDC41E9BB9FAC.ashx.
14. Catherine Collins, "8 Things the Rich Spend Money on That Poor and Middle Class People Don't," *Yahoo Finance*, November 10, 2023, https://finance.yahoo.com/amphtml/news/8-things-rich-spend-money-200117237.html.
15. Johannes Schmieder, Till von Wachter, and Stefan Bender, "The Causal Effect of Unemployment Duration on Wages: Evidence from Unemployment Insurance Extensions" (National Bureau of Economic Research, October 2014) https://www.nber.org/papers/w19772.

16. The Conversation, "Why NASA's Mars Rover Could Inspire a More Ethical Future for AI," *Fast Company*, September 2023, https://www.fastcompany.com/90956177/nasa-mars-rovers-artificial-intelligence-ethics.

Myth 26: Digital Copying Is Victimless

Since the earliest days of the digital economy, many have claimed that making and sharing copies of books, music, movies, software, and other digital content is "fair use" and all part of the new economy where "information wants to be free." The reality is that violating copyrights is a form of theft that seriously harms the digital ecosystem.

Nearly ubiquitous broadband and mobile Internet access coupled with cheap data storage have propelled the growth of digital content, but have also enabled digital piracy to flourish around the world. Piracy is the unauthorized copying and distribution of music, movies, television programs, software, video games, books, and photos. It is often quick and easy. Unfortunately, many critics of copyright law believe that most piracy is a "victimless crime." They are wrong.

Piracy defenders still recycle the same baseless claims that copying unlicensed software or getting movies or music from unlicensed streaming or so-called file-sharing services is victimless. They claim that people who steal software and content aren't real customers, thus nothing is lost; they say that people steal content because they can't access the content at a price they can afford, and that copying only affects the rich (e.g., big movie studios and software firms). Some even argue that piracy eventually leads to *more* content purchases. All of these ideas are both wrong and misguided, as if the price or creator of a product justifies stealing it online, even though that clearly would not be the case offline.[1] These narratives imply that governments shouldn't really worry about stopping digital piracy.

© The Author(s), under exclusive license to Springer Nature Switzerland AG 2024

R. D. Atkinson and D. Moschella, *Technology Fears and Scapegoats*, https://doi.org/10.1007/978-3-031-52349-6_27

Lawrence Lessig summed up this view when he said "Copying—for a digital network—is like breathing to us."[2] This is why he can write an essay entitled "In Defense of Piracy."[3] I wonder if Larry would like you to only read pirated versions of his 15 books.[4]

But it's not just academics who hold the view that it's okay for users instead of creators to decide how works are used, advocacy groups like the Library Copyright Alliance do as well. An association that has as one of its two members the American Library Association, which recently elected as its president an avowed Marxist,[5] claims that "online infringement no longer poses an existential threat to the content industries, to the extent it ever did."[6] This is like saying that "shrinkage" (retail store theft) no longer poses an existential threat to retailers because its "only" about $95 billion a year.[7]

Research continues to show that piracy remains rampant. For example, one study by Akamai estimated that global piracy that there were 3.7 billion visits to websites offering unlicensed access to movies and television shows, through a browser, mobile application, or downloads between January and September 2021.[8]

Creators, artists, and developers invest considerable effort and resources into producing software, music, movies, books, and other creative works. They depend on the revenue generated from selling these products to sustain their livelihoods and continue producing new content. However, as the saying goes, "It's hard to compete with free." Illegally copying software or copyrighted content deprives creators of their rightful income. It also impacts the many people that support them, such as technicians, engineers, song writers, producers, and myriad other administrative and support staff.

This financial loss can be substantial, especially in the digital age where illegal content can spread rapidly online around the world, making it challenging (if not impossible) for creators to address all instances of piracy. But even if digital piracy had no financial impact on creators, that still doesn't make it ethical. If I go on vacation and someone breaks into my house to live in while I am gone, it doesn't necessarily affect me economically, but it is still unethical and illegal.

Common Justifications

For many years the "free content" critics claimed that they pirate content because they can't access the content they want. For example, the Electronic Frontier Foundation (EFF) argues that "Infringement went down when the industry (Hollywood) adapted and gave people what they wanted: convenient, affordable, and legal alternatives. But recently, corporations have given up on affordability and convenience."[9] Really? Spotify? Apple Music? Netflix? Amazon Prime movies? There are now more than 140 legitimate video streaming services providing a range of content at different prices; consumers have never had so many legal options.

But this gets at a key, and disingenuous, tactic of anti-IP opponents: They demand perfection in order to justify their "communal" views. For them, it's always Hollywood's fault. They should let more content be copied. They make too much money. They don't give enough legal choices. It's all a smoke screen for the fact that many such critics do not see intellectual property as about the balance between access and protection. Absolute access is the ultimate goal.

Real Damage

Piracy sites divert users who might otherwise use legal streaming services like Netflix, HBO, Disney, Hulu, and Amazon. It remains prevalent around the world.[10] Studies of legal injunctions that block user access to the major piracy sites show that they divert users from piracy to legal content sites.[11] A 2016 United Kingdom study showed that blocking access to 53 major piracy sites caused a 10 percent increase in user visits to legal ad-supported streaming sites such as the United Kingdom's BBC and Channel 5.[12] It also caused an estimated 6 percent increase in visits to paid legal subscription-based streaming sites such as Netflix. This is similar to the 12 percent increase in visits to subscription-based sites in an earlier 2013 study.[13] These studies disprove the argument that people who engage in piracy aren't real customers since they would never pay for the content anyway.

Piracy apologists act as if the economic evidence about the impact of piracy is mixed, but it isn't. After 20-plus years of research and debates, with near unanimity, the peer-reviewed literature confirms what many advocates for content creators and software developers have been claiming for years—that online piracy harms both creators and consumers.[14] The creative industry is a significant employer, encompassing a wide range of professionals, including artists, writers, designers, developers, editors, and more. A 2019 United States Patent and Trademark Office (USPTO) study estimates copyright-intensive industries accounted for $1.3 trillion of U.S. economic activity and 6.6 million jobs.[15] Also, a 2019 study of online video piracy estimated that it cost $29.2 billion in lost U.S. revenues, 230,000 lost American jobs, and $47.5 billion in reduced GDP.[16]

Piracy apologists try to justify the "victimless" nature of piracy by saying that it only hurts major movie studios and software firms, and that's fine as they're big and "rich." Indicative of this, EFF states that "Illegal downloading and streaming are not the cause of Hollywood's woes. They're a symptom of a system that is broken for everyone except the few mega corporations and the billionaires at the top of them."[17] But a firm's size should not justify piracy.

Even worse, these apologists ignore the fact that piracy also affects small businesses and independent creators who have fewer resources to combat the illegal copying of their work. For example, in 2017, the National Endowment for the Arts reported that there are approximately 2.5 million artists in the American workforce and that nearly 35 percent were self-employed.[18] The task facing small firms and independent creators in their fight against piracy is daunting given the volume and reach of online infringement. Without an affordable, accessible, and effective set of legal tools to fight digital piracy, it is essentially impossible for small firms and independent creators to defend their work online.

Piracy also hurts law-abiding consumers who in effect have to pay higher prices to compensate for those who prefer to steal. Perhaps most importantly, society is especially hurt by unlicensed content and software as it often lacks the necessary updates, patches, and support, opening the door to malware, viruses, and other cybersecurity threats.

Similarly, we often hear that piracy is done by otherwise law-abiding individuals, but this is simply not true.[19] Not only is piracy not victimless, it directly supports criminals.[20] The majority of piracy websites are in it for one reason: to make money, often by showing ads directing consumers to other shady sites that often load malware on their devices.[21] For example, the owners of The Pirate Bay, a notorious online clearinghouse for unlicensed content, were earning $3 million a year, according to Swedish prosecutors.[22] U.S. law enforcement stated that one of the world's most popular piracy sites—KickassTorrents—was making $16 million annually from advertising.[23]

The Importance of Copyright

At the highest level, digital piracy harms society by reducing the economic incentives for investment in creative and innovative outputs.[24] That's why America's Founders included the so-called Copyright Clause in the U.S.

Constitution: "To promote the Progress of Science and useful Arts, by securing for limited Times to Authors and Inventors the exclusive Right to their respective Writings and Discoveries." The Founders knew that innovation is driven, in no small part, by the potential for financial gain. Creators and businesses invest in research and development and creative endeavors because they anticipate a return on their investment.

Piracy discourages investment in new technologies and creative works as the incentives are either reduced or eliminated. It also hurts the ability of content producers to create legitimate business models for selling digital content and undermines the incentive for companies to invest in user experience improvements, customer support, and ongoing updates for software and digital services. If creators can't profit from their creations, why would they invest time and resources into developing new and better products, business models, and services?

Ultimately, there is no reason for piracy web sites to exist: They should be shut down or blocked and their owners prosecuted. Online piracy is nothing more than digital looting. Rationalizations that they're not really stealing, and no one is any worse off need to be finally put to rest. These spurious arguments distract from good faith efforts to enact and enforce better laws and regulations to protect and promote creative individuals and firms. While there is no "silver bullet" that will solve the piracy problem, there are many actions that can reduce it. This is where policymakers should focus, not on the bogus arguments that anti-IP proponents have been peddling for decades.

—RA

Notes

1. "The Ethics of Piracy" (Stanford University), https://cs.stanford.edu/people/eroberts/cs181/projects/software-piracy/ethical.html; "What Does 'Piracy Is Not a Victimless Crime' Mean? Who Are the Victims?" *Quora*, https://www.quora.com/What-does-piracy-is-not-a-victimless-crime-mean-Who-are-the-victims; Peter Sunde, "The Pirate Bay's: It's Evolution, Stupid," *Wired*, February 2021, https://www.wired.co.uk/article/peter-sunde-evolution; "Is Downloading Really Stealing? The Ethics of Digital Piracy," *The Conversation*, https://theconversation.com/is-downloading-really-stealing-the-ethics-of-digital-piracy-39930.

2. Lawrence Lessig, "The Code of Privacy," Proceedings of the American Philosophical Society, vol. 151(3) (September 2007), 283.

3. Lawrence Lessig, "In Defense of Piracy," *Wall Street Journal*, October 2008, http://saeta.physics.hmc.edu/courses/h1/uploads/Main/Lessig.pdf.

4. Lawrence Lessig, https://www.amazon.com/stores/Lawrence-Lessig/author/B001HCW3ZK.

5. Tyler Kingkade, "Top Librarian Calls 'Marxist Lesbian' Tweet Backlash 'Regrettable'," *NBC News*, August 2023, https://www.nbcnews.com/news/us-news/american-library-association-president-marxist-lesbian-rcna98254.

6. Jonathan Band, "Library Copyright Alliance Statement of Interest in Participating in Consultations Concerning Technical Measures," *Regulations*, February 2022, https://www.regulations.gov/comment/COLC-2021-0009-4898.

7. "NRF Reports Retail Shrink Nearly a $100B Problem," *National Retail Federation*, September 2022, https://nrf.com/media-center/press-releases/nrf-reports-retail-shrink-nearly-100b-problem.

8. "The High Stakes of Innovation: Attack Trends in Financial Services," Akami, 2023, https://www.akamai.com/our-thinking/the-state-of-the-internet.

9. Katharine Trendacosta, "Hollywood's Insistence on New Draconian Copyright Rules Is Not About Protecting Artists" (Electric Frontier Foundation, September 2022), https://www.eff.org/deeplinks/2022/09/hollywoods-insistence-new-draconian-copyright-rules-not-about-protecting-artists; Mike Masnick, "Senators Leahy & Tillis to Team Up to Suggest Destroying the Internet for Hollywood's Sake," *Techdirt*, March 2022, https://www.techdirt.com/2022/03/21/senators-leahy-tillis-to-team-up-to-suggest-destroying-the-internet-for-hollywoods-sake/.

10. "Theme Report," Motion Picture Association, 2019, https://www.motionpictures.org/wp-content/uploads/2020/03/MPA-THEME-2019.pdf.

11. Brett Danaher, et al., "The Effect of Piracy Website Blocking on Consumer Behavior" (SSRN, August 2019), https://papers.ssrn.com/sol3/papers.cfm?abstract_id=2612063.

12. The analysis of the results for access to ad-support and subscription video services was based on an analysis of coefficients from a regression analysis and showed that the estimate for the change in access to ad-supported video site was measured with 95 percent confidence, while the estimate for access to subscription services was measured with 75 percent confidence.

13. The study into the website blocks of 2013 did not have data on visits to ad-supported legal content sites.

14. Michael Smith, "The Truth About Piracy" (Technology Policy Institute, February 2016), https://techpolicyinstitute.org/publications/int ellectual-property/copyright-and-piracy/the-truth-about-piracy/.

15. Andrew Toole, et al., "Intellectual Property and the US Economy: Third Edition," United States Patent and Trademark Office, March 2022, https://www.uspto.gov/ip-policy/economic-research/int ellectual-property-and-us-economy.

16. David Blackburn, Jeffrey Eisenach, and David Harrison, "Impacts of Digital Video Piracy on the US Economy" (Global Innovation Policy Center, June 2019), https://www.theglobalipcenter.com/wp-content/ uploads/2019/06/Digital-Video-Piracy.pdf.

17. Katharine Trendacosta, "Hollywood's Insistence on New Draconian Copyright Rules Is Not About Protecting Artists" (Electronic Frontier Foundation, September 2022), https://www.eff.org/deeplinks/2022/ 09/hollywoods-insistence-new-draconian-copyright-rules-not-about-protecting-artists.

18. "Artists and Other Cultural Workers: A Statistical Portrait" (National Endowment for the Arts, April 2019), https://www.arts.gov/sites/def ault/files/Artists_and_Other_Cultural_Workers.pdf.

19. Ardi Janjeva, Alexandria Reid, and Anton Moiseienko, "Taking the Profit Out of Intellectual Property Crime: Piracy and Organised Crime" (RUSI March 2021), https://rusi.org/explore-our-research/ publications/whitehall-reports/taking-profit-out-intellectual-property-crime-piracy-and-organised-crime; Gregory Treverton, et al., "Film Piracy and Its Connection to Organized Crime and Terrorism" (RAND, 2009), https://www.rand.org/pubs/research_briefs/RB9417. html.

20. "At a Glance: Taking the Profit Out of Intellectual Property Crime" (RUSI, March 2021), https://ik.imagekit.io/e0tlm8mqux/stage/s3fs-public/2021-04/whr_ip_crime_aag_web_version.pdf.

21. Michael Smith and Rahul Telang, "Piracy and Malware: There's No Free Lunch" (Technology Policy Institute, March 2018), https://tec hpolicyinstitute.org/2018/03/13/piracy-and-malware-theres-no-free-lunch/.

22. Ernesto Van der Sar, "Pirate Bay Admins Charged with Assisting Copyright Infringement," *Torrent Freak*, January 2018, https://torrentfreak. com/pirate-bay-team-charged-080131/.

23. United States v. Artem Valum, Criminal Complaint, July 2016, https://www.justice.gov/usao-ndil/file/877591/download.

24. Brett Danaher and Michael Smith, "Digital Piracy, Film Quality, and Social Welfare," George Mason Law Review, vol. 24(4), 2017, https://www.cmu.edu/entertainment-analytics/documents/impact-of-piracy-on-sales-and-creativity/digital-pirac-film-quality.pdf.

Myth 27: U.S. Broadband Lags Behind Other Developed Nations

As part of a long-standing crusade to establish government-managed broadband networks, or at least turn private providers into regulated utilities, anticorporate advocates have spread the view that, compared to other modern nations, America's private-sector broadband networks are too slow, expensive, and/or scarce. The data shows that these claims are false.

Ever since Samuel Morse developed the telegraph in 1848, mass communications in America—telegraph, telephone, television, radio, cable TV, wireless telephony, and now broadband Internet—have been provided almost exclusively by the private sector.[1] Sometimes, as was the case with telephony, it has been via a regulated monopoly, but more often, services are offered by multiple companies competing with each other. This contrasts with many nations, where—at least until recently—communications networks have often been operated by government-run corporations.

But even though most Americans have supported the private-sector-led model, there have always been opponents.[2] For example, in the 1890s, the Populist Party ran on a plank of nationalizing railroads along with the telegraph and telephone systems.[3]

Similarly, in the last few decades (in part because of the generous foundation funding for progressive advocacy groups and think tanks), the calls have grown louder for government ownership—or at least a reversion to regulated monopolies. Accompanying this push has been a concerted effort to depict current U.S. broadband as severely lacking. After all, if it ain't broke, why fix it?

© The Author(s), under exclusive license to Springer Nature Switzerland AG 2024
R. D. Atkinson and D. Moschella, *Technology Fears and Scapegoats*,
https://doi.org/10.1007/978-3-031-52349-6_28

In straining to make the case for greater government involvement, these advocates claim that U.S. broadband prices are too high, speeds too low, and service too limited, particularly in neighborhoods with marginalized subsets of the population. If only there were more competition ("competition" here functioning as a codeword for the government building competing broadband networks) or regulation (turning broadband into a public utility), all would be well.

One of the leading advocacy groups against business-run broadband is Free Press, an organization founded by professor Robert McChesney, who wrote in the Marxist journal *Monthly Review* that "any serious effort to reform the media system would have to necessarily be a part of a revolutionary program to overthrow the capitalist political economy."[4] Progressive academic Susan Crawford claims that "American Internet service is falling behind other nations because cable companies have such dominance in many markets."[5] And fueled by misleading analyses from anti-corporate groups like the Open Technology Institute, popular news sources now routinely repeat that claim that "people in the U.S. pay more for slower internet than [their] counterparts" in peer nations.[6]

Conveniently, these problems often come with a ready-made solution: government-owned broadband networks. Advocates argue that "community-led broadband is the best option for promoting economic prosperity, improving quality of life, and ensuring access for everyone across income and background."[7] If only the government-owned and operated broadband networks, every home in America would be wired at gigabit-per-second speeds with extremely low prices. But if prices were actually low, it would only be because consumers would be paying in their role as taxpayers providing subsidies.

Competitive Speeds

But in their ideological opposition to corporations, and even capitalism, advocates paint a dark picture—and a misleading one—of U.S. broadband performance. They start with broadband speeds, claiming that U.S. speeds lag those of other nations, particularly those whose governments either provide the service or regulate a monopoly provider.

The reality is quite different. Until March, 2024, the Federal Communications Commission (FCC) defines broadband as a reliable connection to speeds of at least 25 Mbps down and 3 Mbps up (25/3).[8] That makes U.S. broadband comfortably fast: By the end of 2022, broadband at 100/

20 (including fixed and licensed fixed wireless networks) passed 90 percent of households.[9] Networks reaching 250/25 covered 87 percent.[10] On the wireless front, high-speed 5G—which can hit 100 Mbps down—reached 62 percent of the population in 2022.[11] By 2022, 55 percent of subscribers were in the 200 to 400 Mbps download speed tier.[12]

With robust high-speed deployment and high levels of adoption—plus the fact that U.S. providers often exceed their advertised speeds—U.S. broadband services consistently rank near the top of international speed tests.[13] As of August 2023, the U.S. fixed average was 6th highest in Ookla's Speedtest Global Index, at 210 Mbps download—Singapore, in first place, was only slightly faster at 255 Mbps down.[14] The U.S. mobile average meanwhile comes in 19th place at a solid 85 Mbps download speed, compared to the median speed of 31 Mbps.[15]

For comparison, the bandwidth needed for a high-quality Zoom call is 3 Mbps down and 3.8 up.[16] Streaming Netflix in Ultra HD requires a minimum of 15 Mbps down.[17] In short, even the way broadband is often used today—for multiple users and multiple connected devices—U.S. speeds generally exceed everyday households' usage requirements, often substantially.

Reasonable Prices

But the myth of low speeds is just one of the charges critics level against the U.S. private-sector broadband system. The other main critique is that U.S. prices, and by definition profits, are unreasonably high compared to other countries. Price is a complicated topic, but the reality is that U.S. broadband prices are not inordinately high. Analyses that rank them poorly often fail to normalize for national income, or compare different plans, clouding assessments of the global broadband marketplace.[18]

In analyses that *do* attempt to normalize for country-level differences, U.S. broadband ranks quite well. The FCC's Communications Marketplace Report has, over two iterations, ranked U.S. fixed prices among the cheapest of over two dozen offerings when quality and demand-side factors are accounted for.[19] An Oxford Economics study in 2022 found U.S. mobile prices were similarly affordable relative to other countries' plans.[20]

To the extent that U.S. prices are higher than those in some other countries, different broadband cost structures play the biggest role.[21] The fact that only Australia and Canada have more suburban and exurban geography than the United States means that it costs broadband providers a lot more to wire the average U.S. household than it does in more densely populated places like

Singapore, Korea, Japan, and most of Europe. Wiring a 20-story apartment complex in Seoul is vastly cheaper than wiring 200 houses spread across a remote part of Wyoming, and overall prices often reflect that.

Moreover, if U.S. prices were unreasonably high because of a lack of competition, then U.S. broadband providers' profits would be inordinately high. But to the contrary, U.S. providers' profits are solidly unremarkable. Net margins for U.S. cable TV and wireless providers are lower than the average market margins for all publicly traded U.S. corporations, and profits for the telephone industry are just 4 percentage points higher.[22]

Average U.S. broadband providers' profits from 2019 to 2022 were only a bit higher than those in Europe (8.4 percent vs. 6.5 percent) where there is mandated unbundling to create more competition.[23] U.S. mobile providers' profit margins were 16 percent below those of European providers.[24] Moreover, prices for broadband services offered by municipal broadband networks are not much lower than those of U.S. private-sector providers, despite the fact that municipal providers do not pay taxes.[25]

Additionally, U.S. broadband isn't untethered from global norms or from other goods in the way that we would expect if there were rampant monopoly pricing. The International Telecommunication Union (ITU) benchmarks broadband prices against an affordability limit of 2 percent of gross national income per capita (GNIpc), and U.S. prices for fixed and mobile broadband service come in at 0.9 and 0.7 percent of GNIpc, respectively.[26] The U.S. fixed average is even somewhat cheaper than average for high-income countries in the ITU dataset. Some broadband prices have even managed to buck the economic trend and *decreased* in the face of inflation.[27]

This is not to say that U.S. broadband service is cheap—and it is certainly true that some households find it unaffordable—but the evidence suggests that prices are about as low as they can sustainably be without some additional revenue source, and U.S. customers are getting quite a bit of bang for their buck. Moreover, U.S. deployment generally outpaces Europe's, where service competition has broadened the pool of competitors; U.S. 5G coverage, for example, hit 93 percent of the population in 2021, far ahead of the European average (62 percent).[28] Overall U.S. adoption rates are squarely in line with those in the European Union.[29]

Real Competition

Finally, critics of the U.S. broadband market see more competition as the magic elixir. But in fact, broadband competition is adequate. The United States is certainly a concentrated broadband market, but not among the global frontrunners. The majority of U.S. households are in areas passed by at least two options for broadband reaching 100 Mbps download.[30]

Out of 11 economies included in a recent global broadband assessment, the U.S. mobile market ranks right in the middle of the pack, according to the Herfindahl–Hirschman index (which assigns higher scores to more concentrated markets).[31] For context, the United States rates lower than Japan, Singapore, and Korea; it ranks higher than the United Kingdom.[32] And emerging broadband technologies, like Elon Musk's Starlink satellite broadband and new 5G fixed wireless offerings, are now providing even more competition to incumbent providers.

Contrary to what we often hear, concentration is not the opposite of competition, and competition doesn't always correlate with consumer welfare. In some industries with certain qualities, fewer firms can actually do a better job serving consumers while providing more benefits to all.

The market structure of broadband argues against maximizing competition at all costs.[33] Some competition is certainly necessary to keep down prices and ensure quality, but it does not follow that more firms are always better. For one, a firm interested in providing broadband must invest significant resources upfront, which means it is highly motivated to attract and retain customers.[34] An industry with high fixed costs can therefore generate fierce competition even among a few firms.[35]

Second, broadband is characterized by scale economies: Since the marginal costs of providing broadband decrease as firm size increases, providers naturally grow and therefore become more efficient, which benefits consumers.[36] Third, there are negative repercussions to overbuilding—i.e., building broadband infrastructure where it already exists—which is what happens when too many providers compete for one population of customers. In the long term, fewer customers supporting a broadband network with large upfront costs will tend to raise prices, not lower them. It also might come full circle—push some firms out of business altogether, leaving the same number of competitors as before, but wasting resources along the way.

There is solid evidence that there is not always a one-to-one correlation between competition and consumer welfare, particularly in the broadband marketplace. Average mobile speeds in the United States are faster than those in, for example, Italy, India, and the U.K., all of which are less concentrated according to the Herfindahl–Hirschman index.[37] Meanwhile, South Korea and Singapore, both technological frontrunners, are fairly concentrated.[38]

The current U.S. model has also encouraged technological advancements and improvements leading to real intermodal competition—namely, the convergence of the fixed, mobile, and satellite industries. 5G is capable of speeds rivaling wireline, and T-Mobile's fixed wireless offering is the fastest-growing home broadband service in the United States.[39] Low-earth-orbit (LEO) satellite solves most of the speed and latency issues of its satellite forerunners and now can offer a viable form of service in the most expensive-to-serve places.[40] And growing pressure from a variety of new entrants, including fixed wireless providers, led wired broadband providers to invest $86 billion in new infrastructure in 2021, the largest amount in 20 years.[41]

A Healthy Situation

In short, the U.S. private-sector-led, intermodal broadband system is healthy. The two areas where there are challenges—lack of adequate broadband in rural areas, and limited broadband adoption among low-income households—are not problems that nationalizing broadband companies would directly solve. Congress is addressing the first problem with the $70 billion lawmakers appropriated for rural broadband deployment in the recent bipartisan infrastructure law.

To address the second challenge, Congress should reform the current Universal Service Fund by shrinking its redundant hodgepodge of federal broadband programs and using that funding to increase the Affordable Connectivity Program (ACP), which is the single most effective broadband access program because it provides direct, flexible support to individuals who need it.[42]

In short, the evidence shows that America's private-sector model has created a healthy and competitive U.S. broadband industry that will only get stronger if policymakers work with it, not against it. Today's false claims about speeds, costs, and availability point policy in the wrong direction, and the various proposed remedies would fail to improve today's largely satisfactory broadband situation.

—RA

Notes

1. Carleton Mabee, "Samuel F.B. Morse," Britannica, updated July 24, 2023, https://www.britannica.com/biography/Samuel-F-B-Morse.
2. Michael A. Janson and Christopher S. Yoo, "The Wires Go to War: The U.S. Experiment with Government Ownership of the Telephone System During World War I," *Texas Law Review*, vol. 91 (2013), 983, Univ. of Pennsylvania Institute for Law and Economics, Research Paper Series, No. 13–14, TRPC: 2012, https://papers.ssrn.com/sol3/papers.cfm?abstract_id=2033124.
3. Many populists considered railroads and telegraph systems to be natural monopolies that needed heavy regulation, or even public ownership. Source: "Another Feature of our Platform," cartoon of the Omaha Platform, Populist Cartoons, Missouri State University courses, accessed August 2023, https://courses.missouristate.edu/bobmiller/Populism/pcartoon/pcartoon17.htm.
4. Robert W. McChesney, "The U.S. Media Reform Movement: Going Forward," Monthly Review, September 2008, https://monthlyreview.org/2008/09/01/the-u-s-media-reform-movement-going-forward/.
5. "Author: When It Comes to High-Speed Internet, U.S. 'Falling Way Behind'," *NPR: All Tech Considered*, February 2014, https://www.npr.org/sections/alltechconsidered/2014/02/06/272480919/when-it-comes-to-high-speed-internet-u-s-falling-way-behind.
6. Charlotte Morabito, "People in the U.S. Pay More for Slower Internet Than European, Canadian, and Asian Counterparts, According to the Open Technology Institute," *CNBC*, October 2021, https://www.cnbc.com/2021/10/06/heres-why-high-speed-internet-is-so-expensive-in-the-us.html.
7. Institute for Local Self-Reliance, Community Networks, "Our Vision," accessed July 2023, https://communitynets.org/content/our-vision.
8. Tyler Cooper, "The FCC Definition of Broadband: Analysis and History," BroadbandNow, updated May 8, 2023, https://BroadbandNow.com/report/fcc-broadband-definition/.
9. Federal Communications Commission, FCC National Broadband Map, Area Summary, last updated July 2023, https://broadbandmap.fcc.gov/area-summary/fixed?version=dec2022&zoom=4&br=r&speed=25_3&tech=1_2_3_7.
10. Ibid.
11. Jessica Dine and Joe Kane, "The State of US Broadband in 2022: Reassessing the Whole Picture" (ITIF, December 2022), https://itif.org/publications/2022/12/05/state-of-us-broadband-in-2022-reassessing-the-whole-picture/.

12. Jessica Dine and Joe Kane, "Broadband Myths: Is U.S. Broadband Service Slow?" (ITIF, January 2023), https://itif.org/publications/2023/01/11/broadband-myths-is-us-broadband-service-slow/.

13. Ibid.

14. Ookla, Speedtest Global Index, Median Country Speeds August 2023, accessed September 2023, https://www.speedtest.net/global-index.

15. Ibid.

16. Zoom Support, "Zoom System Requirements: Windows, macOS, Linux," last updated February 17, 2023, https://support.zoom.us/hc/en-us/articles/201362023-Zoom-system-requirements-Windows-macOS-Linux.

17. Netflix Help Center, "Internet Connection Speed Recommendations," accessed July 2023, https://help.netflix.com/en/node/306?ba=Swifty peResultClick&q=speed%20requirements.

18. Doug Brake and Alexandra Bruer, "Broadband Myths: Are High Broadband Prices Holding Back Adoption?" (ITIF, February 2021), https://itif.org/publications/2021/02/08/broadband-myths-are-high-broadband-prices-holding-back-adoption/.

19. *2020 Communications Marketplace Report*, Appendix G: International Broadband Data Report Appendices (Washington, DC: FCC, December 2020), Docket No. 20–60, https://www.fcc.gov/document/fcc-releases-2020-communications-marketplace-report; *2022 Communications Marketplace Report*, Appendix G: International Broadband Data Report (Washington, DC: FCC, December 2022), Docket No. 22–203, https://www.fcc.gov/document/2022-communications-marketplace-report; https://www.fcc.gov/reports-research/reports/consolidated-communications-marketplace-reports/CMR-2022.

20. Oxford Economics, "Unpacking the Cost of Mobile Broadband Across Countries" (Oxford, November 2022), https://www.oxfordeconomics.com/wp-content/uploads/2022/11/CTIA-Oxford_Economics_Report-Cost_of_Mobile_Broadband.pdf, 9.

21. Jessica Dine and Robert D. Atkinson, "Apples vs. Oranges: Why Providing Broadband in the United States Costs More Than in Europe" (ITIF, July 2022), https://itif.org/publications/2022/07/11/apples-vs-oranges-why-providing-broadband-in-the-united-states-costs-more-than-in-europe/.

22. Aswath Damodaran, "Damodaran Online," Margins by Sector (US), data as of January 2023, https://pages.stern.nyu.edu/~adamodar/New_Home_Page/datafile/margin.html.

23. Damodaran, "Damodaran Online," Data: Archived, Operating and Net Margins by Industry Sector, updated January 2022, https://pages.stern.nyu.edu/~adamodar/New_Home_Page/datacurrent.html.

24. "Damodaran Online," Data: Current, Operating and Net Margins by Industry Sector, updated January 2023, https://pages.stern.nyu.edu/~adamodar/New_Home_Page/datacurrent.html.

25. Doug Brake and Alexandra Bruer, "Broadband Myths: Does Municipal Broadband Scale Well to Fit U.S. Broadband Needs?" (ITIF, June 2021), https://itif.org/publications/2021/06/24/broadband-myths-does-municipal-broadband-scale-well-fit-us-broadband-needs/.

26. ICT Price Baskets (International Telecommunication Union, accessed July 2023), https://www.itu.int/en/ITU-D/Statistics/Dashboards/Pages/IPB.aspx.

27. Dine and Kane, "The State of US Broadband in 2022."

28. "STATE OF DIGITAL COMMUNICATIONS: 2022" (Brussels: European Telecommunications Network Operators' Association, February 2022), https://etno.eu/downloads/reports/state_of_digi_2022.pdf.

29. Dine and Kane, "The State of US Broadband in 2022."

30. "2022 Communications Marketplace Report" (FCC, 2022), 9.

31. International Broadband Scorecard 2022: interactive data (London: Ofcom, December 2022), https://www.ofcom.org.uk/research-and-data/telecoms-research/broadband-research/eu-broadband-scorecard/international-broadband-scorecard-2022-interactive-data.

32. Ibid.

33. Doug Brake and Robert D. Atkinson, "A Policymaker's Guide to Broadband Competition" (ITIF, September 2019), https://itif.org/publications/2019/09/03/policymakers-guide-broadband-competition/.

34. Ibid., 4.

35. Ibid. For example, consider the theoretical economic model of Bertrand competition: If two firms producing homogenous goods only compete through price and face no capacity constraints, those two competing firms can reach the same end result as would an endless number of competing firms.

36. Ibid.

37. Ookla, Speedtest Global Index, Median Country Speeds June 2023; International Broadband Scorecard 2022: interactive data.

38. Ibid.

39. Monica Alleven, "T-Mobile Marks 1 M Home Internet Customer Milestone," *Fierce Wireless*, April 2022, https://www.fiercewireless.com/wireless/t-mobile-marks-1m-home-internet-customer-milestone.

40. Sabine Neschke, "Exploring the Potential of LEO Satellites for Broadband Access" (Bipartisan Policy Center, December 2022), https://bipartisanpolicy.org/blog/leo-satellites-broadband-access/.

41. "2021 Broadband Capex Report" (USTelecom: The Broadband Association, July 2022), https://ustelecom.org/research/2021-broadband-capex-report/.

42. Joe Kane, "Sustain Affordable Connectivity By Ending Obsolete Broadband Programs" (ITIF, July 2023), https://itif.org/publications/2023/07/17/sustain-affordable-connectivity-by-ending-obsolete-broadband-programs/.

Myth 28: The Internet Is Destroying Journalism

The decline of many national, regional and local newspapers has led to predictable handwringing about the future of the news business. However, both history and recent events suggest that such fears will prove unwarranted. Like many other industries, the news business is being restructured as it becomes much more specialized.

It's a familiar economic pattern. Industries tend to become more specialized and less vertically integrated over time. In the early decades of the automobile and aerospace businesses, Ford and Boeing made most of the key parts of their cars and planes. Similarly, in the 1960s and 1970s, IBM and other major computer companies built hardware, wrote software, and provided supporting services. But eventually, market and competitive pressures restructured all three industries into vast ecosystems of focused, global suppliers—for tires, jet engines, disk drives, and countless other components.

The Internet is bringing similar restructuring to the news industry. For decades, newspapers published many different types of news—reporting, opinions, weather forecasts, sports coverage, business and classified ads, obituaries, TV listings, event calendars, entertainment reviews, and more. But during the twenty-first century, specialized online services have pulled apart this highly integrated model—through ESPN, The Weather Channel, Yelp, eBay, Carvana, Zillow, Rotten Tomatoes, cable TV providers, memorial websites, search engines, content aggregators, and a vast array of specialized news and opinion providers.

© The Author(s), under exclusive license to Springer Nature Switzerland AG 2024
R. D. Atkinson and D. Moschella, *Technology Fears and Scapegoats*,
https://doi.org/10.1007/978-3-031-52349-6_29

We witness the inefficiency of the traditional newspaper structure every year as hundreds, even thousands, of media representatives descend upon events such as the Superbowl, the COP climate conference, and the Davos gabfest, all covering pretty much the same thing. In contrast, focused information providers have scale economies that make both high efficiency and rapid innovation possible. Not surprisingly, many consumers find these mostly free offerings more appealing than relying on a single paid newspaper subscription. As eyeballs migrate to the digital world, money inevitably follows, and the newspaper industry's wealth and power declines.

All of this is well known. But what, if anything, does the shift from vertically integrated newspapers to specialized information service providers tell us about the state of journalism? After all, the car, aerospace, and computing industries all became much bigger, more efficient, and more global after they adopted a focused-supplier approach, and these changes mostly benefited consumers. The restructuring of the news business will likely do the same.

Journalism vs. Journalists

Just as we should adopt a broad definition of "news" that encompasses its many forms, we also need to decide what we mean by "journalism." The American Press Institute defines it as: "the activity of gathering, assessing, creating, and presenting news and information. It's also the product of these activities." Using this definition, more journalism is being produced than ever before. Reporters, researchers, subject matter experts, and topic enthusiasts of all sorts are providing important news and analysis in every field, and via every means—tweets, blogs, podcasts, guest articles, journals, books, magazines, white papers, TikTok, YouTube and other videos, newsletters, Substack postings, FAQs, fact checking, content moderation, editing, analytics, and now even generative AI. Some of this work is of the highest quality and some is poor, but taken together the volume of output dwarfs that of traditional newsrooms.

Yet despite this explosion of news and information, we often hear that journalism is in decline. But this is what happens when we equate journalism with journalists. For example, in 2021 Pew Research made headlines by revealing that the number of journalists had fallen 26 percent since 2008. However, Pew was basically counting journalists working in newsrooms. While this is an interesting number, it's no longer an accurate journalism activity metric. It's mostly a measure of the rate of decline within the old newspaper-led order. It says a lot about the number of self-identified "professional" journalist employees, but little about the creation, flow, and influence of information in the wider world. Many prominent journalists—such as Matt Taibbi, Glen Greenwald, and Bari Weiss—no longer work for traditional news publications.

These definitional and measurement problems are further complicated by the fact that journalism isn't a profession in the typical use of the term. When we talk about the "professions," we are usually referring to doctors, lawyers, accountants, architects, professors, and others who have certified understanding of an agreed upon body of knowledge. Electricians, plumbers, nurses, and others with certified skills can also fall into the professional category. They all have, and need, a license to practice.

While journalism has its own professional schools, societies, and practices, they aren't mandatory, and there is no required certification. Prominent figures—including Walter Cronkite, Peter Jennings, Carl Bernstein, Seymour Hersch, Nina Totenberg, Maureen Dowd, Rachel Maddow, and a great many others—don't have degrees in journalism. Similarly, subject matter experts and informed citizens can also do journalism, which is why we now have a lot more journalism, even as there are fewer people who see themselves purely as journalists. The lack of a clear journalist definition also explains why deciding who should be given press credentials now often seems so arbitrary.

Are You Being Served?

Given that both the financial weakness of newspapers and the declining number of journalists working in newsrooms can be misleading indicators, the best way to assess the state of journalism today is to focus on how well the public is being served. Although this is a complex and subjective topic, the conventional wisdom is that the media and journalism are failing in this regard at both a national level and local level. Yet these complaints are almost entirely limited to investigative and hard news reporting. No one says that consumers of opinions, sports, weather forecasts, entertainment reviews, classified ads, obituaries, and similar information are poorly served. In these areas, they are served better than ever. When one compares Internet services to traditional newspapers, it's important to keep this broader set of news offerings in mind.

Too Much National News

At a national level, there is arguably too much, not too little, news. In addition to all of the major newspapers, television stations, and social media, there's Politico, Slate, the Huffington Post, the Daily Beast, the Atlantic, the Hill, the Federalist, Real Clear Politics, Breitbart, newcomers such as Substack and the Free Press, and countless other offerings. This surplus of competitors requires everyone to vie for attention and revenues, which helps explain why many news outlets put so much emphasis on controversies, opinions, and gotchas, as opposed to balanced in-depth investigations and reporting.

This dynamic is made worse by the shift from advertising to subscriber revenue. Although reliance on advertising brings its own set of biases, it had the virtue of incentivizing newspapers to reach as many eyeballs as possible. In contrast, today's growing reliance on digital subscribers puts the emphasis on subscription sign-ups and renewals. If most of your subscribers lean left or right, there is a strong incentive to feed them stories that they want to hear, and little incentive to do otherwise. Subscribers to Fox Nation are generally not going to subscribe to the New York Times, and vice versa. The shift to a subscription model is an underappreciated driver of increasing media bias.

As opinions rise in importance and the incentive to serve a broad audience declines, it's hardly surprising that news providers become more polarized. Things have reached such a state that some media figures now argue that journalists should move away from traditional notions of objectivity and balance altogether. If "my side" speaks the truth, why should we give airtime to the others? This growing one-sidedness (of both liberal and conservative outlets) inevitably leads to vast differences in what is covered, as well as less reliable information, and a loss of trust among those whose opinions and priorities differ. As we have argued, journalistic bias creates more societal distrust than social media, despite countless claims to the contrary.

Not So Deserted Locally

The local news situation has raised even more dire alarms than those heard nationally. We are increasingly warned about the dangers of "news deserts," regions that no longer have a local newspaper. A widely cited study claimed that some 2200 local U.S. newspapers (about a quarter of the total) ceased publication between 2005 and 2020. There are similar worries about "ghost newspapers," which still exist but are now a shadow of their former selves.

These trends and terms speak to real change; many regional and local papers are now thinner, less frequent, online only, or closed entirely.

However, as with the national situation, it's easy to overlook the improvements. Anyone with an Internet connection can now access all the global reporting, opinions, and analyses they wish. This certainly was not the case in the pre-Internet era, and represents a massive consumer gain. Likewise, news about local sports, real estate listings, restaurants, weather, jobs, etc., is also generally available freely online, through a variety of sources. In both of these cases, the decline of local newspapers mostly affects those without online access. However, lack of online access is much more of a universal service challenge than a critique of journalism; it's also a much more solvable problem, as over time the number of people unwillingly disconnected from the Internet will trend toward near zero.

Those who fear for the future of local news are mostly talking about investigative and in-depth reporting at a local level. As traditional newspapers weaken, this area is clearly under pressure. There are currently four main suggested ways to close the gap:

1. Local news could be subsidized, either through tax incentives or direct public funding. Several bills along these lines have been floated in Congress, although none have passed. States, cities, and towns could also launch their own subsidy initiatives if so inclined.
2. Philanthropists and sponsors could fund local news coverage in the same way that billionaires have done for national media, including Laurene Powell Jobs (The Atlantic), Jeff Bezos (The Washington Post), and John Henry (The Boston Globe). Local support of this nature seems certain to increase.
3. Lawmakers could require the major Internet platform companies to pay news outlets for linking to their stories, as Australia has done, Canada has attempted, U.S. Sen. Amy Klobuchar (D-CA) proposed in her thus far failed Journalism Competition and Preservation Act (JCPA), and California is now considering. Payments could also be made voluntarily between parties as Google has been doing with the New York Times.
4. Social media platforms, community TV, and new local news players could grow to meet citizen information needs in areas such as regional development, town planning, local elections, schools, police and fire reports, taxation, community events, and traffic control.

Items one and two seek to protect newspapers and newsrooms as we have always known them. They are almost a form of nostalgia and will likely be difficult to broadly sustain over time. The third option is mostly unfair. News publishers are under no obligation to list their content with Google News or other online platforms, and there are technical controls they could use to prevent tech companies from indexing their articles. But most publishers choose not to do this because they benefit from the traffic that the platforms generate. So basically, they are asking to be paid for something they benefit from. Moreover, why should newspapers be compensated for links to their content when no other Internet content providers are?

The fourth option is the more forward-looking and potentially sustainable over time. We have shown that people with an Internet connection don't need a local newspaper for national and international news, nor for many day-to-day information services. They mostly need it for local news and reporting. The question is whether path number four can meet this need. Fortunately, the answer seems to be yes.

Today, Facebook, X, and cable TV can and are used to serve local communities. But there is also much more going on with local news initiatives than is readily visible nationally. Rather than top-down Gannett-style local and regional papers, there are now a great many bottom-up efforts—some for profit and some not. There are more than 270 local initiatives in Massachusetts alone. Additionally, the online news media company Axios has launched local newsletters serving more than two dozen cities across the country, with more on the way. Of course, such efforts tend to be in relatively well-off areas, but this was true for local newspapers as well. Given the growing number of citizens and groups who can create and post informed online content, the potential for active civic-mindedness and participation remains high.

Restructuring for the Future

The shift from vertically integrated companies to specialized providers has served consumers well in many important industries. Although the news business is still in the middle of this restructuring, the pattern seems likely to hold once again. We often hear that the decline of traditional newspapers is a "threat to democracy," but what's really happening is that the news business is being democratized, resulting in more information, more voices, and more choices, with all of the benefits, challenges, and complexities that diversity creates. The claim that the Internet is reducing the quality and quantity of journalism and societal information will be increasingly proven false.

—*DM*

Myth 29: Market Concentration Is at an All-Time High

A relatively new, but fast-growing narrative is that the economy is experiencing a "crisis of market concentration," with dominant players stifling competition in industry after industry. That belief is the pretext for a push to radically restructure antitrust policy. But newly released Census data mostly contradicts this claim. Market concentration has generally fallen.

It has long been recognized that, during the Industrial Revolution, firms raised living standards and cut prices by consolidating and mass-producing manufactured goods.[1] But today, the narrative that scale is efficient is being pushed aside in favor of a new one, that big is bad for consumers because in the words of Senator Elizabeth Warren, "big companies [have been] abusing their market power to price gouge consumers and crush workers and small business."[2]

This narrative is based on the claim that big business is getting bigger.[3] This "fact" of rising concentration, and even monopoly power, has been picked up by many commentators. Brookings' analyst David Wessel wrote, "There's no question that most industries are becoming more concentrated. Big firms account for higher shares of industry revenue and are reaping historically large profits relative to their investment."[4] Former chairman of the Council of Economic Advisors Jason Furman testified that market concentration has increased since 1997.[5] Economist Paul Krugman wrote that "growing monopoly power is a big problem for the U.S. economy."[6] The neo-Brandeisian (individuals who oppose large corporations) advocacy group Open Markets has referred to "America's concentration crisis."[7] And

© The Author(s), under exclusive license to Springer Nature Switzerland AG 2024
R. D. Atkinson and D. Moschella, *Technology Fears and Scapegoats*,
https://doi.org/10.1007/978-3-031-52349-6_30

the Center for American Progress has written about "America's monopoly problem."[8]

Why Does This Matter and Where Did It Come From?

The "growing monopoly" myth matters because it can fuel misguided policies targeting market concentration—specifically antitrust enforcement and reform. For instance, the Biden-Sanders unity task force in August 2020 released a list of recommendations for the purpose of "Tackling Runaway Corporate Concentration." The task force emphasized:

> Democrats are concerned about the increase in mega-mergers and corporate concentration across a wide range of industries, from hospitals and pharmaceutical companies to agribusiness and retail chains. We will direct federal regulators to review a subset of the mergers and acquisitions that have taken place since President Trump took office, prioritizing the pharmaceutical, health care, and agricultural industries, to assess whether any have increased market concentration, raised consumer prices, demonstrably harmed workers, increased racial inequality, or reduced competition, and assign appropriate remedies. Democrats will direct regulators to consider potential effects of future mergers on the labor market, on low-income and racially marginalized communities, and on racial equity. And as a last resort, regulators should consider breaking up corporations if they find they are using their market power to engage in anti-competitive activities.[9]

The myth of "growing monopoly" came about because of a few recent studies. One study, led by Gustavo Grullon, looked at firm-level data from the Center for Research in Security Prices and Compustat between 1972 and 2014 and concluded that since the late 1990s, over 75 percent of U.S. industries experienced an increase in concentration at the three-digit North American Industry Classification System (NAICS) level.[10] Typical three-digit industry levels would be textile mills and food and beverage stores. Weighting the concentration in each industry by its proportion of sales, the median increase in the Herfindahl–Hirschman Index (a measure of industry concentration), between 1997 and 2014, was 41 percent, while the average increase was 90 percent.[11] They concluded, "Results suggest that the US product markets have undergone a shift that has potentially weakened competition across the majority of industries."[12]

A 2016 report by the Council of Economic Advisors (CEA) indicates that between 1997 and 2012, the revenue share of the top 50 firms increased in 10 of 13 two-digit NAICS industries (e.g., construction, wholesale trade). In the case of both transportation, warehousing, and retail trade, the increase exceeded 11 percentage points. The report cites this increase as a key indicator pointing toward a decline in competition.

Autor et al. also used Census data to measure concentration in several industries at the four-digit NAICS level and found "a remarkably consistent upward trend in concentration in each sector."[13] Between 1992 and 2012, the C4 ratio increased by 5 percentage points in manufacturing, 9 percentage points in finance, 4 percentage points in services, and 15 percentage points in retail trade. However, they assert that this reflects the effects of competition in which more efficient firms gained market share.

Finally, Covarrubias, Gutiérrez, and Philippon used data on individual public companies and Census data to measure concentration ratios for the top eight firms at the four- and six-digit NAICS code levels going back to 1980.[14] They found concentration ratios in both manufacturing and non-manufacturing industries have increased by roughly 4 to 8 percent since 1987, and, during the 1990s, market concentration was driven by tougher price competition, intangible investment, and increased productivity of market leaders. However, they also concluded that, since 2000, concentration reflects decreased competition and rising barriers to entry—a trend they linked to lower investment, higher prices, and lower productivity growth.

Why This Is a Myth?

One key problem in these analyses is that they relied on misleading market concentration measurements. Philippon, for instance, used 3-digit NAICS codes to state concentration was up in his widely publicized book, *The Great Reversal*.[15] These NAICS codes break down the economy into just over 70 industries.[16] They combine unrelated companies under a single umbrella and consider them competitors. "Agricultural products" (NAICS code 111), for instance, is a single industry in 3-digit NAICS even though it combines industries as different as apples (NAICS code 111331), tobacco (NAICS code 111910), and cotton (NAICS code 111910).[17] But firms only gain market power when there are few substitutes for their products, so measuring market power requires well-defined industries. The 3-digit NAICS codes are not that.

NAICS's 6-digit codes are the most specific industry categories that the U.S. government provides. The Census Bureau divides the economy into over one thousand industries in this classification. Using 6-digit NAICS Census data, a groundbreaking ITIF report found that the average C4 ratio (the share of sales captured by the top four firms in an industry) increased by just 1 percentage point from 2002 to 2017, from 34.3 percent to 35.3 percent.[18] Only 4 percent of U.S. industries were highly concentrated in 2017, with the share of industries with low concentration growing by around 25 percent from 2002 to 2017. Additionally, the more concentrated an industry was in 2002, the more likely that industry was to become less concentrated by 2017. In short, there was no evidence that concentration has been growing overall at the national level.

Recent studies also confirm that concentration is not rising at the local level, which is the most relevant for many industries, including restaurants and retail shopping. Kevin Rinz of the U.S. Census Bureau used the federal government's Longitudinal Business Database and W-2 Forms to measure labor market concentration within 4-digit NAICS industries in separate commuting zones. From 1976 to 2005, local industrial concentration declined by approximately 25 percent.[19] These lower concentration levels were tied to higher incomes and decreased inequality. After 2005, local concentration, as assessed by the Herfindahl–Hirschman Index, grew marginally but remained far lower than its 1976 level.

Rinz concluded that the pattern of declining concentration reflected national chains such as restaurants and supermarkets opening up new stores in local markets. If a national top four supermarket opens a store in a new retail market, it increases the C4 concentration ratio at the national level. However, it also decreases concentration, and increases competition, at the local level, which is the most relevant in this case.[20]

Another study looked at product markets in a broad range of industries between 1990 and 2014, and found that the positive trend in national concentration levels became negative when they focused on local concentration levels.[21] This trend was more pronounced when looking at narrower geographic areas, such as counties or zip code levels, and at industries with narrower Standard Industrial Classification codes. When weighted by employment, markets in which concentration was declining accounted for 78 percent of total employment and 72 percent of sales.[22]

In sum, the most recent statistics indicate that concentration has not increased nationally or locally. This fact is a major blow to the foundational tenet of the narrative that big business is getting bigger. Although neo-Brandeisians attribute numerous problems in the U.S. economy to a general increase in market power, these explanations are invalid if market concentration hasn't actually risen.[23]

So Where Are We?

The new "anti-monopoly movement" has been gaining traction, even in unlikely circles. Once mostly the domain of technocrats, antitrust issues have been proposed and debated by presidential candidates, political parties, and voters alike. Unlike recent past elections, antitrust issues were front and center among the many Democratic contenders in the 2020 primaries, and are now an important part of the Biden administration's overall economic policy.[24]

The now widely accepted view is that U.S. industrial concentration has increased significantly in the last two decades—and for many, to dangerously high levels. But as better national and local data have shown, there is virtually no support in the data for this view. So, what explains this divergence between conventional wisdom and evidence? There are at least three main reasons.

First, many people, even economists, tend to generalize from personal experience. We see this in how so many experts argue, without any real evidence, that the pace of technological innovation is accelerating, just because they see the pace of innovation in smartphones.[25] The same dynamic occurs with regard to views toward changes in concentration. Many Americans use Google, Amazon, and an iPhone, and fly on the four major airlines, and simply assume that concentration must be endemic.

Second, people's attention is asymmetrical: Whenever a major merger is announced, there is usually a widespread reaction advancing the narrative of galloping concentration. But when companies announce divestitures that reduce concentration, it is like the proverbial tree falling in the forest: silence. For example, recent divestitures such as AT&T's divestiture of Time Warner, and those by Astra Zeneca and 3M have received relatively little attention.[26] Yet, according to Ernst and Young, private equity-backed divestitures have increased 40 percent from 2020 to 2021.[27] Likewise, the growth of smaller companies into larger ones that take market share away from the largest companies in a particular industry is rarely factored in. For example, companies such as Salesforce, Netflix, Biogen, and Gilead were much smaller a decade ago but now challenge traditional leaders.[28]

Finally, and most importantly, the key reason the "monopoly" narrative has become dominant is that neo-Brandeisians seek a wholesale change in antitrust law to break up large companies and weaken the political power of business, and the narrative of out-of-control monopolization is a critical part of this campaign.

This has led to a proliferation of progressive screeds against bigness: Tim Wu's *The Curse of Bigness*, Matt Stoller's *Goliath: The 100 Year War Between*

Monopoly and Democracy, Jonathan Tepper's *The Myth of Capitalism: Monopolies and the Death of Capitalism,* Zephyr Teachout's *Break 'Em Up: Recovering our Freedom From Big Ag, Big Tech and Big Money,* Barry Lynn's *Cornered: The New Monopoly Capitalism and the Economics of Destruction,* and perhaps the book with the catchiest, if not the most eloquent, title, Sally Hubbard's *Monopolies Suck: 7 Ways Big Corporations Rule Your Life and How to Take Back Control.*

But when it comes to market concentration, not only have these authors misdiagnosed the problem, they often offer cures that are worse than the symptoms. Deconcentrating markets in pursuit of a fanciful small business economy would seriously damage the competitiveness of U.S. companies. If American firms can no longer compete with larger foreign rivals, Americans will lose high-paying jobs and the U.S. will lose its global leadership. And as small businesses are on average less productive and pay lower wages, the result would be a decline in living standards. That's not to say that monopoly power is never a problem and that antitrust is useless. But antitrust is not a magic cure-all for stagnant wages, low productivity growth, and income inequality as many allege. Instead, policymakers must address these issues with other tools like higher minimum wages, higher income taxes, and stronger investment incentives.[29]

—RA

Notes

1. "Work in the Late 19th Century," Library of Congress, accessed August 17, 2023, https://www.loc.gov/classroom-materials/united-states-history-primary-source-timeline/rise-of-industrial-america-1876-1900/work-in-late-19th-century/.
2. "Warren, Jones Introduce Bicameral Legislation to Ban Anticompetitive Mergers, Restore Competition, and Bring Down Prices for Consumers," Elizabeth Warren, accessed August 18, 2023, https://www.warren.senate.gov/newsroom/press-releases/warren-jones-introduce-bicameral-legislation-to-ban-anticompetitive-mergers-restore-competition-and-bring-down-prices-for-consumers.
3. German Lopez, "Big Business Gets Bigger," *The New York Times,* July 21, 2023, https://www.nytimes.com/2023/07/21/briefing/microsoft-activision-ftc-corporate-concentration.html.

4. David Wessel, "Is Lack of Competition Strangling the US. Economy?" *Harvard Business Review* (March–April 2018), https://hbr.org/2018/03/is-lack-of-competition-strangling-the-u-s-economy#.

5. Jason Furman, "Prepared Testimony to the Hearing on 'Market Concentration'," OECD, May 2018, DAF/COMP/WD(2018)67, https://www.oecd.org/daf/competition/market-concentration.htm.

6. Paul Krugman, "Robber Baron Recessions," *The New York Times*, April 18, 2016, https://www.nytimes.com/2016/04/18/opinion/robber-baron-recessions.html.

7. "America's Concentration Crisis: An Open Markets Institute Report," Open Markets Institute website, June 2019, https://concentrationcrisis.openmarketsinstitute.org/.

8. "America's Monopoly Problem: How the Growing Concentration of Economic Power Affects the Economy, Innovation, and Democracy," Center for American Progress Action Fund, March 2019, https://www.americanprogressaction.org/events/2019/02/27/173322/americas-monopoly-problem/.

9. "Biden-Sanders Unity Task Force Recommendations: Combating the Climate Crisis and Pursuing Environmental Justice," Joe Biden campaign website, accessed April 15, 2021, https://joebiden.com/wp-content/uploads/2020/08/UNITY-TASK-FORCE-RECOMMENDATIONS.pdf.

10. Gustavo Grullon, Yelena Larkin, and Roni Michaely, "Are US Industries Becoming More Concentrated?" *Review of Finance*, vol. 23(4) (2019), https://doi.org/10.1093/rof/rfz007. The study excluded the financial and utility sectors.

11. Gustavo Grullon, Yelena Larkin, and Roni Michaely, "Are US Industries Becoming More Concentrated?" *Review of Finance*, vol. 23(4) (2019), 702, https://doi.org/10.1093/rof/rfz007.

12. Gustavo Grullon, Yelena Larkin, and Roni Michaely, "Are US Industries Becoming More Concentrated?" *Review of Finance*, vol. 23(4) (2019), 697, https://doi.org/10.1093/rof/rfz007.

13. David Autor et al., "Concentrating on the Fall of the Labor Share," *American Economic Review: Papers & Proceedings*, vol. 107(5) (2017), https://doi.org/10.1257/aer.p20171102.

14. Matias Covarrubias, Germán Gutiérrez, and Thomas Philippon, "From Good to Bad Concentration? US. Industries Over the Past 30 Years" (NBER Working paper No. 25983, September 2019), http://nber.org/papers/w25983.

15. Thomas Philippon, *The Great Reversal: How America Gave Up on Free Markets* (Belkamp Press, 2019).

16. Executive Office of the President Office of Management and Budget, "North American Industry Classification System," https://www.naics.com/wp-content/uploads/2022/07/2017_NAICS_Manual.pdf, 27.

17. "Commodity Description Lookup," U.S. International Trade Commission, accessed March 28, 2023, https://dataweb.usitc.gov/classification/commodity-description/NAIC/3.

18. Robert Atkinson and Filipe Lage de Sousa, "No, Monopoly Has Not Grown" (ITIF, June 2021), /publications/2021/06/07/no-monopoly-has-not-grown.

19. Kevin Rinz, "Labor Market Concentration, Earnings Inequality, and Earnings Mobility" (Center for Administrative Records Research and Applications, US. Census Bureau, Working Paper 2018, September 2018), https://www.census.gov/library/working-papers/2018/adrm/carra-wp-2018-10.html.

20. Ibid., 5.

21. Esteban Rossi-Hansberg, Pierre-Daniel Sarte, and Nicholas Trachter, "Diverging Trends in National and Local Concentration" (Federal Reserve Bank of Richmond, Working Paper Series 18-15R, February 27, 2019), https://doi.org/10.21144/wp18-15.

22. Ibid.

23. Gábor Koltay and Szabolcs Lorincz, "Competition Policy Brief" (Brussels: European Commission, November 2021), https://competition-policy.ec.europa.eu/system/files/2021-12/Competition%20Policy%20Brief%202-2021_Industry%20concentration%20and%20competition%20policy.pdf; Pauline Affeldt et al., "Market Concentration in Europe: Evidence from Antitrust Markets" (DIW Berlin Discussion Paper, January 2021), https://papers.ssrn.com/sol3/papers.cfm?abstract_id=3775524.

24. Michael Levenson, "Price Gouging Complaints Surge Amid Coronavirus Pandemic," *N.Y. Times* (March 2020), https://www.nytimes.com/2020/03/27/us/coronavirus-price-gouging-hand-sanitizer-masks-wipes.html; Stephanie Zimmerman, "Illinois Attorney General Calls for Amazon, Other Sellers to Police Coronavirus Price-Gouging," *Cihi. Sun Times* (March 2020), https://chicago.suntimes.com/coronavirus/2020/3/25/21194411/illinois-attorney-general-raoul-coronavirus-price-gouging-sanitizer-masks-amazonfacebook-walmart; Geneva Sands and Priscilla Alvarez, "Feds Target Price Gouging as States and Hospitals Swarm Private Market for Supplies," *CNN* (April

2020), https://www.cnn.com/2020/04/25/politics/fema-doj-price-gou ging-supplies/index.html.

25. Robert D. Atkinson, "The Nonsense of Techno-Exponentialism" (ITIF, May 2014), https://itif.org/publications/2014/05/10/nonsense-techno-exponentialism/.

26. Amber Tong, "After a Brief Break, AstraZeneca Is Back at Divesting— Handing Off Hypertension Meds for $350 M," *Endpoints News*, January 2020, https://endpts.com/after-a-brief-break-astrazeneca-is-back-at-divesting-handing-off-hypertension-meds-for-350m/; Norbert Sparrow, "3 M Divests Most of Its Drug-Delivery Business in $650-Million Deal," *Plastics Today*, December 2019, https://www.plasticst oday.com/medical/3m-divests-most-its-drug-delivery-business-650-million-deal.

27. Andrew Wollaston et al., "How Private Equity Is Refining Exit Strate-gies for Stronger Valuations: 2021 Global Private Equity Divestment Study," EY, May 2021, https://www.ey.com/en_us/divestment-study/private-equity.

28. Thomas C. Frohlich and Evan Comen, "America's Fastest Growing Companies," *USA TODAY*, October 2016, https://www.usatoday.com/story/money/business/2016/10/08/americas-fastest-growing-com panies/91728104/.

29. Hadi Houalla and Aurelien Portuese, "The Great Revealing: Taking Competition in America and Europe Seriously" (ITIF, May 2023), https://itif.org/publications/2023/05/15/the-great-reveal ing-taking-competition-in-america-and-europe-seriously/.

Myth 30: Big Pharma Is Driving High Healthcare Costs

In recent years, there has been growing political pressure to transform the pharmaceutical industry by regulating drug prices and/or turning drug development into more of a government-run system. To build support for this cause, many advocates argue that U.S. drug profits are excessive, that drug prices are driving up healthcare costs, and that drug companies spend too little on developing new drugs. All three claims are wrong. Moreover, implementing advocates' proposals would reduce the development of new treatments and cures, and thus weaken America's current global leadership.

Many of the myths related to U.S. innovation industries such as broadband, Internet services, and AI seek to gain support for regulations that would give government more control of the industry. This is arguably even more the case with pharmaceuticals, an industry that America leads globally. Many want to fundamentally transform the sector by imposing strict price controls, weakening patents, and/or instituting a government-run drug development system, all of which would slow the development of important new drugs.

The calls for radical change are legion. The liberal Center for American Progress has proposed a wide array of policies to reduce drug prices, including price controls and reducing the period of data exclusivity (the time which companies can keep data proprietary).[1] Progressive economist Dean Baker has urged lawmakers to "expand the public funding going to NIH or other public institutions and extend their charge beyond basic research to include developing and testing drugs and medical equipment."[2] Liberal commentator Robert Reich has proposed reducing drug patent terms from 20 years to three, while Knowledge Ecology International, a leading drug populist organization,

© The Author(s), under exclusive license to Springer Nature Switzerland AG 2024
R. D. Atkinson and D. Moschella, *Technology Fears and Scapegoats*,
https://doi.org/10.1007/978-3-031-52349-6_31

wants to eliminate drug patents, especially in developing economies.[3] (Eliminating patents would make available more generic versions of today's drugs, but alas, fewer new drugs.)

To justify such a dramatic shift, proponents need to discredit the current private-sector-led model that has made America the world leader in pharma and biopharma innovation.[4] They must convince policymakers and the public that the drug industry no longer serves the public interest of effectively delivering new drugs. To do this, they claim that the industry earns excess profits from rapidly rising drug prices, spends too much money on stock buybacks and advertising, and too little on new drug development. If the populists can advance these claims and show that the free-market system has failed, fundamentally transforming the industry becomes much easier. But the facts show otherwise.

Normal Profits

Start with profits. The left argues that there is plenty of money for the industry to develop drugs, even if its revenues are significantly lowered as a result of price controls or reduced intellectual property protection. They rationalize this assertion with claims of excess profits and wasted spending.

U.S. Rep. Katie Porter (D-CA), deputy chair of the Congressional Progressive Caucus, issued a scathing report in 2021 titled "Killer Profits," attempting to make the case that the industry makes too much money.[5] Two years earlier, the Center for American Progress made the same claim that "Big Pharma Reaps Profits."[6] More recently, the self-described "democratic socialist" Senator Bernie Sanders (VT) has claimed that "Greedy pharma firms rip off Americans."[7]

The reality is that, when adjusting for risk and comparing it to other industries, pharmaceutical firms' profits are not excessive, nor are drug prices driving up overall healthcare expenditures. Researchers Sood, Mulligan, and Zhong compared excess profits of pharmaceutical companies and S&P 500 firms.[8] They defined excess profit as "higher than expected profits given the risk associated with their investments" and found that pharmaceutical companies' excess profits were actually 1.7 percentage points *lower* than the 3.6 percent average among S&P 500 firms.[9]

By contrast, researchers found that the excess profits of middlemen in the U.S. biopharmaceutical supply chain—insurers, pharmacy benefit managers, and retailers—averaged 5.9 percent from 2013 to 2018. Moreover, an analysis in *PLosONE* found that pharmaceutical "returns were substantially lower than [those of] the other eight health care industries."[10] Despite today's rhetoric, prescription medicines have accounted for only about 14 percent of U.S. healthcare spending in recent years, and that share is expected to remain stable going forward.[11] Similarly, the research firm Altarum found in a 2020 report that the *retail* pharma share will likely remain stable in the 9 percent range through most of this decade, with non-retail expenditures also roughly stable in the 4.5 to 4.9 percent range. (Fig. 1.) This puts the United States right in line with other OECD nations.[12]

Others, such as Dean Baker, attack the industry for spending too little money on R&D for drug development and too much on stock buybacks and marketing. In arguing that the industry wastes money on marketing, Baker notes that industry marketing costs are comparable to research expenditures, and that if the industry just reduced advertising, it could reduce drug prices. This sentiment is no doubt fueled by pharma's extensive use of television advertising.

Yet, over the last 10 years, the annualized return on the Standard & Poor's (S&P) Biotech Index averaged 7.95 percent and the Pharmaceutical Select Index averaged 3.29 percent, both lower than the S&P 500 index return of 12.49 percent, which undercuts the argument that stock buybacks are being used to "prioritize short term financial returns," as one article contended.[13]

When it comes to marketing, the charge is just as specious. An analysis in *JAMA Network*, which included all promotional activities, physician education, advertising, and unbranded disease awareness campaigns as "medical marketing," puts the total of these activities (many of which have significant

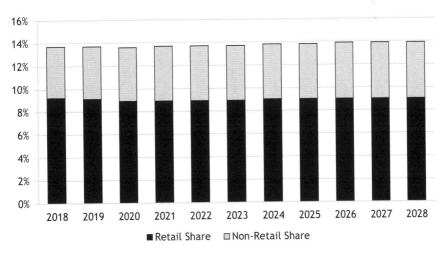

Fig. 1 Projected prescription drug share of national healthcare expenditures[14]

value to patients) at one-third of R&D expenditures.[15] When looking just at pharmaceutical advertising, total spending reached was $6.58 billion in 2020, a small fraction of the $122 billion the industry invested in R&D in the United States that year.[16]

Opponents of large drug companies also claim that the companies are not investing in R&D. The progressive think tank Roosevelt Institute has argued that, "as prices have skyrocketed over the last few decades, these same companies' investments in research and development have failed to match this same pace."[17] In reality, from 2012 to 2016, drug sales increased $5.8 billion a year, while R&D actually increased $6.8 billion a year.[18]

Drug companies in America are highly R&D intensive and have become even more so, with their R&D-to-sales ratio increasing from 11 percent in 2006 to 20 percent in 2018.[19] The ratio for the top 20 U.S. drug companies increased from 15 percent in 2006 to 23.6 percent.[20] Further, while drug revenues increased 56 percent from 2006 to 2018 (in nominal dollars), R&D increased by 85 percent, and it is the largest firms, not the smallest, that are the most R&D intensive.[21] The non-partisan Congressional Budget Office reports that "In 2019, the pharmaceutical industry spent $83 billion dollars on R&D. Adjusted for inflation, that amount is about 10 times what the industry spent per year in the 1980s."[22]

In fact, America's pharmaceutical industry is the most R&D-intensive industry in the world, investing over 20 percent of its sales into R&D each year, which accounts for 18 percent of the total U.S. business R&D investment.

Pricing Realities

The populists tell us that prices are rising way too fast because of "corporate greed." The Kaiser Family Foundation rails that "Prices Increased Faster Than Inflation for Half of all Drugs Covered by Medicare in 2020."[23] But of course that means that prices increased less than inflation for the other half. Three professors of medicine at Harvard agree, claiming that drug prices are "skyrocketing."[24]

To be sure, there are cases where individuals confront large and sudden medical bills: One study found that nearly 40 percent of commercially insured individuals incurred half of their annual out-of-pocket drug spending on one purchase, and 26 percent incurred 90 percent of their annual healthcare spending in only one or two encounters.[25] (This is why policies such as "smoothing" Medicare beneficiaries' out-of-pocket costs over the course of a year are often warranted.)[26] Yet overall, the data shows that American consumers' out-of-pocket expenditures on drugs over the past two decades have grown much less than their overall healthcare and health insurance expenditures.

Furthermore, the distinction between net prices and list prices is critical because while list prices may be on the rise, the share of expenditures being paid to drug manufacturers in recent years is lower than before. For instance, Andrew Brownlee at the Berkeley Research Group found that the share of revenues accruing to drug manufacturers for all drugs decreased by over 17 percentage points from 2013 to 2020, from 66.8 percent to 49.5 percent, while the share going to intermediaries (wholesalers, pharmacies, Pharmacy Benefit Managers (PBMs), and insurance companies) increased from 33.2 to 50.5 percent.[27]

In other words, less than half of every dollar Americans spend on drugs actually goes to the companies developing and making them. Overall, Brownlee found that brand manufacturers retain just 37 percent of total spending on all prescription medicines.[28] Similarly, researchers at the University of Southern California examined the "net price" of insulin and found that list prices did increase between 2014 and 2018, but that the share of insulin drug sales flowing to manufacturers decreased, with more than half of insulin expenditures going to intermediaries by 2018.[29] Indeed, there has been a 140 percent increase in insulin list prices over the past eight years, but net prices actually declined by 41 percent, casting a new light on Angelis and colleagues' argument that "old and common drugs" like insulin "have seen inexplicable price increases."[30] Meanwhile, the Biden administration has used the assertion that America's biopharmaceutical industry is excessively concentrated to justify policies such as expanding Bayh-Dole Act march-in rights to control the price of resulting products. For instance, the administration palpitates that America's 25 largest pharmaceutical companies command around 70 percent of industry revenues. Yet that is hardly evidence of an overconcentrated market. To see one that truly is, just look at the pharmacy benefit managers (PBM) market, where just four companies—Express Scripts, OptumRx, Prime Therapeutics, and Kaiser Pharmacy—commanded 68 percent of the revenue in 2021. That's a concentrated market; America's pharmaceutical sector is not. Thus, as noted, America's PBM market is both substantially more concentrated and profitable than America's pharmaceutical sector, yet it's investing a scant fraction of its revenues back into R&D, let alone creating innovative products that substantially benefit quality and longevity of life.

Early Access

Moreover, by focusing solely on prices, drug populists neglect to mention that Americans enjoy access to innovative medicines far earlier than citizens in other nations do.[31] For instance, 87 percent of new medicines launched globally from 2011 through year-end 2019 were available first in the United States, a wide gap over Germany and the United Kingdom, where only 63 and 59 percent of medicines were available similarly fast, with percentages declining to as low as 46 percent in Canada and 39 percent in Australia.[32]

Considering the percentage of drugs available within one year of their global launch, U.S. residents again enjoyed the greatest access, with 80 percent of drugs available to them first, followed by Germany and the United Kingdom at 47 and 41 percent, respectively, and then Canada and Australia trailing at 26 percent and 19 percent, respectively.[33] For these medicines, the average delay in availability averaged 0 to 3 months from launch in the United States, 10 months in Germany, 11 in the United Kingdom, 15 in Canada, 16 in Japan, 18 in France, and 20 in Australia. These are huge differences.

The Pace of Development

Finally, to press the case for dismantling the U.S. drug development system, opponents argue that the system is not effectively performing its core function: producing effective treatments and cures. Given that the leading drug companies came up with Covid-19 vaccines in record time, using break-through technologies, this case is much harder to make now. But undeterred, the Porter report states, "Rather than producing breakthrough, lifesaving drugs for diseases with few or no cures, most companies focus on small, incremental changes to existing drugs in order to kill off generic threats to their government-granted monopoly patents."[34]

But in reality, new drug approvals have significantly accelerated. The FDA's Center for Drug Evaluation and Research's five-year rolling approval average stood at 44 new drugs per year in 2019, double the five-year rolling average of 22 drugs approved, as happened in 2009. And the number of drugs in development globally increased from 5,995 in 2001 to 13,718 in 2016.[35] Moreover, the share of drugs that are new has risen since the 1970s, not fallen.[36]

At the end of the day, the America's private-sector-led drug development system, coupled with the support of university research and the National

Institutes of Health, has made the United States the medicine chest of the world, responsible for more new drugs than any other nation. As much as the drug populists would like us to think otherwise, the truth is the current system is not just working; it's the envy of the world.

— RA

Notes

1. The Center for American Progress (CAP), "The Senior Protection Plan: $385 Billion in Health Care Savings Without Harming Beneficiaries" (CAP Health Policy Team, November 2012), https://cdn.ame ricanprogress.org/wp-content/uploads/2012/11/SeniorProtectionPlan-3.pdf.
2. Dean Baker, "Malpractice" (Center for Economic Policy Research, May/June 2009), http://cepr.net/publications/op-eds-columns/malpra ctice.
3. James Love, "Groups, individuals write to Senator Wyden, appalled at pressure on India over drug patents," *Knowledge Ecology International,* June 2017, https://www.keionline.org/?s=drug+patents.
4. Stephen Ezell, "Ensuring U.S. Biopharmaceutical Competitiveness" (ITIF, July 2020), https://itif.org/publications/2020/07/16/ensuring-us-biopharmaceutical-competitiveness/.
5. Office of Congresswoman Katie Porter, "Killer Profits: How Big Pharma Takeovers Destroy Innovation and Harm Patients" (January 2021), https://porter.house.gov/uploadedfiles/final_pharma_ma_and_innovation_report_january_2021.pdf.
6. Abbey Meller and Hauwa Ahmed, "How Big Pharma Reaps Profits While Hurting Everyday Americans," (CAP Health Policy Team, August 2019), https://www.americanprogress.org/article/big-pharma-reaps-profits-hurting-everyday-americans/.
7. Bernie Sanders, "Greedy Pharma Firms Rip Off Americans while Pfizer, Moderna Swim in Profits," (Senator Bernie Sanders, January 2023), https://www.sanders.senate.gov/op-eds/greedy-pharma-firms-rip-off-americans-while-pfizer-moderna-swim-in-profits/.
8. Neeraj Sood, Karen Mulligan, and Kimberly Zhong, "Do Companies in the Pharmaceutical Supply Chain Earn Excess Returns?" *International Journal of Health Economics and Management* Vol. 21, No. 1 (2021), https://doi.org/10.1007/s10754-020-09291-1.
9. Ibid.

10. Ge Bai et al., "Profitability and Risk-Return Comparison Across Health Care Industries, Evidence From Publicly Traded Companies 2010–2019," *PLoS ONE* Vol. 17, Issue 11 (November 16, 2022), https://journals.plos.org/plosone/article?id=10.1371/journal.pone.0275245, 1.

11. Rabah Kamal, Cynthia Cox Twitter, and Daniel McDermott, "What Are the Recent and Forecasted Trends in Prescription Drug Spending?" (Peterson Center on Healthcare and Kaiser Family Foundation, February 2019), https://www.healthsystemtracker.org/chart-collection/recent-forecasted-trends-prescription-drug-spending.

12. Organization for Economic Cooperation and Development, "Pharmaceutical Spending as % Total Health Spending, 2020," https://data.oecd.org/healthres/pharmaceutical-spending.htm.

13. S&P Biotechnology Select Industry Index (accessed August, 2023), https://www.spglobal.com/spdji/en/indices/equity/sp-biotechnology-select-industry-index/#overview; S&P Pharmaceuticals Select Industry Index (accessed August, 2023), https://www.spglobal.com/spdji/en/indices/equity/sp-pharmaceuticals-select-industry-index/#overview.

14. Altarum, "Projections of the Non-Retail Prescription Drug Share of National Health Expenditures," September 2020, https://altarum.org/publications/projections-non-retail-prescription-drug-share-national-health-expenditures. 3.

15. Lisa M. Schwartz and Steven Woloshin, "Medical Marketing in the United States, 1997–2016" *Journal of the American Medical Association* Vol. 321, Issue 1 (2019): 80–96, https://doi.org/10.1001/jama.2018.19320.

16. Beth Snyder Bulik "The Top 10 Ad Spenders in Big Pharma for 2020," *Fierce Pharma*, April 2021, https://www.fiercepharma.com/special-report/top-10-ad-spenders-big-pharma-for-2020.

17. Ibid., p. 5.

18. *Scrip 100* (In Vivo Informa Pharma Intelligence, 2018), https://invivo.pharmaintelligence.informa.com/outlook.

19. Ibid.

20. Ibid.

21. Ibid.

22. "Research and Development in the Pharmecutical Industry," (Congressional Budget Office, April 2021) https://www.cbo.gov/publication/57126.

23. Juliette Cubanski and Tricia Neuman, "Prices Increased Faster Than Inflation For Half of all Drugs Covered by Medicare in 2020," (KFF,

February 2022) https://www.kff.org/medicare/issue-brief/prices-increa sed-faster-than-inflation-for-half-of-all-drugs-covered-by-medicare-in-2020/.

24. Benjamin Rome, Alexander Egilman, and Aaron Kesselheim, "Prices for New Drugs Are Rising 20 Percent a Year. Congress Needs to Act," *New York Times*, June 2022, https://www.nytimes.com/2022/06/08/opinion/us-drug-prices-congress.html.

25. Alan Goforth, "Time to Revisit Out-of-Pocket Expenses Calculations? Consumers Burn through Their Share in a Matter of Days," *ALM Benefits Pro*, February 2021, https://www.benefitspro.com/2021/02/04/time-to-revisit-out-of-pocket-expenses-calculations-consumers-burn-through-their-share-in-a-matter-of-days/.

26. Stephen Ezell, "Testimony to the Senate Finance Committee on 'Prescription Drug Price Inflation'," (ITIF, March 2022), https://itif.org/publications/2022/03/16/testimony-senate-finance-committee-prescription-drug-price-inflation/.

27. Andrew Brownlee and Joran Watson, "The Pharmaceutical Supply Chain, 2013–2020," (Berkeley Research Group, 2022), https://www.thinkbrg.com/insights/publications/pharmaceutical-supply-chain-2013-2020/, 3.

28. Ibid.

29. Karen Van Nuys et al., "Estimation of the Share of Net Expenditures on Insulin Captured by US Manufacturers, Wholesalers, Pharmacy Benefit Managers, Pharmacies, and Health Plans From 2014 to 2018" *Journal of the American Medical Association* Vol. 2, Issue 11 (2021), https://jamanetwork.com/journals/jama-health-forum/fullarticle/2785932.

30. Adam Fein, "Drug Channels News Roundup, March 2020: Sanofi's Gross-to-Net Bubble, Drug Pricing Findings, Amazon Replaces Express Scripts, and Drug Channels Video," *Drug Channels*, March 2021, https://www.drugchannels.net/2020/03/drug-channels-news-roundup-march-2020.html.

31. Kevin Haninger, "New Analysis Shows that More Medicines Worldwide Are Available to U.S. Patients," *The Catalyst*, June 2018, https://catalyst.phrma.org/new-analysis-shows-that-more-medicines-worldwide-are-available-to-u.s.-patients; Patricia M. Danzon and Michael F. Furukawa, "International Prices and Availability of Pharmaceuticals In 2005" *Health Affairs* Vol. 7, No. 1 (January/February 2008), https://www.healthaffairs.org/doi/abs/10.1377/hlthaff.27.1.221.

32. PhRMA analysis of IQVIA Analytics Link, U.S. Food and Drug Administration (FDA), European Medicines Agency (EMA), Japan's Pharmaceuticals and Medical Devices Agency (PMDA), Health Canada and Australia's Therapeutic Goods Administration (TGA) data. June 2020. Note: New active substances approved by FDA, EMA, PMDA, Health Canada and/or TGA and first launched in any country between January 1, 2011 and December 31, 2019.
33. Ibid.
34. Robert Atkinson and Stephen Ezell,"Five Fatal Flaws in Rep. Kelly Porter's Indictment of the US Drug Industry, (ITIF, May 2021), https://itif.org/publications/2021/05/20/five-fatal-flaws-rep-katie-por ters-indictment-us-drug-industry/.
35. In Vivo: *The Business and Medicine Report*, Vol 34, No. 1 (January 2016), 25, https://invivo.pharmaintelligence.informa.com/outlook/ industry-data/-/media/marketing/Outlook%202019/pdfs/2016.PDF (subscription only).
36. Ibid.

Global Competition & Strategy

Myth 31: Small Businesses Create Most New Jobs and Innovations

Since at least the 1970s, the conventional wisdom among policymakers across the ideological spectrum has been that small businesses are the main source of jobs and innovation in America. Ergo, it's okay for policy to be indifferent to, or even harmful toward large businesses. But the reality is that large corporations play important roles in both innovation and job creation. While small businesses do create many new jobs, they eliminate nearly as many.

In 1979, economist David L. Birch wrote a report titled "The Job Generation Process" that became hugely influential in economic policy circles. The report was prepared by the MIT Program on Neighborhood and Regional Change for the U.S. Commerce Department's Economic Development Administration.[1] In it, Birch argued that small businesses are the most important job creators in America. This assertion has since taken on mythic proportions, to the point that it is no longer even questioned. It served as the foundational premise for President Obama's budget in 2013, which stated flatly: "Small businesses are the engine of job growth in our economy."[2]

Particularly in the Internet era, small businesses have also gained a reputation as innovators that run circles around big, stodgy, bureaucratic corporations, desperately trying to hold onto their existing market shares. Such claims are mostly wrong. But that does not stop small-is-beautiful advocates from continually repeating them. Indeed, job creation is the ace in the hole for anti-corporate advocates. Even if they lag large businesses on every other performance indicator, small business advocates can always assert that at least small firms create the lion's share of jobs.

© The Author(s), under exclusive license to Springer Nature Switzerland AG 2024
R. D. Atkinson and D. Moschella, *Technology Fears and Scapegoats*,
https://doi.org/10.1007/978-3-031-52349-6_32

However, more recent research has shown that it is not small firms per se that create most jobs, only new businesses. Haltiwanger, Jarmin, and Miranda found that after controlling for firms' age, "the negative relationship between firm size and net growth disappears and may even reverse as a result of relatively high rates of exit amongst the smallest firms."[3]

Indeed, a widely cited study for the Kauffman Foundation, which is devoted to supporting entrepreneurship, found that all net job growth comes from firms less than one year old—meaning start-ups.[4] But the problem is that these new firms also destroy jobs, because so many go out of business soon after they start. As Ryan Decker and coauthors have written, "Most business startups exit within their first ten years, and most surviving young businesses do not grow but remain small."[5] In 1986, Jonathan Leonard concluded, "The obvious pattern, and one that has been largely ignored in previous studies, is that small establishments account for most net job loss just as surely as they account for most net job gain."[6]

In other words, lots of new firms hire workers, but lay them off when they go out of business. This is why Haltiwanger and his colleagues at the U.S. Census Bureau have found that the median net employment growth for young firms is "about zero."[7] According to the Small Business Administration (SBA), just one-third of new businesses survive to their tenth year.[8] Indeed, Zoltan Acs has explained it this way: "Some industries can be best characterized by the model of the conical revolving door, where new businesses enter but where there is a high propensity to subsequently exit from the market."[9]

One study concluded that the smallest firms generate a slightly greater share of new jobs than their share of overall jobs (35.1 percent relative to a 27.2 percent employment share), though "there is stronger evidence that the smallest firms also generate a disproportionate share of gross job destruction (33.9 percent, relative to the 27.2 percent employment share)."[10] This is why the correlation between the start-up rate and the failure rate across industries at the three-digit industry code level is 0.77. In other words, industries that have the highest rates of firm start-ups also have the highest rates of firm failures.[11] Davis, Haltiwanger, and Schuh have rightly pointed out that "a common confusion between net and gross job creation distorts the overall job creation picture and hides the enormous number of new jobs created by large employers."[12]

Age Matters

The majority of small companies actually shed jobs after their first year. One study found that among small companies in their second, third, fourth, and fifth years of business, more jobs were lost to bankruptcy than were added by those still operating. This is why the mean number of workers per firm actually goes down every year after a firm is born. According to the SBA, the mean number of workers in a new firm in its first year is 3.07. But by year 5 this figure declines to 2.36, and to 1.94 in year 11. Or, as the SBA has put it, "Employment gains from growing businesses are less than employment declines from shrinking and closing businesses."[13] In short, small firms create lots of jobs, but they also destroy lots of jobs.

This shouldn't be surprising. "One study of a representative sample of the founders of new businesses started in 1998 showed that 81 percent of them had no desire to grow their new businesses."[14] Another study found that 50 percent of small business owners did not start their business principally to make money.[15] A NBER working paper by Hurst and Pugsley noted in 2015 that when asked about their ideal firm size, the median response of new business owners was that they wanted their businesses to have just a few employees.[16] This makes sense given that the overwhelming majority of small business owners in the United States are skilled craftsmen (e.g., plumbers, electricians, painters), professionals (e.g., lawyers, dentists, accountants, insurance agents), or small shopkeepers (e.g., dry cleaners, gas stations, restaurants).[17]

This, combined with the fact that so many new firms fail within ten years, is why economist Scott Shane has found that it takes forty-three start-ups to end up with just one company that employs anyone other than the founder after ten years.[18] And on average, that surviving start-up will have just nine employees. To be sure, there are always the Amazons and Teslas, start-ups that get very big, but they are statistically rare.

Who Are the Real Innovators?

What about innovation? Surely what small businesses lack in terms of job creation they make up for by building better mousetraps, right? Their defenders argue that "the dynamic contributions made by small firms far offset" their lower levels of productivity and wages."[19] If this were true, it might compensate for small businesses' sub-par performance on wages and productivity. But it is not true.

While small firms account for 49 percent of U.S. employment, they account for just 16 percent of business spending on R&D, while firms of more than 25,000 workers account for 36 percent.[20] Likewise, small firms account for 18.8 percent of patents issued, while the largest firms account for 37.4 percent of patents.[21] Also note that the top 1.5 percent of patenting firms were responsible for 48 percent of all patents from 1999 to 2008. In 2011, 108,626 utility patents of U.S. origin were granted. Just fifty U.S. companies (all large) were responsible for over 30 percent of these patents. The reality is, only a tiny fraction of the nation's 6 million small firms—such as those in Silicon Valley—patent or innovate.[22]

Average R&D spending per worker also increases with company size. Firms with five to ninety-nine workers spend around $790 per worker in, while firms with 5,000 or more workers spend around $3,370 per worker.[23]

As the innovation scholar Luc Soete has found, "Inventive activity seems to increase more than proportionately with firm size."[24] Other research suggests that even among firms that patent, the assumption that small firms are more innovative is not that simple, in part because of the focus on patents as a measure of innovation. In a 1996 paper, Wesley M. Cohen and Steven Klepper found that R&D and firm size are closely related, as large firms invest more in R&D as a share of sales.[25]

Further, "By applying the fruits of their R&D over a larger level of output, larger firms not only have a greater incentive to undertake R&D than smaller firms but they also realize a greater return from their R&D than smaller firms."[26] In 2016, business professors Anne Marie Knott and Carl Vieregger explained how previous studies got the data wrong.[27] Historically, innovation scholars have relied on product or patent counts as a proxy for innovation output. But doing so overemphasizes product innovation and underestimates process innovation (innovation in how something is produced)—activities that large firms engage in more but rarely involve a patent filing.

The recent development of the Business Research and Development and Innovation Survey allowed the National Science Foundation to better analyze incremental and process innovation. NSF estimates that a 10 percent increase in the number of employees increases R&D by 7.2 percent, and that a 10 percent increase in firm revenues increases R&D productivity by 14 percent. These conclusions show that large firms invest more in R&D activities and enjoy higher returns on innovation output per dollar invested in R&D.

Small Business Motivations

One reason for these low figures is that very few new businesses have any intention or capability to innovate. In a 2011 study, Erik Hurst and Benjamin Wild Pugsley found that most small businesses do not intend to grow or innovate.[28] Most small business owners cited nonpecuniary reasons, such as being their own bosses or having flexible schedules, as their motives for starting a company; only 41 percent had a new business idea or sought to create a new product ("new" here does not mean new to the United States, only that the owner thought that his or her idea was new).[29] Only 15 percent of new businesses surveyed planned "to develop proprietary technology, processes, or procedures in the future."[30] This is not to say that tech start-ups and small R&D-intensive firms are not important to driving innovation, but these firms are a very small share of small businesses overall.

The Bottom Line

All of these findings support the view that tax incentives for business investment should treat large and small firms the same, as policymakers should have no strong preference for one over the other. More importantly, they mean that in responding to the China technology challenge, policymakers shouldn't assume that America can stay ahead simply by generating high-tech start-ups. We need both innovative small firms and powerful established ones.
— RA

Notes

1. David L. Birch, "The Job Generation Process," 1979, unpublished report prepared by the MIT Program on Neighborhood and Regional Change for the Economic Development Administration, U.S. Department of Commerce, Washington, DC.
2. White House, Office of Management and Budget, "Supporting Small Businesses and Creating Jobs," ObamaWhiteHouseArchives.gov, n.d., https://obamawhitehouse.archives.gov/omb/factsheet/supporting-small-businesses-and-creating-jobs.
3. Haltiwanger, Jarmin, and Miranda, "Who Creates Jobs?," *The Review of Economics and Statistics*, Vol. 95, no. 2 (May 2023), 30.

4. Tim Kane, "The Importance of Startups in Job Creation and Job Destruction" (Kansas City, MO: Kauffman Foundation, July 2010), http://www.kauffman.org/~/media/kauffman_org/research%20repo rts%20and%20covers/2010/07/firm_formation_importance_of_star tups.pdf.

5. Ryan Decker, John Haltiwanger, Ron Jarmin, and Javier Miranda, "The Role of Entrepreneurship in U.S. Job Creation and Economic Dynamism," *Journal of Economic Perspectives,* vol. 28, no. 3 (Summer 2014).

6. Jonathan S. Leonard, "On the Size Distribution of Employment and Establishments," NBER Working Paper 1951 (Cambridge, MA: National Bureau of Economic Research, June 1986), http://www.nber. org/papers/w1951.pdf.

7. John Haltiwanger, Ron S. Jarmin, Robert Kulick, and Javier Miranda, "High Growth Young Firms: Contribution to Job, Output, and Productivity Growth," US Census Bureau, Center for Economic Studies Working Papers, vol. 16, no. 49, November 2016, 30.

8. US Small Business Administration (SBA), Office of Advocacy, "Frequently Asked Questions" (Washington, DC: SBA, September 2012), https://www.sba.gov/sites/default/files/FAQ_Sept_2012.pdf.

9. Zoltan J. Acs, *Are Small Firms Important? Their Role and Impact* (Boston: Kluwer Academic, 1999), 32.

10. David Neumark, Brandon Wall, and Junfu Zhang, "Do Small Businesses Create More Jobs? New Evidence for the United States from the National Establishment Time Series," IZA Discussion Paper 3888 (Bonn: Forschungsinstitut zur Zukunft der Arbeit, Institute for the Study of Labor, December 2008), ftp://repec.iza.org/pub/SSRN/pdf/ dp3888.pdf.

11. Scott A. Shane, *The Illusions of Entrepreneurship: The Costly Myths That Entrepreneurs, Investors, and Policy Makers Live By* (New Haven, CT: Yale University Press, 2010).

12. Stephen J. Davis, John C. Haltiwanger, and Scott Schuh, *Job Creation and Destruction* (Cambridge, MA: MIT Press, 1996).

13. SBA, Office of Advocacy, "Frequently Asked Questions."

14. Shane, *The Illusions of Entrepreneurship,* 43.

15. Ibid., 66.

16. Erik G. Hurst and Benjamin W. Pugsley, "Wealth, Tastes, and Entrepreneurial Choice," National Bureau of Economic Research, working paper 21,644, October 2015, https://www.nber.org/papers/ w21644.

17. Hurst and Pugsley, "What Do Small Businesses Do?" National Bureau of Economic Research, working paper, 17,041, December 2011, https://www.nber.org/papers/w17041.

18. Shane, *The Illusions of Entrepreneurship*, 154.

19. David B. Audretsch, "Small Firms and Efficiency," in *Are Small Firms Important? Their Role and Impact*, ed. Zoltan J. Acs (New York: Kluwer Academic, 1999), 22.

20. National Science Foundation,"Business Research and Development and Innovation: 2012" (Table 5. Worldwide R&D Paid for by the Company and Performed by the Company and Others, by Industry and Company Size: 2012), https://nsf.gov/statistics/2016/nsf16301/#chp2 (accessed March 5, 2017).

21. Ibid.

22. Justin Hicks, "Knowledge Spillovers and International R&D Networks" (Information Technology and Innovation Foundation, May 2012), http://www2.itif.org/2012-knowledge-spillover-hicks.pdf.

23. Michael Mandel, "Scale and Innovation in Today's Economy" (Washington, DC: Progressive Policy Institute, December 2011), http://progressivepolicy.org/wp-content/uploads/2011/12/12.2011-Mandel_Scale-and-Innovation-in-Todays-Economy.pdf, 3.

24. Luc L. G. Soete, "Firm Size and Inventive Activity: The Evidence Reconsidered," *European Economic Review*, vol. 12, no. 4 (October 1979), 319–340, https://ideas.repec.org/a/eee/eecrev/v12y1979i4p319-340.html.

25. Wesley M. Cohen and Steven Klepper, "A Reprise of Size and R & D," *Economic Journal*, vol. 106, no. 437 (July 1996), 948, http://www.jstor.org/stable/2235365.

26. Ibid.

27. Anne Marie Knott and Carl Vieregger, "Reconciling the Firm Size and Innovation Puzzle," Center for Economic Studies Paper 16–20 (Washington, DC: US Census Bureau, March 2016), https://www2.census.gov/ces/wp/2016/CES-WP-16-20.pdf.

28. Hurst and Pugsley, "What Do Small Businesses Do?" 73.

29. Ibid., 75.

30. Ibid., 96.

Myth 32: We Have All the Technology We Need to Fight Climate Change

It's often said the biggest climate change challenge is simply one of political will. The prevailing view in policymaking circles is that we have all the clean-energy technologies we need to replace fossil fuels at little or no additional cost. We just lack the political courage to accelerate the shift to today's clean technology options. But the stark reality is that the world does not yet have all the capabilities it needs, and believing that we do diverts attention from the hard work and investments required to develop and commercialize more advanced and affordable energy technologies.

In November 2021, as the Biden administration was gearing up for COP26 in Glasgow (the UN's annual climate change assembly), it published a white paper setting forth how the United States could cut emissions by investing in renewables, along with other measures.[1] The paper asserted that the administration's strategy would produce a net economic benefit by 2050. It cited eleven studies from energy think tanks, environmental organizations, and universities in support of this conclusion. This view that we can decarbonize with existing technologies and save money in the process has become the conventional wisdom in the climate debate.

Stanford professor Mark Jacobson is perhaps the leading advocate espousing the view that most, if not all clean technologies are already at price-performance parity with fossil fuels.[2] The title of his book—"No Miracles Needed: How Today's Technologies Can Save Our Planet and Clean Our Air"—is downright Pollyannaish. In it, he writes:

Bill Gates said we have to put a lot of money into miracle technologies. But we don't—we have the technologies that we need. We have wind, solar,

© The Author(s), under exclusive license to Springer Nature Switzerland AG 2024
R. D. Atkinson and D. Moschella, *Technology Fears and Scapegoats*,
https://doi.org/10.1007/978-3-031-52349-6_33

geothermal, hydro, and electric cars. We have batteries, heat pumps, and energy efficiency. We have 95% of the technologies right now that we need to solve the problem.[3]

Alejandro DeLa Garza, a climate reporter for *Time,* agrees: "Scientists and engineers have already created the technologies that can save us. What we need now is the courage to use them," whatever "courage" means.[4] Of course, this narrative is not new; it got its biggest initial boost in Al Gore's 2006 documentary, *An Inconvenient Truth,* in which he claimed that "we have all the technology we need."[5] But saying so doesn't make it true.

Climate Hopes

Rather than grappling with the technological and economic realities of fighting climate challenge, Jacobson and the others have opted to play "let's pretend." Let's pretend not just that the green transition will be cost-free, but that we will actually become richer while deploying it, since the massive investments required will be paid back within just 6 years via cost savings. Let's just pretend that the variability problems of wind and solar will suddenly vanish, and that "a well-connected electrical transmission system" will magically spring up across the globe (when it has not yet done so in 100 years of grid deployment). And let's pretend that all these new technologies, like electric vehicles, provide the same or superior user experience as their fossil fuel alternatives.

Indeed, as in many fairy tales in which everyone lives happily ever after, this is a comforting thought. No need to wait for technology to provide solutions. No need to shift from subsidizing expensive clean technologies to supporting research, development, and demonstration of breakthrough technologies that companies and consumers will want to buy in the free market because they perform better and are cheaper than existing technologies.

For most climate change activists, assuming that we have all the technology we need—and that it costs the same or less than traditional energy—leads to the conclusion that the main task of climate policy is to aggressively deploy these already-affordable technologies. We should simply mandate that everyone uses heat pumps, electric vehicles, and LED light bulbs. Just ban coal-fired power plants, gas stoves, and even drilling for oil. Everything will follow from there.

Harsh Realities

But what the Biden administration neglected to say in its white paper, and the studies it cited failed to make clear, is that the delivery of net economic benefits is contingent on renewable energy costs continuing to decline steadily, as well as the continuation of heavy government subsidies. Yes, for example, if lithium-ion batteries prices fall a lot more and EVs continue to get hefty $7,500 purchase subsidies, it could make economic sense for drivers to switch from internal combustion engines. But do we really want to bet the future of the climate on questionable assumptions and continued government largess?

For example, these studies project the cost of offshore wind to drop 25 to 43 percent by 2030. With higher capacity and fewer land-use constraints than traditional onshore wind, offshore wind is seen as vital to a high-renewable grid. Similarly, utility-scale battery storage is projected to decline in cost by between 33 and 60 percent by 2030. What the Biden administration did not say is that if the energy transition models relied on today's costs rather than these projected declines, the system transition would, rather than providing a net benefit, be very costly. Few citizens in low-income nations would support such cost increases, and not many in rich countries would either.

As investment companies like to say, past performance is no guarantee of future performance: Just because many technologies have gotten cheaper does not mean their costs will continue to fall. In fact, all technologies eventually plateau at some point. Some further cost declines are likely as more units are deployed and revenues drive innovation in design, deployment, and management. However, scale and learning effects eventually exhaust themselves, and history suggests they can do so unexpectedly. The recent uptick in renewable costs should serve as a wake-up call, even if it proves to be transitory. The International Energy Agency, for example, notes that the total cost for utility-scale wind and solar projects could increase by as much as 25 percent over the next few years before inflationary pressures in global commodity markets subside.[6]

It's Not Just About Houses and EVs

The "we have all the technology we need" myth mostly refers to electricity production through renewables and the economics of electric vehicles. But the narrative glosses over a host of industries that are hard to decarbonize, including sectors such as steel, chemicals, cement, trucking, shipping, and aerospace.

Take medium and heavy-duty trucks (MHDTs), which emit 30 percent of the U.S. transportation sector's CO_2. Reducing the total cost of ownership (TCO) of battery-electric and hydrogen fuel-cell MHDTs to be on par with or below the TCO of diesel MHDTs remains the biggest obstacle to adoption because the current TCO for these options is two to three times that of diesel.[7]

The same is true in aviation. Sustainable aviation fuels (SAF) come at a huge premium—an average of 3 to 5 times the cost of conventional fuel, depending on the type.[8] In an optimistic scenario, where the cost of SAF falls to 2 times that of Jet A (the current fuel), it would still cost the world $180 billion a year to subsidize replacing the 95 billion gallons Jet A consumed each year with SAF.[9]

The iron and steel sector is another one without sufficient technology. Their production makes up 8–10 percent of total global emissions, the largest single industrial source of traded product emissions. There are several established technologies and promising pathways that could drastically reduce GHG emissions from the steelmaking process. However, these new production processes and technologies come at a significant cost premium. They need to become much more cost competitive with traditional steel production methods to be widely adopted, especially in low-income nations.[10]

Similarly, many climate advocates pin their hopes on green hydrogen, a close-to-zero-emissions fuel produced with renewable energy. But green hydrogen is now and is expected to remain considerably more expensive than regular hydrogen or other alternatives. One study found that by 2050 it would still be higher than natural gas prices today—and six-times higher than thermal coal prices.[11]

Facing Reality

Climate advocates advance the myth that we have all the clean-energy technologies we need because they worry that if they told the full truth—that getting to net-zero with what we have would cost a lot of money—then people would resist policies to force, induce, or subsidize higher-cost energy solutions. And they would likely be right. Polling has found that 43 percent of Americans are not willing to pay even one dollar more on their electricity bill to combat climate change.[12] The problem is not that people are dumb or don't care about climate change: They just have other more pressing financial priorities, especially people making below the median income level.

But as depressing as it might be to climate activists who demand change now, continued investment in technology innovation is crucial to achieving a low-carbon future. Telling Americans we can make a green transition with today's technology and not pay more for it is not only misleading, it makes it harder to generate support for critically needed science and technology policies that might generate needed breakthroughs.

This is why "we have all the tech we need" is such a disastrous message. It says that we just need to focus our efforts and we will find the sunlit uplands of a green economy that is cheaper and cleaner than today's.[13] We just have to urge people to ditch their gas stoves, junk their second most expensive asset (cars), and install a heat pump. We just need energy providers to store energy at scale and build smart grids that can manage the daily, seasonal, and annual variability of wind and solar. We can then replace 136,000 TWh of fossil fuels,[14] and generate enough green hydrogen to decarbonize heavy industries and transportation. It's an easy lift that requires no sacrifice or significant new technologies, just the will to save the planet. Unfortunately, this vision remains a fantasy, easily undercut by reality.

—RA

Notes

1. "The Long-Term Strategy of the United States: Pathways to Net-Zero Greenhouse Gas Eissions by 2050," United States Department of State and the United States Exective Office of the President (November 2021) https://www.whitehouse.gov/wp-content/uploads/2021/10/US-Long-Term-Strategy.pdf

2. Mark Z. Jacobson et al., "Low-Cost Solutions to Global Warming, Air Pollution, and Energy Insecurity for 145 Countries," Energy & Environmental Science, vol. 15, no. 8 (2022): 3343–3359, https://doi.org/10.1039/D2EE00722C.

3. Bill Gates, "We Need Energy Miracles," GatesNotes blog post, June 25, 2014, https://www.gatesnotes.com/energy-miracles.

4. Alejandro De La Garza, "We Have the Technology to Solve Climate Change. What We Need is Political Will," Time, April 2022, https://time.com/6165094/ipcc-climate-action-political-will/.

5. The White House, "FACT SHEET: Biden-Harris Administration Races to Deploy Clean Energy That Creates Jobs and Lowers Costs," The White House, January 12, 2022, https://www.whitehouse.gov/briefing-room/statements-releases/2022/01/12/fact-sheet-biden-harris-administration-races-to-deploy-clean-energy-that-creates-jobs-and-lowers-costs/.

6. "What is the impact of increasing commodity and energy prices on solar PV, wind and biofuels?" International Energy Agency, December 2021, https://www.iea.org/articles/what-is-the-impact-of-increasing-commodity-and-energy-prices-on-solar-pv-wind-and-biofuels.

7. Hoyu Chong and Ed Rightor, "Closing the Trucking Gaps: Priorities for the Department of energy RD&D Portfolio," ITIF, June 2023, https://itif.org/publications/2023/06/20/closing-the-trucking-gaps-priorities-for-the-department-of-energys-rd-and-d-portfolio/.

8. Eric G. O'Rear, et al., "Sustainable Aviation Fuels: The Key to Decarbonizing Aviation," (Rhodium Group, December 2022), https://rhg.com/research/sustainable-aviation-fuels/.

9. Hannah Boyles, "Aviation Decarbonization and the Gap to Price Parity" (ITIF, June 2023) https://itif.org/publications/2023/06/14/aviation-decarbonization-and-the-gap-to-price-parity/.

10. Hannah Boyles, "Climate-Tech to Watch: Clean Steel" (ITIF, June 2023) https://itif.org/publications/2023/06/07/climate-tech-to-watch-clean-steel/.

11. Lize Wan and Paul Butterworth, "Energy from Green Hydrogen will be Expensive, Even in 2050," (CRU Group, February 2023,) https://sustainability.crugroup.com/article/energy-from-green-hydrogen-will-be-expensive-even-in-2050; See also Robin Gaster: "A Realist Approach to Hydrogen", (ITIF, January 2024), https://itif.org/publications/2024/01/16/a-realist-approach-to-hydrogen/.

12. "Is the Public Willing to Pay to Help Fix climate Change?" The Energy Policy Institute at the University of Chicago and The AP NORC Center, November 2018, https://apnorc.org/projects/is-the-public-willing-to-pay-to-help-fix-climate-change/.

13. Jacobson et al., "Low-Cost Solutions to Global Warming, Air Pollution, and Energy Insecurity for 145 Countries." *Energy & Environmental Science*, vol. 15, no. 8 (2022): 3343–3359, https://doi.org/10.1039/D2EE00722C.

14. "Fossil Fuels." Our World in Data, Accessed June 1, 2023, https://ourworldindata.org/fossil-fuels.

Myth 33: China Has Invented a New Form of Capitalism

China's economy is best viewed as a giant Asian Tiger. China's great success stems mostly from its vast size and its adoption of the proven Asian development model. Claims that it's mostly the result of unfair state-sponsored enterprises and human rights violations distort U.S. priorities and policies. A more liberal China might be an even more competitive economic, geopolitical and societal rival.

As competition and tensions between the U.S. and China rise, it's all too easy for the West to focus on the things it most objects to: predatory trade practices, massive subsidies for its firms, weak environmental regulations, the use of forced labor, and the oppression of its citizens through brutality, censorship, and propaganda. Many have claimed that these practices amount to a new and dangerous form of state-sponsored capitalism. But if heavy-handed government intervention was enough to make a nation thrive economically, the world would be full of prosperous authoritarian capitalists. It isn't.

China has lifted its people out of poverty by adopting an economic model similar to that of Japan, South Korea, Taiwan, and Singapore in their early development years. But whereas their populations are 125 million, 51 million, 23 million, and 5.4 million, respectively, China's is 1.4 billion—seven times the other four combined. This scale has allowed China to add a new tool that the other Asian countries did not have: using access to its market as a cudgel to demand concessions from foreign firms. It's this combination of vast size and successful Asian development model that best explains why China is now an economic, military, and financial rival to the United

© The Author(s), under exclusive license to Springer Nature
Switzerland AG 2024
R. D. Atkinson and D. Moschella, *Technology Fears and Scapegoats*,
https://doi.org/10.1007/978-3-031-52349-6_34

States. By focusing mostly on the role of China's state-sponsored capitalism and authoritarian social policies, American leaders have often lost sight of vital U.S. economic and competitive interests and realities.

Revisiting the "Asian Miracle"

During the second half of the twentieth century, there was a great deal of international debate about why many Asian economies were developing so much faster than other countries around the world. But the reasons were always easy enough to identify. The formula for Asian economic development was both articulated and implemented by Lee Kwan Yew (LKY), who served as Prime Minister of Singapore from 1959 to 1990. LKY is widely seen as the father of Singapore. But because of his unapologetic belief that developing nations are best served by a strong and effective one-party state, he has been called the father of modern China as well.

All of the tigers relied on the same basic building blocks: effective mass education, elite technical and managerial training, a compliant and low-cost workforce, an export and manufacturing focus backed up by export subsidies and import limitations, access to foreign investment and IP, modern infrastructure, high savings rates, social stability, low crime, a willingness to initially serve the commodity end of the value chain, the nurturing of strategic industry sectors, and efforts to move up the value chain and become world class over time, all backed by a strong, engaged, and effective state. China ticks all of these boxes, but its vast size has resulted in much greater global influence and power, especially the power to force companies to share technology in exchange for market access and to mostly stay silent regarding sensitive political and economic issues.

The Tigers' approach has been especially important in computer and related hardware markets (including consumer electronics), most of which have evolved from the bottom up. Japan, Korea, Taiwan, and China all began with the low-end manufacturing of keyboards, mice, printers, and similar commodities. But over time they used this experience to move up the value chain into semiconductors, networking equipment, storage devices, high-resolution displays, and other forms of advanced, high-volume production. World leadership has now been achieved in most manufacturing areas.

In contrast, U.S. technology firms have primarily focused on the upper ends of the value chain—system design, software, customer experience, etc. While this top-down approach has been very successful in capturing the most profitable market segments, it's vulnerable to innovation and supply chain bottlenecks from below, as commodity suppliers move up the value chain. America's lack of its own manufacturing capacity and its dependence on rare earth minerals are now making these risks obvious.[1]

Democracy as an Output

Although Asia's economic miracle was generally applauded, it had one dimension that the West often found uncomfortable: authoritarian, one-party, sometimes brutal government. Despite Singapore's growing prosperity, many in the West criticized Lew Kwan Yew for not tolerating dissent. Similarly, South Korea didn't become a stable democracy until 1987, the same year that Taiwan ended martial law, while Japanese industry initially developed during its imperial era. In all four nations, multiparty democracy came relatively late, and thus was more the output of economic success than a necessary input. In the post-World War II era, American leaders mostly overlooked Asia's lack of Western-style democracy because all four countries were anticommunist allies. Obviously, this is not the case with China.

The realization that the political liberalization of Asia came after economic success explains why many experts believed that China would follow a similar path, and there's still a chance that someday it will. Although many global leaders are reluctant to admit it, the fact that democratic elections around the world have often failed to improve national prosperity also reinforces the democracy-as-output view. Both the fundamental building blocks and a strong, engaged, and effective state have been required. This is the essence of the Asia model.

Open China's Potential

At this stage of its development, China might be even more successful if it becomes more open, as there are growing downsides to its authoritarian practices, just as there were with the other Asian Tigers at roughly similar stages. Oppressive practices make China a less attractive place for foreign professionals to live and work; they discourage international students from attending China's universities; they reduce tourism and limit the global appeal of China's culture, language, and brands. They also make it difficult for Chinese professionals, scientists, and students to engage with their counterparts around the world, increasing the risks of groupthink while dividing and diminishing the influence of the vast Chinese diaspora. Most importantly, they limit the creativity and innovation of the Chinese people. To gauge the lost potential, imagine Taiwan operating at China-like scale.

And it's not as if liberalization would put an end to having a strong, effective, and engaged state. Significant state involvement is now more the rule than the exception. Like China, just about every nation oversees its *commanding heights* to at least some extent in areas such as energy, transportation, aerospace, banking, insurance, natural resources, schools, media, and health care. Consider the way that China has rolled out more EV charging stations than the rest of the world combined.[2] Governments in every developed nation hope to sponsor similar success, believing that it's essential to both the transition to electric vehicles and EV manufacturing competitiveness. Through the CHIPS and Science Act, the Inflation Reduction Act, and other initiatives, the U.S. Congress has significantly increased the level of U.S. government economic engagement, especially in semiconductors and clean energy. But it's not yet clear whether this is a one-time initiative, or a fork in the road for the United States.

Living with a Giant Tiger

America and its allies should continue to push back against many mercantalist Chinese trade and economic practices, but putting so much emphasis on hard-to-change issues such as censorship, human rights, and the use of coal has taken the focus off of challenges that more directly affect the United States, especially: China's domination of the market for many rare earth minerals, its rapid advances in many industries that challenge U.S. capabilities, its investments around the world to gain economic and political influence, and perhaps most importantly how the United States allowed itself to become so dependent on Taiwanese-made semiconductors. These and other vital U.S. interests will continue to be at risk regardless of the extent of China's authoritarianism, especially as a more open and "normal" China might make for an even greater competitive challenge.

China's size and the power of the Asian development model will continue to be the two main issues going forward. In terms of the latter, America would be wise to look at the factors that have enabled the Asian miracle over the last 60 years and ask itself how well it follows this proven formula, much of which is relevant to developed and developing economies alike. Given America's many internal tensions and divides, its cultural belief in laissez-faire economics, and its weaknesses at the lower and middle levels of so many value chains, it won't always be a pleasant experience. While some have argued that in an age of robots, AI, and automation, the Asian development formula will become less effective over time, there's little evidence that this is the case, as the success of Vietnam demonstrates.

As for size, China is—or is destined to be—the world's largest market, the world's biggest supplier, America's toughest competitor and its main geopolitical rival, regardless of whether it liberalizes or not. America needs a strategic mindset that acknowledges these four realities as expanded upon below:

1. To remain as world leaders, American companies must succeed in the Chinese domestic market to an extent that is broadly comparable to China's success in the United States (Many Chinese companies now thrive in the U.S. market even though many consumers are unaware of their national ownership.). Failure to sell in China would put American firms at a distinct global disadvantage. Reciprocity—i.e., if the U.S. government allows TikTok to operate in America, then American social media firms should be allowed to operate in China—should be the overall mindset. If China is limiting U.S. company access, then America should limit similar access to its markets. Any technology transfers between the United States and China should also be broadly reciprocal in nature. And if China is competing unfairly to access allied nations markets, the latter should respond in kind and limit Chinese firms access their markets.

2. America doesn't have to eliminate all of its China dependencies, but it needs to develop enough mutual interdependence that major conflicts are unattractive to both sides. Other than in the most advanced digital areas, America is currently much more dependent on China than China is on America, and this is a destabilizing dynamic that requires a systematic and sustained national response. American cannot afford to lose any more advanced industry leadership to Chinese companies. One possible, but politically delicate, answer is to have more Chinese factories in the United States, replacing many imports. This is the primary way that trade tensions with Japan and Korea have been reduced.

3. The United States and its allies must either lead or maintain parity in strategic industries and technologies. China, of course, feels the same way. Peaceful co-existence and interdependence require that neither side be an outright winner in all major categories. As with interdependence, technology leadership also requires a much more coherent U.S. national effort, one that embraces a full value-chain perspective in key industry sectors.

4. Geopolitical stability depends upon the reciprocity, mutual interdependence, and value-chain mindsets above; it cannot be assured via military strength and international alliances alone.

Rising U.S./China tensions should worry everyone, and both nations' overriding goal must be to avoid military conflicts and major supply chain disruptions. Toward this end, any liberalization by China should be warmly welcomed as it could reduce U.S./China tensions by taking some of the cultural, moral, and emotional issues off the table. But liberalization alone won't reduce China's challenges to vital American interests; it might even increase them.

By viewing China more as a giant Asian tiger that we need to live with and compete with through more effective technology industry practices and policies, and less as an unfair aberration that must be resisted, America can shift its course from trying to change and limit China to trying to support, and where needed, protect its advanced industry firms. By following the liberalization path of its Asian predecessors, China could also reduce tensions. Unfortunately, neither nation is fully stepping up to this challenge.

— *DM*

Notes

1. Robert D. Atkinson, "The Hamilton Index: Assessing National Performance in the Competition for Advanced Industries" (ITIF, June 2022), https://itif.org/publications/2022/06/08/the-hamilton-index-assessing-national-performance-in-the-competition-for-advanced-industries/.
2. Peter Brown, "China Leads World in EV Charging Stations," Electronics 360, July 1, 2022, https://electronics360.globalspec.com/article/18338/china-leads-world-in-ev-charging-stations.

Myth 34: American Manufacturing Is Roaring Back

When it comes to restoring U.S. manufacturing, ambitious and supportive government action is constrained by the fact that many in Washington believe that U.S. manufacturing is both healthy and roaring back. This wrong and Pollyannish belief limits the industrial policy initiatives needed to compete in today's multipolar global economy.

In their zeal to head off any kind of domestic trade protectionism, Washington free-trade pundits and other elites advance the myth that U.S. manufacturing is strong and that virtually all the lost jobs were due to automation, not offshoring and foreign competition. Their fear is that if the extent of U.S. manufacturing decline is acknowledged, tariffs, "America first" and other forms of protectionism will be the result. Better to advance the narratives that American manufacturing is just fine, or that the U.S. is naturally evolving into a services economy.

Consider *Washington Post* columnist Catherine Rampell's 2022 op-ed: "The myth of the manufacturing comeback" where she parrots the conventional inside the beltway wisdom about U.S. manufacturing:

"Contrary to myths that we've stopped 'making' things in the United States, we already manufacture a lot of stuff here. In fact, we manufacture nearly the most 'stuff' on record, as measured by the inflation-adjusted value of those products."[1] A *Wall Street Journal* article is titled "America Is Back in the Factory Business."[2] Likewise, the U.S. Chamber of Commerce writes that "American manufacturing is alive and well."[3]

Likewise, when it comes to explaining the 25 percent loss of U.S. manufacturing jobs over the last 22 years (at a time when total U.S. employment

© The Author(s), under exclusive license to Springer Nature
Switzerland AG 2024
R. D. Atkinson and D. Moschella, *Technology Fears and Scapegoats*,
https://doi.org/10.1007/978-3-031-52349-6_35

increased 14 percent), former Bush administration economist and now Columbia University economist R. Glenn Hubbard reflects the standard view: "The decline in U.S. manufacturing employment is explained by rapid growth in manufacturing productivity."[4]

Much of this naively builds on Daniel Bell's seminal 1973 book *The Coming of the Post-Industrial Society*. But Bell was clear headed, and argued only that services jobs would increase (as they have) and that "the post-industrial economy, is preeminently, a high technology economy," including with ICT and computer production.[5] But Rampell and current manufacturing deniers go much further, arguing that "the United States is—and has long been—an overwhelmingly services-based economy."[6] This is akin to saying that people are overwhelming beer drinkers, if most of the wine drinkers have died.[7]

In other words, they are telling us that U.S. manufacturing output is near its all-time peak and the massive loss of manufacturing jobs over the last two decades was not because manufacturing moved offshore or closed down because of foreign competition, it was because U.S. manufacturers were so productive, they didn't need all those workers anymore. Ignore the loss of one-quarter of U.S. manufacturing jobs over the last 24 years, at a time when total private-sector employment increased by 22 percent, they counsel. That's a sign of strength, not weakness.

Manufacturing's Decline

But this is highly misleading. For example, the data that Rampell cites actually shows that the year the U.S. produced the most "stuff" was actually 15 years ago (2007), and by 2022 inflation-adjusted manufacturing output had fallen 4 percent. But even that raw number understates the decline because over that period real GDP grew 28 percent. So, if manufacturing output had remained at a constant share of GDP, it would have had to grow 28 percent, rather than declining 4 percent. This is relevant because as GDP grows, so does demand for manufactured goods: cars, computers, clothes, furniture, etc. If GDP grows 28 percent, unless manufacturing output also grows 28 percent, manufacturing will shrink as a share of the overall economy.

Another way of thinking about this is to compare the United States to a nation like South Korea. The United States produces more manufacturing goods than S. Korea, but that's because its economy is some 16 times larger. The real question is how big U.S. manufacturing is relative to other nations and over time. On both fronts it's not a good picture. Not only is manufacturing output going down, but manufacturing as a share of GDP is smaller than 24 out of 26 OECD nations.[8]

Measurement Distortions

The best way to measure manufacturing health is to look at real (adjusted for inflation) value-added growth (the amount of final sales subtracting inputs like electricity and component parts). But U.S. government manufacturing value-added statistics are overstated for two reasons. First, as offshoring has grown, the U.S. Bureau of Economic Analysis' ability to differentiate between the value added of manufacturing here vs. overseas has not kept up, with foreign value added often incorrectly attributed to domestic, making it look like U.S. output is much higher than it actually is.[9] In other words, as more final goods (e.g., computers, lawn mowers, etc.) are made with foreign parts, the government undercounts the value of those parts, making it look like there was more manufacturing in the United States than was in fact the case.

Second, to measure productivity in any sector (e.g., output per hour of work) BEA must control for inflation. If a car costs 4 percent more this year, how much of that increase was due to inflation as opposed to the new model being more technologically advanced or higher quality. If it's due to inflation, then real car manufacturing value added did not increase.

An even bigger measurement problem is how BEA accounts for changes in value added in the computer and electronics sector (known in official tables as NAICS 334). With Moore's Law at work (computing power doubling every 18 to 24 months), BEA treats semiconductor and computer output as if it doubled, rather than just the speed of the computer or smart phone doubling. In other words, if a new iPhone is 50 percent more powerful (in memory, processing speed, etc.; all due to Moore's law) BEA counts it as Apple boosting phone output by 50 percent.

Using this highly dubious method shows that from 1990 to 2010, the real gross output for computers and electronic products grew by 570 percent, 20 times faster than the growth rate for the rest of manufacturing. But nominal shipments of computer and electronic products from U.S. factories grew just 24 percent between 1992 and 2011, while between 2000 and 2010, they actually fell by about 70 percent. Using this highly exaggerated data suggests that total U.S. manufacturing value added increased by 13 percent from 2007 to 2021, leading many to claim that manufacturing output is at an all-time high.

But if we leave out the overstated NAICS 334 data, real output increased just 3 percent, 22 points less than real GDP growth. This statistical over-statement is so massive that it leads to an overestimate of GDP growth by approximately 25 percent in the 2000s.[10] In other words, if computers and electronics output was measured more appropriately, measured GDP growth in the 2000s would be 25 percent less. Sadly, all of the supposed health of U.S. manufacturing stems from this one totally misused factor: computers getting constantly faster.

Moreover, real manufacturing value added as a share of GDP for 18 of 19 U.S. manufacturing industries (leaving out NAIC 334: computers and electronics), actually declined from around 12 percent in 2006 to around 10 percent in the second quarter of 2021.[11] If this annual rate of decline continues, it will certainly dash any hopes for strategic self-sufficiency and resiliency. Today's growing interest in reshoring and bringing jobs back home clearly has a long way to go.

Weak International Comparisons

Finally, no assessment of U.S. manufacturing is comprehensive unless it looks at other nations. As ITIF has shown in its Hamilton Index of Advanced-Industry Performance (that looks at U.S. performance in phar-maceuticals; electrical equipment; machinery and equipment; motor vehicle equipment; other transport equipment; computer, electronic, and optical products; chemicals, fabricated metals; and information technology and information services),[12] U.S. performance is weak and declining.

U.S. global market share in advanced industries has fallen since 1995 from 5 percent under the size-adjusted global average to 13 percent, and 25 percent below when software is not included. China's share in advanced industries is 47 percent higher than the global average, Japan 21 percent, Germany 39 percent, South Korea 77 percent, and Taiwan more than double (110 percent). To match the advanced-industry share of China's economy, U.S. manufacturing output would have to nearly double.

Scapegoating Automation

When it comes to the massive job loss in U.S. manufacturing (declining from 17.4 million in 1999 to 12.9 million in 2023 (and from 16.5 percent of private-sector jobs to 9.8 percent) the deniers are not deterred because they argue that automation was the cause. From 1965 to 2000, manufacturing employment was more or less stable, hovering between 19.5 and 16.5 million jobs. But the 2000s saw this number plummet by more than 5 million—a rate faster than in the Great Depression. But undeterred, Rampell states, "We just happen to make that stuff with fewer workers than we used to, because technological advances have led to huge productivity gains."

That's not true. If high productivity were the cause of manufacturing job decline, how can we explain that U.S. manufacturing productivity gains were higher in the 1990s than in the 2000s, but manufacturing jobs declined just 3 percent in the 1990s compared to 33 percent in the 2010s? The difference was China joining the World Trade Organization in 2001, and U.S. companies offshoring millions of manufacturing jobs to China, Mexico, and elsewhere.

Rampell doubles down on her culprit of automation, stating: "U.S. factories still make things, but those things are increasingly produced by robots." In fact, when controlling for manufacturing wage levels, the United States ranks 16th in robots per 1,000 workers,[13] behind number one Korea, which has not seen any manufacturing job loss.[14] Moreover, over the last 13 or so years, U.S. manufacturing labor productivity has grown more slowly than overall economy-wide productivity, hardly a sign of "increasingly produced by robots."[15]

If manufacturing productivity was the driving factor behind job losses, then we should expect to see above-average rates of investment by manufacturers in machines and other fixed assets. In fact, while manufacturing fixed investment grew 5.3 percent per year from 1950 to 1999, it fell by 1.8 percent per year in the 2000s. This is why the United States ranked 25th of 29 OECD countries in the rate of manufacturing fixed investment in the 2000s.[16]

Moreover, U.S. manufacturing productivity (measured in real output per hour of labor) was lower at the end of 2022 than in 2020. In contrast, productivity increased by 0.5 percent for the non-manufacturing, non-farm business sector. More generally, U.S. manufacturing productivity has been in a secular decline. Between 2011 and 2021, it fell by 2.8 percent, hardly a sign of strength.[17]

Finally, if manufacturing is so strong, why does the United States run a massive trade deficit in manufactured goods, in absolute terms and as a share of GDP?[18] (Fig. 1) Similarly, if manufacturing is strong then the U.S. share of global manufacturing output should have grown, or at least remained stable. In fact, controlling for the value of the dollar, U.S. manufacturing output dropped from 25 percent of world share in the early 2000s to 18.4 percent in 2014.[19] It has no doubt fallen further since.

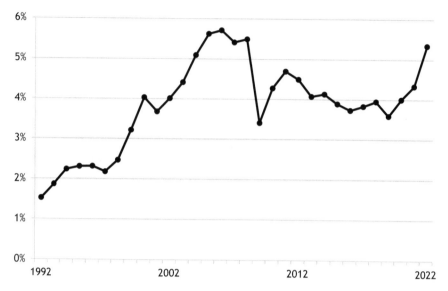

Fig. 1 Manufacturing trade deficit (minus food, beverage, and tobacco manufacturing) as a share of GDP[20]

In short, these myths let people maintain the comforting belief that globalization still works, and that we don't need a dreaded "industrial policy." But it's well past time for Washington to take America's manufacturing decline, especially in advanced sectors, much more seriously. This means ignoring those who say that manufacturing doesn't matter, that seeking to restore U.S. manufacturing is a form of nostalgia, that manufacturing is healthier than ever, or that we should fully embrace an emerging services economy. Instead, policymakers need to face today's stark manufacturing realities, and do something about them.

— *RA*

Notes

1. Catherine Rampell, "The Myth of the Manufacturing Comeback" *Washington Post,* September 2022, https://www.washingtonpost.com/opinions/2022/09/08/biden-manufacturing-made-america/.
2. John Keilman, "America Is Back in the Factory Business," *Wall Street Journal*, April 8, 2023, https://www.wsj.com/articles/american-manufacturing-factory-jobs-comeback-3ce0c52c.

3. John G. Murphy, "'We Don't Make Anything Anymore' and Other Myths About U.S. Manufacturing," U.S. Chamber of Commerce, October 2023, https://www.uschamber.com/international/trade-agr eements/we-dont-make-anything-anymore-and-other-myths-about-u-s-manufacturing.

4. Peter Whoriskey, "Productivity Gains in Manufacturing Are Overstated, Economists Say in New Report," *Washington Post*, March 2012, https://www.washingtonpost.com/business/economy/econom ists-offer-more-pessimistic-view-on-manufacturing-in-upcoming-rep ort/2012/03/19/giqakspzns_story.html.

5. Daniel Bell, "The Coming of the Post-Industrial Society," The Educational Forum, 1976, https://canvas.harvard.edu/files/3747690/download?download_frd=1.

6. Catherine Rampell, "The Real Problem with 'Bidenomics'," *The Washington Post*, September 10, 2023, https://www.washingtonpost.com/opinions/2023/09/10/biden-bidenomics-manufacturing-economy-jobs/.

7. Industrial Production: Manufacturing (NAICS) FRED ST Louis Federal Reserve, July 2023, https://fred.stlouisfed.org/series/IPMAN.

8. Manufacturing Value added (% of GDP)—OECD members, https://data.worldbank.org/indicator/NV.IND.MANF.ZS?locations=OE.

9. Susan Houseman et al., "Offshoring Bias in US Manufacturing" (Upjohn Institute for Employment Research, 2011), https://ideas.repec.org/p/upj/weupjo/snh20112.html.

10. Robert Atkinson et al., "Worse Than the Great Depression: What the Experts Are Missing About American Manufacturing Decline" (ITIF, March 2012), https://itif.org/publications/2012/03/19/worse-great-depression-what-experts-are-missing-about-american-manufacturing/.

11. Bureau of Economic Analysis, Industry Data (Value Added by Industry, Value Added by Industry as a Percentage of Gross Domestic Product (A); accessed October 7, 2023), https://www.bea.gov/itable/gdp-by-industry; Bureau of Economic Analysis, Data Archive (Data Archive: Gross Domestic Product by Industry and Input–Output Statistics, 2023, Q1; accessed October 7, 2023), https://apps.bea.gov/histdata/histChildLevels.cfm?HMI=8.

12. Robert Atkinson, "The Hamilton Index: Assessing National Performance in the Competition for Advanced Industries" (ITIF, June 2022), https://itif.org/publications/2022/06/08/the-hamilton-index-assessing-national-performance-in-the-competition-for-advanced-industries/.

13. Robert Atkinson, "Asia Leads in Industrial Robot Adoption. Why Europe and the US Lag Behind?" (Marsh McLennan, April 2019) https://www.brinknews.com/asia-leads-in-industrial-robot-adoption-why-do-europe-and-the-u-s-lag-behind/.

14. Statisa, "Annual Growth Rate of Employment in the Manufacturing Industry in South Korea from 1990–2021," https://www.statista.com/statistics/1323448/south-korea-employment-growth-in-manufacturing/.

15. Robert Atkinson, "US Manufacturing Productivity is Falling, and It's Cause for Alarm," (Industry Week, July 2021) https://www.industryweek.com/the-economy/article/21169426/falling-us-manufacturing-productivity-is-cause-for-alarm.

16. Bureau of Economic Analysis, Data Archive (Data Archive: Fixed Asset, 2020; accessed October 8, 2023), https://apps.bea.gov/histdata/histChildLevels.cfm?HMI=11; OECD Statistics, "8A. Capital formation by activity ISIC rev4," accessed October 8, 2023, https://stats.oecd.org/.

17. Ian Clay, "Fact of the Week: US Manufacturing Labor Productivity Fell by 2.8 Percent between 2011 and 2021," (ITIF, January 2023) https://itif.org/publications/2023/01/30/us-manufacturing-labor-productivity-fell-between-2011-and-2021/.

18. Robert Atkinson, "Korea Should Capitalize on Soaring Dollar," (Korea Times, September 2022), https://www.koreatimes.co.kr/www/opinion/2022/09/784_336032.html.

19. OECD Statistics, TiVA 2022 ed. Principal Indicators (VALU: Value added; C: Manufacturing; Accessed October 11, 2023), https://stats.oecd.org/Index.aspx?DataSetCode=TIVA_2022_C1.

20. USA Trade, "HS District-level Data," HS Codes 27–96, Accessed September 12, 2022, https://usatrade.census.gov/data/Perspective60/Browse/browsetables.aspx?utosid=845c439a95b6a88e9da17e387fd60268&cache=ribd7u; Bureau of Economic Analysis, "National Data: Gross Domestic Product," Table 1.1.5, Accessed September 12, 2022, https://apps.bea.gov/iTable/iTable.cfm?reqid=19&step=2#reqid=19&step=2&isuri=1&1921=survey.

Myth 35: India Will Save the West from China

While the potential synergies between the U.S. and India are real, today's talk of a close, long-term U.S./India alliance to outflank China is likely wishful thinking. India will pursue its own interests, and this means working with both the United States and China. While there is now a great deal of focus on America's dependence on China for physical goods, a similar dependence on India for software and services gets far less attention.

The surface case for India as a counterweight to China is compelling. While the history, politics, and culture of the world's two most populous nations couldn't be much more different, both countries also have much in common: decades-long efforts to lift their people out of poverty, vast domestic markets, huge numbers of skilled scientists, engineers, and technicians, a large and low-cost labor force, a global diaspora of multilingual students, professionals, and entrepreneurs, and deep information technology (IT) capabilities.

The case for closer U.S./India alignment is also compelling. Both are democracies, with strong linguistic, legal, and cultural affinities. Like the United States, India sees China as a geopolitical and military rival. Moreover, India has the potential to become an important global manufacturing hub for Western companies seeking an alternative to China, while U.S. companies such as Alphabet, Amazon, and Meta are currently much better positioned in India than they are in China.

Yet, there is another, much more worrisome parallel. Although America is now all too aware of its dependence on China for many essential manufactured goods, our increasing reliance on India for important hi-tech services

© The Author(s), under exclusive license to Springer Nature Switzerland AG 2024
R. D. Atkinson and D. Moschella, *Technology Fears and Scapegoats*,
https://doi.org/10.1007/978-3-031-52349-6_36

gets far less attention. The similarities between the way American businesses depend on India for IT services and China for manufacturing are striking. Both countries started with relatively low-level products and services, but now provide much more advanced and hard to replace offerings.

Like China, India has its own self-reliance movement (Atmanirbhar Bharat). While India greatly values the ready access to the U.S. market for its large technology services firms. It's also wary of becoming too dependent on America's Big Tech giants, and sees little reason why it shouldn't develop its own firms in these areas. Perhaps most strategically, India will carefully balance its opportunities, dependencies, and tensions with the U.S. and China; it's in India's long-term interest to have stable and productive relationships with both of the world's superpowers.

Growing India Dependency

Except for public sector businesses such as defense and education, nearly every large U.S. industry now relies heavily on Indian IT services in one way or another. Initially this work was mostly focused on back-office operations and support, but over time, India has moved up the value chain into business analytics, process automation, artificial intelligence (AI), research and development, the Internet of things, cloud migration, and other forms of *digital transformation.* There are four main approaches:

1. U.S. companies can contract directly with Indian IT services supplier such as TCS, Infosys, Wipro, HCL, Cognizant, or others. While not exactly household names, these firms are often highly successful. Industry leader, TCS, has a market capitalization of some $170 billion, about the same as IBM.
2. U.S. companies can indirectly get services from India by using Western companies such as Accenture, IBM, Deloitte, DXC, and others who do much of their actual work in India. These four U.S. organizations alone employ some 400,000 people in India, and could not successfully deliver their services without their India operations.
3. U.S. companies can set up their own operations in India. Sometimes this is called "in-sourcing," sometimes Global Capability Centers. But whatever one calls it, over 1,000 U.S. multinational companies now have large India-based operations, employing some one million people.

4. U.S. companies can bring Indian citizens to the United States. There are over 400,000 non-U.S. residents working in the United States through the H1-B visa program. Roughly three quarters of them—overwhelmingly in IT—are from India. Every year, American firms recruit heavily from India's many technical colleges, even in highly strategic areas such as semiconductor design.

The scale and significance of these four business models are not widely understood by American policymakers and isn't captured by traditional services trade data. Today, more than two million people of Indian nationality are now working to meet the IT needs of U.S. corporations. (This figure doesn't even count the vast number of American citizens and permanent residents of Indian heritage now working in tech hubs such as Silicon Valley, research institutes, universities, and other sources of digital innovation.) As only about five million U.S. citizens are IT professionals, it's clear that India is now an indispensable part of America's digital talent ecosystem.

Looking back, the parallels with China over the last twenty years are remarkable. The growth of China was given a huge boost by its admission into the World Trade Organization in 2001. Similarly, India's major IT services companies substantially increased their global business and reputation by doing much of the work needed to manage the "Y2K" challenge that dominated the IT agenda from 1998 to 2000. Since then, both nations have moved steadily up the value chain to the point of matching or even exceeding U.S. capabilities in various technological areas.

In some ways, America's reliance on India is greater than it is on China. It's mostly U.S. manufacturers and retail businesses that are dependent on China, whereas just about every industry sector now relies on India for IT. Many of these industries are doubly dependent on India in that they also rely heavily on Amazon, Microsoft, and Alphabet for cloud computing services, all three of whom have their own dependencies on India for talent, leadership, and ongoing support.

Indeed, many U.S. companies now face three types of dependency: China for physical goods, India for IT services, and the U.S. cloud giants for their core digital infrastructure. All three of these developments have taken place in less than 20 years, and although being dependent on India is not nearly as scary as being dependent on a geopolitical rival such as China, it's dependency, nonetheless.

India's STEM Model

Thus far, we've talked about India mostly as a place—a country where important work gets done. But India is also a people, and the spread of individuals of Indian nationality around the world is now a powerful economic force, especially within the IT industry. Today the CEOs of Microsoft, Alphabet, IBM, Adobe, and many others are of Indian heritage, but this is just the tip of a vast talent iceberg. Although Silicon Valley has long attracted skilled and ambitious individuals from all over the world, India's presence exceeds that of any other nation.

How did this come to be? Americans often seem to think that Indians (and Chinese) are just good at math and science, but the reality is much more systematic than that. In the excellent book, The Other One Percent, Indians in America, the authors describe a "triple selection" process, which historically has worked as follows:

1. India initially provided access to advanced education primarily to those with high social and economic status.
2. Within this pool, India's educational and examination systems selected those individuals best suited for advanced technical education.
3. The U.S. immigration system favored international students and individuals with technical talent, especially in IT and STEM fields.

Given that there were very limited STEM career possibilities within India during the 1970–2000 period, it's understandable that many highly educated people from India chose to move to the United States for either school or work. Despite often facing severe discrimination, people of Indian heritage now have the highest per capita income of any U.S. ethnic group. For example, people of Indian heritage account for just under one percent of the United States population, but over 5 percent of all U.S. physicians.

It's hard to overstate the importance of the triple selection process and the subsequent academic ties between India and the United States. There are now some 200,000 Indian students in the United States, with only China having comparable numbers. The figures within STEM fields are particularly striking, with roughly half of all master's and Ph.D. degrees now going to international students. In computer science it is more than half. Overall, 81 percent of full-time graduate students in U.S. university electrical engineering programs, and 79 percent in computer science, are international students. A 2019 Congressional Research Service report finds that nearly 70 percent of foreign students enrolled in STEM courses came from China and India.[1]

Keeping the Pipeline Flowing

Whether for work or study, most Indian immigrants to the United States initially came and stayed voluntarily—as opposed to fleeing severe hardships and/or oppression. This has created powerful bidirectional dynamics. The Indian community's very strong networks both within America and back to India have helped make talented Indians living in America particularly successful as global executives, managers, and entrepreneurs. In contrast, many Chinese professionals in the United States can't travel or communicate back home nearly as freely. This makes the global Indian diaspora a uniquely valuable community, not just in the United States, but also in the United Kingdom, Australia, Canada, Singapore, Africa, the Mideast, and elsewhere.

It is vital that this pipeline of talent continues to come to the United States, and that many Indian students decide to live and work in America after graduation, especially as the flow of Chinese students to the United States in advanced STEM fields slows due to the current geopolitical tensions. However, many people of Indian heritage—old and young alike—are concerned about America's current cultural tensions, crime, and declining educational standards. America would be seriously diminished if Indian students, teachers, and businesspeople ever decide to stay home or live elsewhere.

India's Neutrality

It's fashionable these days to see the United States and India as natural partners—two democracies working to limit the influence of an authoritarian China. But this is only a recent phenomenon. Throughout the Cold War, India was among the leaders of the so-called Non-Aligned Movement, a group of nations that sought to avoid taking sides in the competition between the United States and the Soviet Union.

As Jawaharlal Nehru noted back in 1946, "We propose, as far as possible, to keep away from the power politics of groups, aligned against one another, which have led in the past to world wars and which may again lead to disasters on an even vaster scale." Additionally, many prominent Indian leaders have long been sympathetic to socialism and often have had an "anti-North" attitude. As evidenced by India's neutrality regarding the war in Ukraine, these inclinations haven't gone away.

It's easy for Americans—but not Indians—to overlook the fact that during the 1980s, the United States was closely aligned with India's most embittered rival, Pakistan. But after the USSR crumbled, Pakistan came to be seen as too close to the Taliban and Al Qaeda; India's IT industry flourished, and China loomed. The United States and India were increasingly drawn together—a development boosted by the seemingly close relationship between Prime Minister Modi and President Trump, and further accelerated by India's border conflicts with China. Given China's currently aggressive military stance in the region, U.S./India defense ties could well strengthen further.

However, U.S./India relations could easily change once again. India's dispute with China over their largely uninhabited border region has already faded somewhat. And although the Quad (Quadrilateral Security Dialog) between the United States, India, Japan, and Australia provides a framework for collective efforts to curb China, its ability to go much beyond the dialog stage is anything but assured. Most importantly, today's U.S./India cooperation will likely prove to be less potent than it currently appears because the potential business interests between China and India are so compelling.

A Worrisome Future?

The nightmare scenario for America's technology industry is that the combination of Chinese manufacturing capacity and India's strengths in software and services creates an industry value chain that is not reliant on the major U.S. tech firms. India has seen how China's technology industry has thrived by blocking the U.S. tech giants and giving its own firms—Alibaba, Tencent, Baidu, and many others—time to develop. It also knows that China can help India become a manufacturing center at least as much as the West can, probably more. These are powerful incentives to once again remain largely neutral in a superpower rivalry. There's no real incentive to choose sides.

Similarly, China can see that India could be a vast new market, largely free from Western pressures and sanctions. It also knows that India strengths in software, services, and semiconductor design can help China reduce or even eliminate its dependence on America. Both India and China would like to break free of the power of Alphabet (Android software), Microsoft (PC and enterprise software), as well as Intel, Arm, Nvidia, and other semiconductor giants. The emergence of the open-source, royalty-free RISC-V system architecture may provide the means to address some of these concerns.

From America's perspective, both China and India present tremendous business opportunities, but also worrisome dependencies. America has clearly woken up to the China challenge. However, this awakening took so long that there are now very few painless options. The options are more appealing with today's more friendly India, but the problems are remarkably similar, and once again America has been largely oblivious to the challenge. It took twenty years for the United States to become highly dependent on China and India, and there is no quick fix in either case. America, China, Europe, and India will define the main dimensions of an emerging multipolar world. Their interests aren't always aligned.

—DM

Note

1. "Foreign STEM Students in the United States," Congresssional Resrach Service, November 2019, https://crsreports.congress.gov/product/pdf/IF/IF11347.

Myth 36: The EU's Digital Rules Are a Model for the World

It's becoming accepted wisdom in the West that the only way to safeguard citizens from the potential harms of artificial intelligence is to embrace a precautionary approach, and regulate AI now. As with digital privacy, European policymakers have been particularly active. But as we saw with privacy, overly strict regulations often do more to raise costs than protect consumers. America needs to adopt a more optimistic and pro-innovation approach.

When the World Wide Web and the commercial Internet emerged in the 1990s, most nations followed the United States' lead and promoted it rather than regulating it. Today, anti-tech advocates don't want to let that "mistake" happen again (although they struggle to say what they would have done differently). Now, they warn, is the time to wrap artificial intelligence in a web of regulations; otherwise, really bad things will happen.

The European Union (EU) has become the pied piper of this narrative, trying to lure the world toward its vision of broad government control over this emerging technology. It has declared its law for AI—the Artificial Intelligence Act (AIA)—to be the "world's first rules on AI" and is touting its approach as a model for countries around the world.[1] The Act is notable for the expansive way it defines AI systems, and the extensive documentation, training, and monitoring requirements it imposes on AI tools. Any company that touches the EU market and develops or wants to adopt machine learning-based software will be affected by the AIA.[2]

The EU has been working hard to evangelize the AI Act in both the East and the West. Officials have reportedly been dispatched to at least 10 Asian countries including India, Japan, South Korea, Singapore, and the

© The Author(s), under exclusive license to Springer Nature Switzerland AG 2024
R. D. Atkinson and D. Moschella, *Technology Fears and Scapegoats*,
https://doi.org/10.1007/978-3-031-52349-6_37

Philippines, but because most of these nations still want innovation and competitiveness, the reception has been lukewarm.[3] Many Asian recognize that new technologies do not necessarily require new laws, and that the harms of new regulations could outweigh any potential benefits. India's Minister of Electronics and Information Technology issued a statement in the spring of 2023 explaining that "the government is not considering bringing a law or regulating the growth of artificial intelligence in the country."[4]

However, the narrative that the risks from AI are so severe that they require major new regulations has resonated with policymakers in North America. Like the European Union, Canada has proposed an AI law called the Artificial Intelligence and Data Act (AIDA) that it hopes will create "a new regulatory system designed to guide AI innovation in a positive direction, and to encourage the responsible adoption of AI technologies by Canadians and Canadian businesses."[5]

The AIDA seems to be premised on the assumption that stronger technology regulation increases consumer trust, and that higher levels of consumer trust will lead to more technology use.[6] But, as past research has shown, there is little evidence to back up that claim.[7] Indeed, fears that a lack of consumer trust may hold back AI adoption appear to be pure conjecture. ChatGPT gained 100 million users in two months, crushing all past records of consumer adoption of a new app.[8]

In the United States, AI alarmists have also struck a chord with policymakers. Exaggerated assertions of potential harms, exemplified by a March 2023 open letter from the Future of Life Institute (FLI), which urged labs to pause the development of advanced AI systems due to unfounded claims of existential risk, have triggered frenetic regulatory activity.

The rhetoric that the United States lags behind the EU in regulating AI has also found attentive ears in the news media, serving as a dog-whistle for action in U.S. policy circles. *The New York Times* has warned, "The United States remains far behind Europe, where lawmakers are preparing to enact an A.I. law." *The Guardian* likewise reported, "The EU is leading the way on AI laws. The US is still playing catch-up."[9] So far the Biden administration has not proposed an EU-style AI Act but it has signaled its interest, including with a draft AI Bill of Rights and a far-reaching executive order on AI regulation.[10] Moreover, several states, including California, Connecticut, Illinois, and Texas, have forged ahead with developing their own laws, and more are likely to follow.

Why Countries Don't Need Sweeping New AI Regulations

The myth that countries need to enact extensive new AI regulations is based on two faulty premises.

The first is that AI is the key factor behind many emerging issues that necessitate new regulations. But many of the concerns underpinning calls for new AI regulation are not actually about AI. For example, the White House's "Blueprint for an AI Bill of Rights" lists concerns such as bias in hiring practices and credit scoring, lack of recourse when unfavorable outcomes occur, and insufficient consumer privacy. Yet, none of those issues are unique to AI.[11] Instead, they are broader problems that (sometimes) have an AI element.

Focusing solely on regulating AI as a solution to such complex, messy, and long-standing social problems is what American philosopher Charles West Churchman called "taming the growl" in 1967. These sorts of solutions, he noted, consist "of 'carving off' a piece of a problem and finding a rational and feasible solution to this piece. ... the taming of the growl may deceive the innocent into believing that the wicked problem is completely tamed."[12] Regulators should focus on the broader problem, not just the part of the problem involving AI. For example, regulators shouldn't just address biased hiring practices involving AI, but rather all biased hiring practices.

The second erroneous assumption is that existing regulations are insufficient to address many of the risks AI poses. But AI does not exempt organizations from following existing rules. Many such laws and regulations, covering areas like worker safety, product liability, and discrimination, apply to AI use as well. For instance, companies must adhere to anti-discrimination laws regardless of whether hiring decisions involve human or AI systems.

To address AI-related concerns, regulators should clarify how they will enforce current rules related to emerging AI products, offer guidance to those adopting these technologies, and solicit public input on potential issues. For example, the U.S. Equal Employment Opportunity Commission (EEOC) and the Consumer Financial Protection Bureau (CFPB) have initiated efforts to address algorithmic fairness within their existing purview and missions.

Regulatory Motivations

It is worth considering why the EU advocates the need for a stringent approach to AI regulation instead of a light-touch approach when doing so could harm innovation and make the bloc less competitive? A paper published in 2021 by an academic at the KU Leuven faculty of law explains:

> ... countries that are the first to adopt regulation on the development and use of AI could arguably gain an advantage over others. The reasoning goes as follows: if country A adopts new regulatory requirements for AI-systems, domestic companies will start learning to abide thereby by necessity. Moreover, any foreign company based in country B that still wishes to serve the market of country A, will need to start abiding thereby too. The companies of country B will however incur costs to ensure compliance with the requirements of country A, a cost that companies in country B who only serve the domestic market do not carry. They will therefore try to eliminate that domestic disadvantage by lobbying the government of country B to adopt similar requirements, ensuring that domestic companies have an equally high burden of regulatory compliance. As a consequence, country B will ultimately adopt similar requirements as country A, but it will be a rule-taker rather than a rule-setter, and its domestic companies will still need to catch up with the new requirements while the companies of country A will already have internalized the relevant costs.[13]

The textbook example of this regulatory first-mover dynamic is the EU's General Data Protection Regulation (GDPR), which went into force in 2018 and quickly became the global standard. Even though many have argued that the GDPR has failed to live up to its promise and that its unintended consequences have been widespread, it is still one of the EU's most successful regulatory export products. Other countries have adopted GDPR-like legislation for various privacy reasons, but they have often done so because they have little choice but to align their regulatory frameworks with the EU's if they want to serve Europe's huge consumer market.

Similarly, the EU's goal is to become "the world's super-regulator in AI," as *The Economist* neatly summed it up in a 2021 headline.[14] A slow regulatory convergence for AI rules, as has happened with GDPR, serves it well. Indeed, the pressure is already on the United States, with European Commissioner for Justice Didier Reynders telling *Wired* in July 2023 that if the EU's forthcoming AI Act isn't matched with comparable U.S. rules for AI, it will be more difficult for U.S. tech giants to be in full compliance.[15]

What Should Policymakers Do Instead?

Regulation is a means to an end, not an end in itself. Because regulation can limit innovation and impose costs on society, policymakers should always seek the most appropriate balance between protection and innovation. Minimizing potential harm from AI systems is an important goal, but so too is maximizing the potential benefits of AI systems. Unfortunately, while policymakers want AI systems that do not cause harm, they have not mastered the art of creating regulations that do not harm AI innovation, as ITIF's Center for Data Innovation explained in a 2023 report.[16]

Designed properly, regulations can spur AI innovation and productivity by reducing uncertainty and rewarding beneficial actions. A good regulatory climate certainly does not mean a simple absence of regulations. Instead, it is one that supports rather than blocks AI innovators and creates the conditions to spur even more innovation, with new products and start-ups entering the market, while at the same time providing more flexibility and efficiency for use in industry.[17] The Center enumerated 10 core responsible yet supportive AI principles:

1. **Avoid Pro-Human Biases**. Allow AI systems to do what is legal for humans (and prohibit what is illegal too).
2. **Regulate Performance, Not Process**. Address concerns about AI safety, efficacy, and bias by assessing outcomes not methods.
3. **Regulate Sectors, Not Technologies**. Set rules for specific AI applications in particular sectors rather than creating broad rules for AI overall.
4. **Avoid AI Myopia**. Address the whole problem rather than fixating on just the portion of a problem involving AI.
5. **Define AI**. Define AI clearly to avoid inadvertently including other software and systems within the scope of new regulations.
6. **Apply Existing Rules**. Hold AI accountable for adhering to existing non-AI regulations.
7. **Ensure Benefits Outweigh Costs**. Consider the full potential costs, not just the benefits of regulations.
8. **Seek Optimization**. Maximize the benefits and minimize the costs of regulations.
9. **Treat Firms Equally**. Apply rules to firms regardless of their size or where they are based.
10. **Leverage Expertise**. Augment regulatory expertise with technical and industry experience.[18]

U.S. policymakers should resist the pressure to harmonize with the EU's AI and privacy rules. If policymakers want to realize the full benefits of AI, they should embrace the hope-based innovation principle, not the fear-based precautionary principle.[19] That is not to say that they should be Pollyannish or libertarian. But the ten innovation principles above can help America maintain its current AI leadership, and provide a global alternative to Europe's more precautionary approach. The time for leadership is now.

—RA

Notes

1. "EU AI Act: First Regulation on Artificial Intelligence" (European Parliament News, June 2023), https://www.europarl.europa.eu/news/en/headlines/society/20230601STO93804/eu-ai-act-first-regulation-on-artificial-intelligence.
2. Benjamin Mueller, "The Artificial Intelligence Act: A Quick Explainer" (ITIF Center for Data Innovation, May 2021), https://datainnovation.org/2021/05/the-artificial-intelligence-act-a-quick-explainer/.
3. "EU Wants AI Act to Be Global Benchmark, but Asian Countries Are Not Convinced" (Reuters in South China Morning Post, July 2023), https://www.scmp.com/tech/tech-trends/article/3228050/eu-wants-ai-act-be-global-benchmark-asian-countries-are-not-convinced.
4. Daniel Castro, "US Policymakers Should Learn from Countries Choosing Not to Regulate AI" (ITIF Center for Data Innovation, May 2023), https://datainnovation.org/2023/05/u-s-policymakers-should-learn-from-countries-choosing-not-to-regulate-ai/.
5. "The Artificial Intelligence and Data Act (AIDA) – Companion document," Government of Canada, March 2023, https://ised-isde.canada.ca/site/innovation-better-canada/en/artificial-intelligence-and-data-act-aida-companion-document.
6. Daniel Castro, "Canada's Reasons for an AI Law Do Not Stand Up to Scrutiny" (ITIF Center for Data Innovation, March 2023), https://datainnovation.org/2023/03/canadas-reasons-for-an-ai-law-do-not-stand-up-to-scrutiny/.
7. Alan McQuinn and Daniel Castro, "Why Stronger Privacy Regulations Do Not Spur Increased Internet Use" (ITIF, July 2018), https://www2.itif.org/2018-trust-privacy.pdf.

8. Dan Milmo, "ChatGPT Reaches 100 Million Users Two Months after Launch," *The Guardian* (February 2023), https://www.theguardian.com/technology/2023/feb/02/chatgpt-100-million-users-open-ai-fastest-growing-app.

9. Cecilia Kang, "In US Regulating AI Is in Its 'Early Days'," *New York Times* (July 2023), https://www.nytimes.com/2023/07/21/technology/ai-united-states-regulation.html; Johana Bhuiyan and Nick Robins-Early, "The EU Is Leading the Way on AI Laws. The US Is Still Playing Catch-Up," *The Guardian* (June 2023), https://www.theguardian.com/technology/2023/jun/13/artificial-intelligence-us-regulation.

10. Daniel Castro, "White House AI Bill of Rights Is All Wrong, Says Center for Data Innovation" (ITIF, October 2022), https://itif.org/publications/2022/10/04/white-house-ai-bill-of-rights-is-all-wrong-says-center-for-data-innovation/; "Executive Order on the Safe, Secure, and Trustworthy Development and Use of Artificial Intelligence," The White House (October 20, 2023), https://www.whitehouse.gov/briefing-room/presidential-actions/2023/10/30/executive-order-on-the-safe-secure-and-trustworthy-development-and-use-of-artificial-intelligence/.

11. Daniel Castro, "Ten Principles for Regulation That Does Not Harm AI Innovation" (ITIF Center for Data Innovation, February 2023), https://www2.datainnovation.org/2023-ten-principles-ai-regulation.pdf.

12. C. West Churchman, "Wicked Problems," *Management Science*, vol. 14(4) (December 1967), https://punkrockor.files.wordpress.com/2014/10/wicked-problems-churchman-1967.pdf.

13. Natalie Smuha, "From A 'Race to AI Regulation': Regulatory Competition for Artificial Intelligence," *Law, Innovation & Technology*, vol. 13(1), 2021 (March 2021), https://papers.ssrn.com/sol3/papers.cfm?abstract_id=3501410.

14. "The EU Wants to Become the World's Super-Regulator in AI" (The Brussels effect, The Economist, April 2021), https://www.economist.com/europe/2021/04/24/the-eu-wants-to-become-the-worlds-super-regulator-in-ai.

15. Paresh Dave, "The EU Urges the US to Join the Fight to Regulate AI" (Wired, July 2023), https://www.wired.com/story/the-eu-urges-the-us-to-join-the-fight-to-regulate-ai/.

16. Daniel Castro, "Ten Principles for Regulation That Does Not Harm AI Innovation" (ITIF Center for Data Innovation, February 2023),

https://www2.datainnovation.org/2023-ten-principles-ai-regulation.
pdf.

17. Hodan Omaar, "US AI Policy Report Card" (Center for Data Innovation, July 2022), https://www2.datainnovation.org/2022-ai-report-card.pdf.

18. Daniel Castro, "Ten Principles for Regulation That Does Not Harm AI Innovation" (ITIF Center for Data Innovation, February 2023), https://www2.datainnovation.org/2023-ten-principles-ai-regulation.
pdf.

19. Daniel Castro and Michael McLaughlin, "Ten Ways the Precautionary Principle Undermines Progress in Artificial Intelligence" (ITIF, February 2019), https://itif.org/publications/2019/02/04/ten-ways-precautionary-principle-undermines-progress-artificial-intelligence/.

Myth 37: Antitrust Actions Are Needed to Curb Big Tech

Antitrust supporters often cite the precedents of IBM, AT&T, Microsoft and Intel. But the history of these cases is complex and shows that targeted remedies are much more effective than sweeping antitrust interventions. The myth that strong antitrust actions have been a major part of technology industry progress could lead to larger interventions than necessary, with serious unintended consequences.

In both Washington and Brussels, the debate over whether or how to reign in Big Tech has become increasingly philosophical in nature. The long-standing view that antitrust interventions are only justified when real consumer harm has been demonstrated is being challenged by those who believe market dominance is inherently a problem. These *Neo-Brandeisians* argue that dominant companies will inevitably treat their competitors unfairly, eventually slowing innovation, and thus be bad for consumers too. They conclude that it's best to intervene early to prevent more serious problems later.

But no matter which side of this debate you are on, the practical questions are the same. Will the marketplace eventually address today's concerns about the size and power of "Big Tech"? If not, what specific policy interventions will do the most good and the least harm? Should these interventions be led by the Courts, Congress, or a federal agency? Perhaps most importantly, will government-imposed changes improve American innovation and global competitiveness over the longer term?

Although history doesn't always repeat itself, 50 years of high-tech antitrust experience suggests a cautious approach. Contrary to what you often hear, the four biggest information technology (IT) antitrust cases thus far have all

© The Author(s), under exclusive license to Springer Nature
Switzerland AG 2024
R. D. Atkinson and D. Moschella, *Technology Fears and Scapegoats*,
https://doi.org/10.1007/978-3-031-52349-6_38

either proved to be unnecessary or have resulted in serious adverse consequences. In contrast, requiring dominant tech companies to modify certain carefully selected business practices has consistently helped the digital world move forward.

The IT industry has a particularly rich body of antitrust experience because IT markets have always had unusually strong winner-take-all tendencies. Whether we are assessing IBM's dominance of the mainframe business, AT&T's control of America's telecom infrastructure, Microsoft's and Intel's influence over personal computers, or the triumphs of Alphabet, Amazon, Apple, and Meta in today's mobility and Internet eras, the pattern is the same. The virtually infinite-scale economies of software and data, the increasing returns that stem from network effects, and customers' desire to make safe choices in complex, risky, and fast-moving technology markets have helped the strong get stronger—at least until the digital paradigm shifts. During each era, complaints about unfair competition and abuse of market power have echoed across Europe and the United States. What can we learn from these experiences?

IBM and AT&T

Over the long history of high-tech antitrust, no date was more momentous than January 8, 1982. On that fateful Friday, the Reagan administration's Justice Department dropped the 13-year-long antitrust suit against IBM— deeming it as "without merit." DOJ also settled its eight-year antitrust battle with AT&T. In a landmark Consent Decree, the telecom giant agreed to divest its local telephone service business into seven new Regional Bell Operating Companies.

DOJ had sought to break up IBM into separate mainframe and small business system companies because it believed IBM was too powerful for other companies to compete against. Throughout the 1970s, it was widely believed that IBM would extend its dominance into satellites, telecommunications, financial services, robotics, and other domains. But by the mid-1980s, IBM had already lost its control of the IT industry. A new paradigm of microprocessor-based systems was rapidly making many proprietary mainframe and minicomputer designs obsolete. By the late 1980s, the idea that IBM needed to be broken up was laughable. Today, the company, while still successful, is a shadow of its once-gigantic self. The government was right to drop this long and expensive case.

Unlike IBM, AT&T was broken up. However, as with IBM, it was changing technology—not antitrust intervention—that led to the biggest industry restructuring. Over the last 30 years, traditional wired telephony services all around the world have been largely replaced by cable/broadband offerings, mobile phone operators, and Internet service providers. These technology shifts were inevitable and have had many great benefits.

But the breakup of AT&T had two major downsides: It led directly to the decline of Bell Labs, once the world's leading research organization. The breakup also helped European and Asian firms dominate the global telecom equipment market, as they do to this day.[1] The demise of Lucent, formerly AT&T's once powerful Western Electric, is another sad chapter in America's manufacturing decline, but it's also a powerful example of adverse unintended consequences. What remains of Bell Labs and Lucent is now owned by the Finnish firm, Nokia, while the global 5G wireless market is dominated by China and Ericsson.

Microsoft's Revitalization

As with IBM, it was widely believed that Microsoft was unstoppable, and in May of 1998 DOJ filed its antitrust suit. Once again, the goal was to break up the market leader, this time by separating Microsoft's applications from its operating system business. But even as the suit was being filed, Microsoft was already on the defensive, as the company missed the early years of both the Internet and mobile phone businesses.

Microsoft and DOJ settled the suit in 2001, with minor, but still helpful, actions such as requiring Microsoft to provide information about its application programming interface to third-party providers. More importantly, Microsoft's steady profits from its applications and operating system businesses enabled it to survive its strategic mistakes and eventually become the essential supplier and potent competitor it is today. A breakup might well have made Microsoft's extraordinary revitalization impossible. Once again, settling the case with only minor changes was the right call.

Undermining Intel

In 1981, IBM chose to use Intel microprocessors in its personal computers, giving Intel a temporary monopoly in this highly strategic market. In 1991, Advanced Micro Devices—a maker of Intel-compatible microprocessors—filed an antitrust suit alleging that Intel "engaged in unlawful acts designed to secure and maintain a monopoly." After much acrimony and numerous related investigations in the United States, Europe, and Japan, the two companies settled in 2009, ending their patent and licensing disputes, with Intel paying AMD $1.25 billion. (There was never any effort to break up Intel since microprocessors are the firm's only dominant business.)

But although a viable and successful AMD clearly helped consumers by lowering PC prices, it weakened Intel's global position. AMD's success made it harder for Intel to compete in capital-intensive semiconductor manufacturing, let alone build factories in the United States. Unlike Lucent, Intel remains a rich and powerful firm, but it's more strategically vulnerable than it's been in decades. Like AT&T, Intel provides a cautionary tale for policymakers who can see how to increase domestic competition in the short run but can't possibly foresee the unintended consequences over the longer, global term.

History Suggests Humility

The IBM and Microsoft stories show that previous high-profile efforts to break up Big Tech were unnecessary. The AT&T and Intel cases highlight the unintended consequences that major government interventions can have. All four histories suggest the need for policymakers to pursue more narrow remedies.

Here, the evidence is on the interventionist's side. IBM, AT&T, Microsoft, and Intel did make life difficult for their competitors, often in very aggressive ways. Rulings and pressures from governments in Europe and the United States effectively addressed some of these concerns. For example, from 1956 to 1996, IBM stayed out of the computer services business; in 1969, it unbundled its hardware and software pricing, making it easier for firms to build and sell IBM-compatible products. AT&T was forced to allow third-party telephones and new long-distance carriers such as MCI to connect to its telephony services. Microsoft and Intel both modified their business practices to treat PC suppliers more even-handedly. These were all significant improvements, with few serious downsides.

Taken together, the failures and successes of the past point the way forward for today. Once again, the case for sweeping antitrust intervention is weak. In both the mainframe and PC eras, there were just two powerful firms—IBM/AT&T and then Microsoft/Intel—neither of which competed directly with the other. Today's claims that five companies—Alphabet, Amazon, Apple, Meta, and Microsoft—are unassailable monopolies are almost self-refuting, especially as these firms increasingly compete with each other and face stiffening competition from China and others, with numerous disruptive scenarios on the horizon.[2]

While it might be tempting to separate Amazon's retail and cloud computing businesses, break up Alphabet into search, email, Android, YouTube, and other businesses, or demand that Meta divest Instagram and/or WhatsApp, this type of armchair chess playing has historically either proved to be unnecessary or had serious unintended consequences. The current antitrust actions against Google, Amazon, and Apple seem likely to repeat the pattern of being launched at the very time these firms are facing increasing competition.

We should also be skeptical of efforts to restrict these firms' future acquisitions or unwind previous ones. Acquiring small companies is an important form of R&D in the tech sector, and an essential part of the start-up and venture capital ecosystems. To spur innovation, new companies need the freedom to sell, ideally to the highest bidder.

Ask yourself: Was it right in 2013 for the FTC to allow the Israeli firm Waze—and its 100 employees—to sell itself to Google for $1.1 billion, or should Waze have been forced into a long battle with Google Maps that this tiny start-up knew it might well lose? If you were one of Instagram's 13 employees in 2012, would you turn down Facebook's $1 billion offer? Ditto for the 55 WhatsApp employees who were no doubt pleased by Facebook's $19 billion offer in 2014. Large acquisitions should still be subject to traditional M&A scrutiny, but acquiring start-ups is a critical part of the Silicon Valley ecosystem.

Rather than sweeping breakups and/or divestments, government oversight should focus on particular business practices and complaints, and as in the past, plaintiffs will sometimes have a compelling case. Companies are not saints, and they inevitably push hard to maximize their interests. It's certainly fair game for regulators to examine Amazon's retail pricing strategies, Apple's app store policies, Google's ad auction dynamics, Facebook's data-usage practices, and similar areas. Such inquiries resemble those that proved helpful in the mainframe, telephony, and PC eras.

The bottom line is that whether you subscribe to the consumer welfare or the Neo-Brandeisian school of antitrust, targeted remedial actions are sometimes justified, and if done well they can result in increased competition. However, as in the past, the biggest transformations will come, not from antitrust interventions, but from shifts in technology and the marketplace. Policymakers need to be humble about how much they should do and very smart about how to do it. This has never been an easy task, and it won't get any easier going forward. Faced with a rising China and the massive investments needed for the future, America's digital economy needs to be nudged forward, not dismantled. History suggests that doing too much is riskier than doing too little.

—DM

Notes

1. Robert D. Atkinson, "Who Lost Lucent?: The Decline of America's Telecom Equipment Industry," *American Affairs*, vol. IV(3) (Fall 2020), https://americanaffairsjournal.org/2020/08/who-lost-lucent-the-decline-of-americas-telecom-equipment-industry/.
2. David Moschella and Robert D. Atkinson, "'Big Tech' Is Not Immune to Creative Destruction" (ITIF Innovation Files, January 2022), https://itif.org/publications/2022/01/07/big-tech-not-immune-creative-destruction.

Myth 38: Federal R&D Crowds Out Private R&D

Many free-market conservatives believe there is only a fixed amount of scientific and engineering research that will be conducted, and thus efforts by government to fund more R&D just "crowds out" more efficient private-sector investments. That isn't true. Both business history and multiple studies show that federal R&D is highly efficient and actually "crowds in" additional private R&D spending.

Both private and public R&D can spur innovation and productivity growth. But because of an abiding faith in "free markets" and a commitment to limited government, many conservatives oppose increases in federal funding of science and engineering research. To justify their position, many claim federal R&D is not additive; it simply crowds out private-sector R&D funding, and we are left with the same amount of R&D as before, just less efficiently done.

As the Heritage Foundation has stated, "By attempting to force government-developed technologies into the market, the government diminishes the role of the entrepreneur and crowds out private-sector investment."[1] If this were true, it would be a powerful argument for government to not increase R&D spending because it wastes scarce public resources on something the private sector would do anyway.

But in making their case, free-market proponents seldom offer much more than ideology. If they did, it would be clear that the evidence directly contradicts their claims. Rather than crowding out business R&D, federal investment "crowds in," business efforts, leading to more company R&D than would otherwise be the case.

© The Author(s), under exclusive license to Springer Nature Switzerland AG 2024
R. D. Atkinson and D. Moschella, *Technology Fears and Scapegoats*,
https://doi.org/10.1007/978-3-031-52349-6_39

The reason is simple: Federal support for basic and applied research complements private research. Knowledge discoveries from publicly supported research provide firms—large and small—with a common platform of basic knowledge, making their own research more productive, effective, and targeted. Indeed, government support for a promising line of research also helps convince firms to boost their own efforts in a particular area.

The Evidence Is In

After reviewing over 60 academic articles on whether public sector R&D crowds out private-sector investments, Cockburn and Henderson concluded:

> There are a number of econometric studies that, while imperfect and undoubtedly subject to improvement and revision, between them make a quite convincing case for a high rate of return to public science in this [life-sciences] industry. It is worth noting that there are, so far as we are aware, no systematic quantitative studies that have found a negative impact of public science.[2]

A 2013 working paper from the World Bank combed through evidence on government funding for R&D, and found that it significantly increases R&D investment.[3] Although there was a large variation in the type of R&D funding examined, the chosen methodologies, and the location of the studies, the results were clear: Government funding boosts R&D spending. The paper also tackled whether government spending "crowds out" private-sector spending, and found the opposite. The data showed public funding incentivizes firms to invest more in R&D.[4]

Another study in 2019 found that government research and development spending has ripple effects, opening doors to new avenues of research. The study looked at patents from 1976 to 2017 that were directly connected to government research and found that a substantial portion of patents (28.2 percent in 2017) relied on government-funded research, and that this figure has increased substantially over time, up from 10 percent in 1975.[5]

Former White House Council of Economic Advisors head Ben Bernanke found that the spillover effects of technologies and research created by the defense sector vastly outweigh any crowding out, with each dollar of defense R&D creating an additional 20–30 cents of private R&D. Another study found that from 1966 to 2003 a 10 percent increase in military procurement led to a 0.7 percent increase in corporate R&D spending and patenting.[6]

For the life-sciences industry, eEconomist Everett Ehrlich found that a dollar of National Institutes of Health (NIH) support for research leads to an increase of roughly 32 cents in private medical research.[7] As an OECD study found, "Direct government funding of R&D performed by firms (either grants or procurement) has a positive effect on business financed R&D (one dollar given to firms results in 1.70 dollars of research on average)."[8] What is more, research has shown there is a strong positive correlation between private R&D investment in a given year and public R&D spending in the previous year.[9]

Public/Private Synergies

The reasoning behind the complementarity nature of private and public R&D is twofold. First, public R&D investment corrects the market failure of the private sector underinvesting in R&D because individual businesses cannot capture all the benefits of their R&D investments for themselves; some of the benefits inevitably flow to competitors and society. Conversely, public R&D dollars expand the knowledge base, which businesses build on by conducting further R&D to create and commercialize new innovations.

Second, businesses that receive federal R&D funding are able to attract more private R&D investments. One reason is that federal R&D grants have a strict evaluation process, which serves as a good indicator of the company's potential for private investors. For example, economist Sabrina Howell found that companies that have received a Small Business Innovation Research award doubled their chances of receiving venture capital in the future.[10]

The Impact on Productivity and Growth

And yet some free-market fundamentalists argue not just that federal R&D substitutes for private-sector R&D, but that it has minimal impact on productivity compared to private-sector R&D. Matt Ridley, in a *Wall Street Journal* op-ed titled "The Myth of Basic Science," cited a U.S. Bureau of Labor Statistics (BLS) article as proof that the return on investment from publicly financed R&D is near zero. Cherry picking from a 2007 article by BLS economist Leo Sveikauskas, Ridley claimed that the evidence showed "that returns from many forms of publicly financed R&D are near zero and that 'many elements of university and government research have very low returns, overwhelmingly contribute to economic growth only indirectly, if at all'".[11]

But what the BLS article actually measured was the impact of that R&D on the productivity of government agencies, which is in fact low. After all, when NIH funds research to treat diabetes or cancer, the results do little to make NIH workers more productive. In fact, the BLS article later concludes that "many advances arising from university or government research eventually have an important indirect effect on growth," and that "programs, especially those in which university scientists compete for grants, such as the National Science Foundation, the National Institutes of Health, some Department of Agriculture programs, and DARPA [Defense Advanced Research Projects Agency] in the Department of Defense, appear to have a remarkable record."[12]

Ridley also misled when he cited an OECD study on the sources of growth among member countries in the 1970s, 1980s, and 1990s as evidence that "whereas privately funded research and development stimulated economic growth, publicly funded research had no economic impact whatsoever. None. This earthshaking result has never been challenged or debunked."[13] Yet, the OECD study Ridley cited immediately qualified that finding with:

> [T]here are important interactions between public and private R&D activities as well as difficult-to-measure benefits from public R&D (e.g., defence, energy, health, and university research) from the generation of basic knowledge that provides technology spillovers in the long run.

Moreover, later and more comprehensive OECD studies found that government-funded research does have a major effect on innovation and growth.[14] This should not be a surprise because virtually every scholarly study examining the issue finds the same thing. For example, Griliches concluded that federal R&D in industry has a positive effect on productivity, though less of an impact than privately financed research.[15] Likewise, Guellec and van Pottelsberghe de la Potterie found that government research expenditures contribute to the rate of economic growth.[16] Another study of the U.K. economy found evidence of spillovers of private R&D and public R&D, with an estimated 20 percent rate of return to public R&D.[17] Similarly, the study examined the number of researchers in the public and private sectors between 1981 and 2017 across 20 OECD countries, and found that a doubling of private researchers increased productivity growth by 4.3–7.2 percent, while doubling public researchers increases productivity growth by 6.1–20.6 percent.[18]

To be clear, some federal R&D, such as the study of black holes, is interesting in its own right and may well be important over the very long term, but has little effect on today's economy. But the real question is whether most federal R&D expenditures are worthwhile within a reasonable timeframe, and here the evidence is definitely yes. It's time to retire the myth that government R&D competes with private R&D, and that the former has limited if any effect on growth. Given that the U.S. federal government invests less in R&D as a share of GDP than it did before Sputnik, greater federal R&D investment would likely have powerful economic benefits.[19] Few areas can more directly affect and improve America's global competition prospects.

— RA

Notes

1. "Blueprint for Balance: A Federal Budget for 2017" (Heritage Foundation, March 2016), http://thf-reports.s3.amazonaws.com/2016/BlueprintforBalance.pdf.

2. Iain Cockburn and Rebecca Henderson, "Publicly Funded Science and the Productivity of the Pharmaceutical Industry" (MIT Press, January 2001), https://www.nber.org/system/files/chapters/c10775/c10775.pdf.

3. Paulo Correa, Luis Andres, and Christian Borja-Vega, "The Impact of Government Support on Firm R&D Investments: A Meta-Analysis," World Bank, July 2013, https://documents1.worldbank.org/external/default/WDSContentServer/WDSP/IB/2013/07/15/000158349_20130715150702/Rendered/PDF/WPS6532.pdf.

4. Ibid.

5. L. Fleming, et al., "Government-Funded Research Increasingly Fuels Innovation," *Science*, June 2019, https://www.science.org/doi/10.1126/science.aaw2373?mc_cid=166197b3cc&mc_eid=%5BUNIQID%5D.

6. Mirko Draca, "Reagan's Innovation Dividend? Technological Impacts of the 1980s US Defense Build-Up," Department of Economics, University College London and Centre for Economic Performance, London School of Economics, February 2012, https://citeseerx.ist.psu.edu/viewdoc/download?doi=10.1.1.295.4170&rep=rep1&type=pdf.

7. Everett Ehrlich, "An Economic Engine: NIH Research, Employment, and the Future of the Medical Innovation Sector" (United for Medical

Research, 2011), http://www.eyeresearch.org/pdf/UMR_Economic% 20Engine_042711a.pdf, 3.

8. Dominique Guellec, Bruno van Pottelsberghe de la Potterie, "The Impact of Public R&D Expenditure on Business R&D" (OECD Science, Technology and Industry Working Papers, 2000/04, June 2000), http://www.oecd-ilibrary.org/science-and-technology/the-imp act-of-public-r-d-expenditure-on-business-r-d_670385851815?cra wler=true.

9. Martin Bailey, "Trends in Productivity Growth" *Technology and Growth: Conference Proceedings, Federal Reserve Bank of Boston* (June 1996), https://www.bostonfed.org/economic/conf/conf40/conf40.pdf.

10. Sabrina T. Howell, "Financing Constraints as Barriers to Innovation: Evidence from R&D Grants to Energy Startups" working paper, Harvard University, Cambridge MA, May 2015, http://scholar.har vard.edu/showell/home.

11. Matt Ridley, "The Myth of Basic Science," *Wall Street Journal,* October 2015, https://www.wsj.com/articles/the-myth-of-basic-sci ence-1445613954.

12. Leo Sveikauskas, "R&D and Productivity Growth: A Review of the Literature," working paper, US. Bureau of Labor Statistics, Washington, DC, 2007, https://www.bls.gov/ore/pdf/ec070070.pdf.

13. "The Sources of Economic Growth in OECD Countries," (OECD, February 2003), https://www.oecd-ilibrary.org/economics/the-sources-of-economic-growth-in-oecd-countries_9789264199460-en.

14. Dan Andrews and Chiara Criscuolo, "Knowledge-Based Capital, Innovation and Resource Allocation" working paper, OECD, Paris, 2013, https://www.oecd-ilibrary.org/economics/knowledge-based-cap ital-innovation-and-resource-allocation_5k46bj546kzs-en.

15. Zvi Griliches, "Productivity, R&D, and Basic Research at the Firm Level in the 1970's," *American Economic Review* (March 1986), 141–154.

16. Dominique Guellec and Bruno van Pottelsberghe de la Potterie, "The Impact of Public R&D Expenditure on Business R&D" (OECD Science, Technology and Industry Working Papers, 2000/04, June 2000), http://www.oecd-ilibrary.org/science-and-technology/the-impact-of-public-r-d-expenditure-on-business-r-d_670385851815.

17. Peter Goodridge, Jonathan Haskell, Alan Hughes, Gavin Wallis, "The Contribution of Public and Private R&D to UK Productivity Growth," Imperial College Business School (discussion paper,

March 2015), https://spiral.imperial.ac.uk:8443/bitstream/10044/1/21171/2/Haskel%202015-03.pdf.

18. Caleb Foote, "Fact of the Week: Doubling the Number of Public Sector Researchers Can Increase Productivity Growth by Up to 21 Percent" (ITIF, July 2020), https://itif.org/publications/2020/07/06/fact-week-doubling-number-public-sector-researchers-can-increase/.

19. Caleb Foote and Robert Atkinson, "Federal Support for R&D Continues Its Ignominious Slide" (ITIF, August 2019), https://itif.org/publications/2019/08/12/federal-support-rd-continues-its-ignominious-slide.

Myth 39: Industrial Policy Is Not the American Way

America's economic strength and national security depend on leading the world in advanced technology industries. And in the fiercely competitive global markets of the 21st century, maintaining leadership requires a concerted effort on the part of government. But the need for strong national industrial policies is widely dismissed by many policymakers as not part of the American tradition. The reality is that for most of U.S. history, state and federal support has been central to America's economic and technological leadership.

John F. Kennedy once said, "The great enemy of truth is very often not the lie, deliberate, contrived and dishonest—but the myth—persistent, persuasive and unrealistic." Perhaps nowhere is this truer than it is with the myth that a laissez-faire tradition has enabled America to lead the world both technically and economically.

In recent years, the U.S. government has taken actions that could be described as "industrial policy" since they have been designed to boost U.S. competitiveness in certain key industries, like semiconductors and electric vehicles. Yet, compared to China and other major competitors, the United States still has an anemic, underfunded, and ad hoc industrial strategy. One big reason is that over the last half-century, many policymakers have come to accept the false premise that America's economic leadership has been due almost entirely to free markets, not industrial policy.

Cases in point: a 2022 *Wall Street Journal* op-ed by former Texas Senator Phil Gramm and Mike Solon, claimed that: "America's success in the world economy has never depended on industrial policy or government subsidies. It has come from the relative absence of government planning and subsidies."[1]

© The Author(s), under exclusive license to Springer Nature Switzerland AG 2024
R. D. Atkinson and D. Moschella, *Technology Fears and Scapegoats*,
https://doi.org/10.1007/978-3-031-52349-6_40

Wall Street Journal Editor-at-Large Gerald Baker echoed that view, stating, "the beauty of the market is, we know from throughout history, particularly history of the last 200 years, when market capitalism has really been allowed to flourish that the market does that much better than government can."[2] Similarly, in their book, *It Didn't Happen Here: Why Socialism Failed in the United States*, Seymour Martin Lipset and Gary Marks write: "The American ideology, stemming from the Revolution, can be subsumed in five words: anti-statism, laissez-faire, individualism, populism, and egalitarianism."[3]

The reality is that from the founding of the Republic until the end of the Cold War, U.S. economic policy was guided by what can best be described as "national developmentalism"; America used government to achieve economic independence from the British, then to become the world's leading industrial nation in the early 1900s, later to defeat the Soviet Union technologically, and then address the 1980s competition from Japan. This tradition, not just laissez-faire economics, is why America became the richest nation on earth. It's also why America must once again embrace national developmentalism to meet today's unprecedented challenge from China.

Government and the Early Republic

Despite a prevailing narrative to the contrary, the Founding Fathers were not followers of Adam Smith. In his history of early American economic policy, Frank Bourgin wrote, "the doctrine of laissez-faire was hardly known to the framers of our Constitution."[4] Rather, they understood that absent developmental policy, the republic was likely to remain a natural resources colony for Britain. For example, the Continental Congress passed a resolution urging every colony to establish "a society for the improvement of agriculture, arts, manufacturers, and commerce."[5]

Alexander Hamilton "believed that in industry lay our great national destiny."[6] He did not want America to remain a "hewer of wood and drawer of water." Indeed, he argued that government should "cultivate particular branches of trade... and to discourage others."[7] That's why the Society of Useful Manufacturers was funded by the state of New Jersey and leading American financiers such as Hamilton were convinced to back it.

Even Thomas Jefferson embraced national developmentalism, including protective tariffs.[8] As president, his goal was to repay the national debt and then use government revenues to fund "rivers, canals, roads, arts, manufacturers, education and other great objects."[9] He "encouraged new branches of industry that may be advantageous to the public, either by offering premiums for discoveries, or by purchasing from their proprietors such inventions as shall appear to be of immediate and general utility, and rendering them free to the citizens at large."[10]

After the War of 1812, Jefferson wrote:

> You tell me I am quoted by those who wish to continue our dependence on England for manufactures. There was a time when I might have been so quoted with more candor, but within the 30 years, which have since elapsed, how are circumstances changed![11]

Indeed, the war heightened calls for more efforts to develop American industry. Henry Clay and other Whigs devised "the American System," consisting of tariffs to protect and promote industry; a national bank to foster commerce; and federal subsidies for roads, canals, and other domestic improvements. When running as a Whig in 1832, Abraham Lincoln stated, "my politics are short and sweet, like the old woman's dance. I am in favor of a national bank... in favor of the internal improvements system, and a high protective tariff."[12]

In fact, tariffs were a key reason the United States industrialized. Congress passed the country's first tariff, the Tariff Act of 1816, for the explicit purpose of protecting U.S. manufacturing from foreign competition. As late as the McKinley administration (1897–1901), the tariff rate on dutiable imports was around 50 percent.[13] Hardly free trade and open markets.

The Role of the States

One reason why the laissez-faire myth arose is that most observers looked only at the federal government for historical evidence of industrial policies. To be sure, these existed. The federal government supported the development of Robert Fulton's steamship, further research into steamboat explosions, and Samuel Morse's telegraph line from Washington, DC to Baltimore.[14]

But until the Civil War, state governments were the major practitioners of national developmentalism. This isn't surprising because the federal government was still so small. As Scheiber writes, "Positive intervention by states has been present continuously. At no time since 1787 does one find that laissez-faire ideology pervasively stood in the way of either promotional or regulatory intervention by the states."[15]

Take New York for example. In 1790, the New York legislature granted a manufacturer of earthenware a loan, because "the establishment of useful manufacturers is closely connected with the public weal." Between 1812 and

1816, the legislature authorized 28 loans to manufacturers.[16] In addition, the state funded "the Society for the Promotion of the Useful Arts" to improve agricultural production.

New York also used the financial surpluses from the Erie Canal to provide capital to banks to lend to manufacturers. The banks extended credit to "millers in Buffalo and Rochester, salt manufacturers in the Syracuse region, and urban commercial interests in Albany and other transshipment cities."[17] In the first half of the nineteenth century, New York "granted bounties to stimulate manufacturers, regulated weights and measures, and levied discriminatory duties on imports entering the port of New York in British ships."[18] Many other states, especially outside the agrarian South, enacted similar policies.

From 1865 to the 1890s, states subsidized railroads through bond-supported aid, land grants, and other assistance. Some states also extended direct cash aid or other benefits "to favored forms of industrial or commercial enterprise." Congress provided critical seed money for Samuel Morse to install the first telegraph line. A decade later, it approved an annual subsidy of $70,000 to lay a telegraph line between New York and Newfoundland, which led the following year to the first cable across the Atlantic.

The Role of the Military

Supporters of the laissez-faire myth also underappreciate the critical role of the military. It was no accident that the Civil War years—when the Democratic agrarian South had no members in Congress—were the most productive in American history for national development policy. Congress passed the Pacific Railway Act, the Homestead Act, the National Banking Act, the Morrill Land Grant Act, the Department of Agriculture Act, and the Morrill tariff.

Moreover, as historian Merritt Roe Smith writes:

Whether one looks at the origins of mechanized production or the latest version of the automatic factory, one finds the imprint of military influence. Computers, sonar, radar, jet engines, swept wing aircraft, insecticides, transistors, fire- and weather-resistance clothing, antibacterial drugs, numerically-controlled machine tools, high-speed integrated circuits, nuclear power—these are but some of the best-known industrial products of military enterprises since WWII. And the list can be greatly extended.[19]

Political scientists William D. Adler and Andrew J. Polsky wrote that in the pre-Civil War period, "The Army did more to shape the pattern and direction of economic development than did any other federal agency, any state government, or any private institution."[20] For example, in the first half of the 1800s, at a time when trained engineers were extremely scarce, the Army supplied them to the private economy.[21] The federal armory system was also central to the development of interchangeable parts. As economic historian David Hounshell has written:

> by specifying interchangeability in its contracts and by giving contractors access to technicians used in the national armories, the [Army] Ordnance Department contributed significantly to the growing sophistication of metalworking and woodworking... in the United States by the 1850s. British observers found these techniques sufficient different from their own and alluded to them as the "American system."[22]

Similarly, Charles Morris stresses that: "… armory practice in machining laid down a substrate of technologies—including gauging, pattern making, profiling and milling—that were seized on later and taken in many different directions by private contractors," including in the sewing machine, bicycle, and auto industries.[23] The Armories were also talent incubators. Henry Leland worked at the Springfield Armory, brought his knowledge to the Browne and Sharpe Manufacturing Company, and then later created the Cadillac and Lincoln Motor Car Companies.[24]

But it didn't stop after the Civil War. As Merritt Roe Smith wrote, "During the 1870s and 1880s… the Naval Ordnance Bureau, with its intense interest in adopting all-steel breechloading guns and armored vessels played an instrumental role in getting firms such as the Midvale Steel Company and Bethlehem Steel company to acquire the latest open-hearth methods and scale up their plants."[25] Indeed the Navy was a major factor in propelling the U.S. steel industry to global leadership.

The Navy also played the key role in creating the Radio Corporation of America, including threatening British Marconi with export controls unless it sold Marconi of America to General Electric. Susan Douglas explained, "Not only did Navy technicians contribute to the development of the art, but private inventors and private manufacturers with their research departments found in Navy patronage the encouragement and inspiration that led them to persevere in their endeavors."[26] The Navy Air Corp also funded General Electric to develop what would become GE's jet engine business.

Later, the Army Signal Corp played a key role in developing transistors through its subsidies, research, engineering development, and plant construction, and standardization requirements. Indeed, the Defense Department's Electronics Production Resource Agency assigned the Corp the task of developing this new technology for military purposes. Military support for the transistor at Bell Labs accounted for 50 percent of Bell funding from 1953 to 1955.[27] The military also funded plants directly, including those of Western Electric, General Electric, Raytheon, RCA, and Sylvania.[28]

In the 1950s and early 1960s, the Navy also played a key role in the development of containerization, while the Air Force played a similar role in numerically controlled machine tools when it created a market for these initially too expensive machines.[29]

Recent Policy Successes

After World War II, the federal government extended its support for advanced industries. By the early 1960s, it spent more on research and development than the rest of the world combined.[30] That fueled an enormous number of breakthroughs, including computers, semiconductors, jet aviation, lasers, numerically controlled machine tools, satellites, relational databases, and of course, the Internet.

In the 1980s, President Reagan supported the creation of the R&D tax credit, and the establishment of SEMATECH, a government-industry R&D partnership that helped restore U.S. leadership in semiconductors. The National Science Foundation launched a series of programs to link university and industry research. And the Reagan administration threatened Japan with tariffs if it didn't open its computer chip market. Congress's 2022 passage of the Chips and Science Act should be seen in this context.

None of this is to say that government alone created U.S. economic leadership. America's vast domestic market enabled unprecedented mass-production; its risk-taking and hard work culture, often enabled by immigrants, was critical, and the fact that, as Calvin Coolidge said, "the business of America is business" meant there were fewer restrictions on U.S. firms than there were on European ones. Nevertheless, without an active developmental state, America's progress would have been much more limited. Given this long and proud developmentalist tradition, the sooner Washington jettisons the laissez-faire myth, the better its chances of effectively competing with China.

—RA

Notes

1. Phil Gramm and Mike Solon, "Peace Through Strength Requires Economic Freedom," *Wall Street Journal* (March 2022), https://www.wsj.com/articles/peace-through-strength-economic-freedom-open-trade-china-ccp-economy-america-competes-act-antitrust-biden-116 46154226.

2. Gerry Baker and Oren Cass, "A New Conservative Economic Philosophy?" *Wall Street Journal Podcasts* (May 2023), https://www.wsj.com/podcasts/opinion-free-expression/a-new-conservative-economic-philos ophy/99a4b802-583a-4afa-94e3-6cfe85532aef.

3. David Boaz, "Nation's Libertarian Roots" (CATO Institute, February 2015), https://www.cato.org/commentary/nations-libertarian-roots.

4. Frank Bourgin, *The Great Challenge* (Harper & Row, 1989), 34.

5. John F. Kasson, *Civilizing the Machine* (New York: Hill and Wang, 1976), 11.

6. Bourgin, *The Great Challenge*, 92.

7. Ibid., 94.

8. John Lauritz Larson, *Internal Improvement: National Public Works and the Promise of Popular Government in the Early United States* (Chapel Hill: UNC Press, 2001), 64.

9. Ibid., 57.

10. Bourgin, *The Great Challenge*, 151.

11. Thomas Jefferson to Benjamin Austin, 9 January 1816, https://fou nders.archives.gov/documents/Jefferson/03-09-02-0213.

12. Michael Lind, *Land of Promise: An Economic History of the United States* (New York: Harper, 2013), 140.

13. "Average Tariff Rates in US (1821–2016)," *Wikipedia* (May 26, 2017), https://en.wikipedia.org/wiki/Tariff_in_United_States_history.

14. Lind, *Land of Promise*, 95.

15. Harry N. Scheiber, "State Law and 'Industrial Policy' in American Development, 1790–1987," *California Law Review*, vol. 75 (1987), 418.

16. Ibid.

17. Scheiber, "State Law and 'Industrial Policy,'" 421.

18. Nathan Miller, *The Enterprise of a Free People* (Ithaca, NY: Cornell University Press, 1962), 10.

19. Merritt Roe Smith, ed. *Military Enterprise and Technological Change* (Cambridge: MIT Press, 1987), 4.

20. William D. Adler and Andrew J. Polsky, "Building the New American Nation: Economic Development, Public Goods, and the Early U.S. Army," *Political Science Quarterly*, vol. 125(1) (Spring 2010), 88, https://www.jstor.org/stable/25698956.
21. Ibid., 105.
22. David Hounshell, *From the American System to Mass Production, 1800–1932* (Baltimore: Johns Hopkins Press, 1983), 332.
23. Ibid., 4.
24. Adler and Polsky, "Building the New American Nation," 106.
25. Smith, *Military Enterprise and Technological Change*, 8.
26. Susan Douglas, "The Navy Adopts the Radio," in Smith, *Military Enterprise and Technological Change*, 118.
27. Thomas Misa, "The Development of the Transistor," in Smith, *Military Enterprise and Technological Change*, 273.
28. Ibid., 275.
29. David Noble, "Military Enterprise and Technological Innovation," in Smith, *Military Enterprise and Technological Change*, 339.
30. Congressional Research Service, "Global Research and Development Expenditures: Fact Sheet," updated September 14, 2022, accessed with CRS reference number R44283 at https://crsreports.congress.gov/.

Myth 40: Industrial Policy Doesn't Work

As political support grows for the U.S. government to assist strategically important industries, many free-market conservatives continue to attack the value
of industrial policy, claiming that it usually fails. Such claims are lacking in
evidence, and their proponents have mostly aimed their fire at straw men.
The reality is that U.S. efforts to bolster industrial competitiveness have often
been highly effective, and they are especially needed in advanced technology
industries.

Every advanced industrial nations—Great Britain, the United States, and all
of the Asian tigers including China—industrialized itself by using specific
policies to shift their economies away from agriculture and low-valued
added manufacturing toward high-value-added production. Yet free-market
economists continue to claim that markets acting alone maximize economic
welfare and that government efforts to spur particular industries mostly make
things worse.

As the United States once again attempts to craft policies to boost advanced
industries, this time in reaction to China, the free-market right has trotted
out its old copies of Adam Smith's *The Wealth of Nations* to belittle any such
efforts, recycling familiar claims about the superiority of limited government
and the inferiority of industrial policy.

Such reactions are predictable. When the United States faced the Japanese
industrial challenge in the 1980s, both Republicans and Democrats wisely
supported policies to spur advanced-industry competitiveness, including
passing the R&D tax credit, creating specialized manufacturing support
programs in the U.S. Department of Commerce, establishing SEMATECH

© The Author(s), under exclusive license to Springer Nature
Switzerland AG 2024
R. D. Atkinson and D. Moschella, *Technology Fears and Scapegoats*,
https://doi.org/10.1007/978-3-031-52349-6_41

(an industry-university-government research program for the semiconductor industry), and placing import restrictions on certain Japanese products, including memory chips.

Free-market advocates vociferously opposed such measures at the time and now mostly ignore their success. Leading the initial charge was Brookings Institution scholar Charles Schultze with his seminal 1983 article, "Industrial Policy: A Dissent."[1] Coming from Brookings, which couldn't easily be accused of being a bastion of free-market ideology, and from Schultze, the chair of President Carter's Council of Economic Advisors, the article played a key role in ensuring that Washington's efforts were limited. It was as if Moses had come down from Mt. Sinai, showing the Lord's truth, and banishing industrial policy heretics from the neoclassical, free-market temple.

Schultze wrote the playbook for today's critics of industrial policy. He denied that the United States was losing industry, as do today's critics. He denied that Japan succeeded because of industrial policy, just as today's critics deny that China succeeds because of their policies. He stood up a straw man to attack, claiming that industrial policy is about supporting "losers," just as today's critics do by always mentioning Solyndra. And like today's critics, he proclaimed that there is no way to outsmart the market in identifying a "winning industrial structure."

Fast-forward to today, as free-market conservatives see, in horror, that Congress has passed the CHIPS and Science Act to support key industries, especially semiconductors. Predictably, they have tarred these efforts as the dreaded government planning. Michael Strain, an economist at the free-market American Enterprise Institute, wrote:

> Current US policies raise all the same old questions that have been asked before about industrial policy. Why should we expect the government to do a good job of picking winners and losers, or to allocate scarce resources better than the market? If the government intervenes in markets, how will it avoid mission creep, cronyism, and corruption?[2]

He went on to claim that "government planners simply lack the control to make an industrial policy succeed over the long term."

Supporting Strategic Industries

Some industries are simply more important than others, especially those that are traded globally, are technologically advanced, and are important to the defense industrial base. Anyone with any objectivity recognizes that industries such as semiconductors, biopharmaceuticals, sophisticated machinery, AI, and autonomous systems are critical to America's economic and military future. They are much more important than, for example, car dealerships and paper products. Contrary to a famous remark by Michael Boskin, once chair of the White House Council of Economic Advisors, potato chips are indeed less important than computer chips.[3]

Strain and other critics fall back on the argument that even if government could identify key industries, politics and bureaucracy will mess it up. But they seldom provide examples or evidence. In fact, U.S. advanced industry policy over the last 75 years at institutions like DARPA, NIH, NIST, and NSF has been consistently successful. For example, NIST's former Advanced Technology Program, which provided funding for particular technologies, was rigorously evaluated and found to be highly effective.[4] DARPA played key roles in developing the Internet, GPS, and other core technologies. And the current Manufacturing USA centers, a network of independent public–private research institutions, have also been found to be effective.[5]

Moreover, other nations have used industrial policy to great success. As Joe Studwell described in his book *How Asia Works*, the only way "Asian Tigers" such as Taiwan and South Korea could move up the industrial value chain was to embrace national industrial strategies.[6] Nations that have adopted smart industrial policies, including Japan, South Korea, Singapore, Taiwan, and now China, have grown dramatically, while many of those that have relied principally on market forces have not.[7]

This is not to say that all policies affecting industry are successful, any more than it is to say all policies affecting housing, health, and education are successful. But there is a significant body of experience and research on how to design effective industrial policies—including requiring industry to have "skin in the game," insulating program decisions from politics, and not picking narrow technologies or single firms as winners. If policy complies with these principles, it has a high chance of success. This is why a recent paper analyzing a significant amount of scholarly literature on industrial policy found "a balanced reading of the emerging literature suggests that it is no longer possible to dismiss industrial policy as ineffective or counter-productive."[8]

Market Inadequacies

One key reason why the free-market camp rejects almost any role for government other than protecting property rights is they believe that markets almost always get things right, and that market failures are rare. In reality, innovation-based industries are subject to a significant number of market failures, including externalities, network failures, system interdependencies, and the public-goods nature of technology platforms.[9]

For example, companies investing in research, on average, capture less than half the returns from that research, even with robust intellectual property protection.[10] The other benefits go to consumers and competitors. This means, absent policies such as an R&D tax credit or pre-competitive R&D grants, companies will tend to underinvest in research relative to the level that would maximize economy-wide returns.

Perhaps most obviously, there can be major market failures related to time. A firm may find it can maximize short-term profits by moving manufacturing overseas or cutting R&D, even if neither is in its long-term interests. As the Business Roundtable has stated, "The obsession with short-term results by investors, asset management firms, and corporate managers collectively leads to the unintended consequences of destroying long-term value, decreasing market efficiency, reducing investment returns, and impeding efforts to strengthen corporate governance."[11]

Finally, most innovation industries are characterized by increasing returns to scale. In such industries, a firm can substantially outcompete its rivals if it gains even a modest advantage in price or performance because that advantage can grow into a much larger one if marginal costs go down and innovation goes up as the business gets bigger. As Michael Lind has noted, "What is true of firms is also true of the nations in which the firms are based. In theory, a single country or trade bloc can monopolize all of the manufacturing in a particular industry."[12] For example, China could make all of the world's telecom equipment; Europe could make all the commercial jets; and Korea and Taiwan could make all the semiconductors. Once achieved, such success is hard to challenge, especially if a competing nation starts from a weak base and is unwilling to institute a sustained and supportive set of industrial development policies.

All of the above is especially true when nations, especially China, are engaged in mercantilist policies and practices targeting innovation-driven industries. Leaving everything to the market runs the real risk of the United States specializing in low-value-added, commodity-based production such as many agricultural products. While free-market economists may see nothing wrong with that—after all if the "market" dictates that the United States produces food and paper, and China produces advanced technology goods, then America would be ill-advised to try to change that outcome. But in such a world, U.S. living standards and national power will surely be diminished.

The Bottom Line

When market failures are rare, and business and national priorities are closely aligned, relying mostly on markets makes sense. But with many advanced industries, it's the other way around. Market failures are frequent, and short-term business and long-term national priorities can sharply differ. In such cases, coherent, effective, and sustained national industrial strategies are often the only way forward. All of America's major competitors know this, and continue to act accordingly.

—RA

Notes

1. Charles Schultze, "Industrial Policy: A Dissent" (The Brookings Review, Fall 1983), https://www.brookings.edu/wp-content/uploads/2016/06/industrial_policy_schultze.pdf.
2. Michael Strain, "Why Industrial Policy Fails" (AEI, August 2023), https://www.aei.org/op-eds/why-industrial-policy-fails/.
3. Robert Atkinson, "Time for a New National Innovation System for Security and Prosperity" (ITIF, March 2021), https://itif.org/publications/2021/03/19/time-new-national-innovation-system-security-and-prosperity/.
4. RT Ruegg, "The Advanced Technology Program, its Evaluation Plan, and Progress in Implementation" (NIST, October 2008), https://www.nist.gov/publications/advanced-technology-program-its-evaluation-plan-and-progress-implementation.
5. Kelly Marchese and Mark Cotteleer, "Manufacturing USA: A Third-Party Evaluation of Program Design and Progress" (Deloitte, January 2017), https://www2.deloitte.com/us/en/pages/manufacturing/articles/manufacturing-usa-program-assessment.html.
6. Joe Studwell, *How Asia Works: Success and Failure in the World's Most Dynamic Region* (Grove Press, New York, 2014).

7. Robert Wade, *Governing the Market: Economic Theory and the Role of Government in East Asian Industrialization* (Princeton, NJ: Princeton University Press, 1990).

8. Réka Juhász, Nathan Lane, and Dani Rodrik, "The New Economics of Industrial Policy" (National Bureau of Economic Research, Abstract, August 2023).

9. The assumption by most economists is that if provided with the right public goods and a "free" market, firms competing with each other will maximize productivity. But in fact, this simplistic assumption is not true. There is an array of reasons why firms may not maximize productivity. The first is the fact that firms cannot capture all the benefits of their own productive activity, meaning they will produce less productivity than is societally optimal. If the actual rate of return to society is greater than to the firms, they will stop investing before the societal rate of return equals the cost of capital. In other words, the inability of firms to capture all the benefits of their own activity means, left on their own, they will invest less in productivity-spurring activities than is optimal. There are other market failures that relate to the fact that many of the social and economic benefits from large-scale deployment of the technology accrue not to those buying or selling products and services, but to competitors through the expansion of network benefits. Another market failure relates to uncertainty. Because increasing productivity often depends on adoption of an emerging, but not yet fully proven, technology, many potential users will disregard the benefits it promises and delay adoption until the technology is proven. Economists refer to this challenge as excess inertia or, more commonly, "the penguin effect"—in a group of hungry penguins, no individual penguin is willing to be the first to enter the water to search for food due to the risk of encountering a predator. Yet if no penguin is willing to test the waters, then the whole group risks starvation. Another market failure relates to time. Rational firms maximize net present value profits. In other words, if a firm can earn $1 in profits this year, but $1.20 next year, the rational firm will choose the latter because it would bring an annual return of 20 percent. But there is considerable evidence that, increasingly, firms, at least in the United States, invest to maximize short-term returns at the expense of higher productivity.

10. Robert D. Atkinson, *Think Like and Enterprise: Why Nations Need Comprehensive Productivity Strategies* (ITIF, May 2016), https://itif.org/publications/2016/05/04/think-enterprise-why-nations-need-comprehensive-productivity-strategies. 47.

11. Dean Krehmeyer, et al., "Breaking the Short-Term Cycle: Discussion and Recommendations on How Corporate Leaders, Asset Managers, Investors, and Analysts Can Refocus on Long-Term Value" (Proceedings of the CFA Centre for Financial Market Integrity and Business Roundtable Institute for Corporate Ethics Symposium Series on Short-Termism, July 2006), https://www.cfainstitute.org/-/media/documents/article/position-paper/breaking-the-short-term-cycle.ashx.

12. Michael Lind, "The Rise of Geonomics," *National Interest*, October 2019, https://nationalinterest.org/feature/return-geoeconomics-87826.

Conclusion

Returning to a Pro-innovation American Agenda

To reinvigorate American innovation and competitiveness, society's belief in the essential role and value of advanced technology must be restored, and numerous economic, technology and policy misconceptions, fears, and scapegoats must be discarded. Faced with rising global competition, both technology companies and policymakers must take specific actions to reverse the inaccurate anti-tech and anti-business narratives of recent years.

The roots of this book go back to 2017 when we first became concerned that most of the increasingly fierce critiques of "Big Tech" were exaggerated, unfair, or flat out wrong. In 2020, we decided to systematically examine each of the major charges to see how well they held up to scrutiny. Our goal hasn't been to dismiss these concerns completely, but rather to defend the value of advanced technology and restore a sense of accuracy and balance. If politicians, policymakers, the media, and the general public have overly negative views of the impact of technology and technology companies on American society, then U.S. innovation and competitiveness will inevitably suffer.

Although there have always been groups concerned about privacy, automation, corporate power and similar issues, today's *Techlash* is much more potent. It first took hold after the UK's Brexit referendum and America's election of Donald Trump in 2016. In both nations the elites needed to find someone or something to blame, and social media was a convenient scapegoat. Since then, there has been a relentless barrage of criticism, with virtually no systematic defense. The digital world is now routinely accused of destroying privacy, spreading misinformation, undermining trust and democracy, eliminating jobs, oppressing workers, targeting and addicting our youth,

R. D. Atkinson and D. Moschella, *Technology Fears and Scapegoats*,
https://doi.org/10.1007/978-3-031-52349-6_42

discriminating by race and gender, accelerating inequality, manipulating consumers, coarsening discourse, reinforcing biases, running roughshod over local languages and cultures, exercising monopoly power, and even threatening the human race. These myths pretty much define today's conventional wisdom.

Additionally, there is a second set of myths that get less media attention but are just as damaging. These are primarily mistakes of economics, history, and policy. Key among these are the widespread beliefs that: Small businesses are more innovative and create more jobs than big ones; productivity gains no longer help workers; corporate profits and industry concentration are at all-time highs; the world is changing faster than ever before; China's success stems mostly from cheating and human rights abuses; we have all the technology we need to address climate change; and government-supported industrial policy doesn't work and is not the American way.

Both sets of falsehoods matter because they make society less willing to develop and adopt new technologies, and less tolerant of any initial problems or failures. They discourage talented people from entering technology fields and make companies more cautious and wary of regulators. They also steer policy in the wrong direction, more focused on slowing things down than accelerating progress, more focused on redistribution than growing the pie. They make policymakers reluctant to even talk about the need to drive progress and innovation.

As has already happened in Europe, anti-business, anti-tech attitudes are making America less competitive, because even as the United States loses its faith in innovation, China and India have not. America's post-World War II dominance of advanced technology industries is being challenged as never before. Staying ahead of the competition requires strong and bipartisan public support, and this requires rejecting a wide array of anti-technology myths and related exaggerations and falsehoods.

This concluding chapter outlines strategies for developing and promoting a much more accurate narrative and pro-innovation hi-tech agenda. While there are no simple answers to these entrenched problems, the overall shape of what needs to be done is clear enough. Companies, policymakers, and the media all have important roles to play in reversing today's myths and re-establishing that—despite real problems and challenges—America unequivocally believes in the past, present, and future of innovation. This is no time to retreat from the world's growing technological imperative.

Defending Thyself

The first step toward establishing a more positive narrative should be made by the technology industry itself. It is far from blameless, and can do many things to improve today's situation, especially along the six lines below:

1. **Pushing Back Against the Criticisms.** During their many congressional appearances in recent years, the leading Big Tech CEOs have mostly acknowledged their company's shortcomings and promised to do better. While being conciliatory is an understandable political tactic, this approach has ceded way too much ground. The longer the many myths in this book go unchallenged, the more entrenched they become—and the more assertive tech's adversaries can be. At some point, the conventional wisdom becomes almost impossible to overturn. It's past time for the technology industry to stop being on the back foot and instead push back against the most damaging charges. If the leading tech companies don't robustly defend AI, automation, targeted advertising, social media, Big Data, facial recognition, autonomous vehicles, and other technologies, why should anyone else?

2. **Aligning with the U.S. National Interest.** Although China remains both a major market and an essential supplier to many of America's leading firms, those dynamics are increasingly outweighed by concerns about China as a military and geopolitical rival. This fundamental shift in U.S. priorities is making the country-neutral mindset of globalization less and less viable. Looking back, the way America's leading tech firms allowed themselves to become so dependent on China and Taiwan is a textbook example of the risks of short-term, country-neutral thinking, and reversing these dependencies will take many years of sustained effort. Chinese companies are legally required to support the Chinese state. America shouldn't go this far. However, even when it affects their short-term business, U.S.-based firms will be increasingly expected to take much more account of America's concerns, whether the issue is returning chip manufacturing to the United States, limiting the export of advanced technologies to China, expanding *friend shoring* to improve U.S. resiliency, overcoming Silicon Valley's traditional resistance to working closely with the Department of Defense, or using their vast cash reserves to directly support American competitiveness.

3. **Restoring Political Neutrality.** America remains a sharply divided country (about as close to 50/50 as possible), but in recent years Big Tech—in particular, social media—has failed to be similarly balanced.

Privately-owned social media companies have the legal right to manage issues such as misinformation and hate speech however they see fit, but they have learned the hard way that they should be humble about their ability to reliably determine which content should be banned or suppressed. Fortunately, there are signs that a more politically neutral digital world may be emerging. Elon Musk says that open political speech will be a fundamental part of X, while Mark Zuckerberg has hinted that Meta might reduce its overall political engagement. Perhaps the censorship that took place during the pandemic will prove to be a largely one-time phenomenon, and we will return to the Internet's more open roots, with content moderation focused on illegal and directly harmful speech. Given today's heightened political polarization, maintaining neutrality won't always be easy or popular, but in the long run it will help establish more bipartisan political and societal support.

4. **Fixing the Main Problems**. Consumers have it right. Their two main digital concerns are information security—identity theft, malware, ransomware, fraud, and similar plagues—and the potential risks to children, especially bullying, pornography, and the obsessive use of social media. In these areas, tech, media, and consumer interests are well aligned, as all three groups agree these are very high priorities. If the tech industry is seen as working hard and making progress in these two challenges, as least some of today's media and political venom would be diminished.

5. **Meeting Long-Term Societal Needs**. The great success of the technology industry thus far has been in the consumer sector—web browsing, mobility, social media, e-commerce, search, maps, apps, etc. But technology has been much less successful in fulfilling the grand promises of the information age—effective and less expensive health care and education, cleaner and more efficient cities and grids, smart products and services, using automation to bring jobs back to the United States, creating a more sustainable and circular economy, and so on. If the digital world is to have a second act as great as its first, it will be because it has addressed these important societal needs. Thus far, technology has helped us stay connected, informed, and entertained, and the public has highly valued these services. But should it also make the world healthier, safer, cleaner, and more sustainable, societal support would be much deeper and long-lasting.

6. **Working Together**. Today, there are almost as many positions on a particular technology issue in Washington as there are technology companies. Whether the topic is patent policy, net neutrality, digital piracy, or trade, companies often spend more political energy lobbying against their

competitors than making common cause against anti-technology forces. Moreover, there is no overarching industry association for innovation. Instead, there is an alphabet soup of trade associations, including AIA, BIO, BSA, CTIA, CompTIA, ESA, ITIC, MPA, NCTA, and USTA. Each is focused on advancing the interests of its members: defense budgets for AIA, telecom regulations for USTA and NCTA, the fallout from NSA revelations for ITIC. It's time for the engine of American economic prosperity to have its own voice: the *American Innovation Industries Association*, with members, small and large, from a wide range of technology-focused sectors, focused on defending and advancing U.S. innovation.

These six strategies can help: (1) rebut the main technology myths and criticisms; (2) demonstrate that U.S.-based firms care about America, not just their own bottom line; (3) rebuild digital trust across the political spectrum; (4) address consumers' most pressing tech concerns; (5) position America's technology industry to take on the challenges of the future; and (6) give technology industry firms a stronger pro-innovation voice. On their own, these steps could blunt much of the anti-tech movement, but they will be much more effective if they are supported by both a pro-innovation technology policy agenda, and corresponding media coverage.

A Pro-innovation Policy Past

Washington politics are so dysfunctional these days that it's easy to forget that smart policies have played a critical role in enabling U.S. technology leadership. Al Gore didn't invent the Internet, but he was an enthusiastic technology supporter in a way that no senior government official is today, and, in retrospect, the Clinton administration deserves high markets for accelerating Internet innovation and adoption, in part by adopting a light-touch regulatory framework. Below are ten of government's most important Internet contributions during the twentieth century:

1. In 1969, Defense Advanced Projects Research Agency (DARPA) developed ARPANET whose underlying technologies became the foundation of the Internet.
2. In 1987, the National Science Foundation contracted with IBM and MCI to build a network of networks, an Internet.

3. In 1989, the hypertext technologies that enabled the Internet to evolve into the worldwide web were developed by Tim Berners-Lee at the European Laboratory of Particle Physics in Switzerland.
4. In 1993, the first graphical Internet browser (Mosaic) was developed by Marc Andreessen and his team at the National Center for Supercomputing in Illinois.
5. In 1995, the U.S. gained World Trade Organization support for the Trade-Related Aspects of Intellectual Property Rights (TRIPS), an important step in the multinational protection of IP rights.
6. In 1996, Section 230 of the Communications Decency Act specified that online service providers are not legally liable for what users post on their services, enabling the rapid expansion of many Internet content services.
7. In 1997, the Clinton administration produced its Framework for Global Electronic Commerce which advocated light regulation and private-sector leadership.
8. In 1998, the Digital Millennium Copyright Act specified that online service providers are not liable for the copyright violations of their users as long as they take prompt action to remove such content once properly notified.
9. In 1998, the Internet Tax Freedom Act established a tax moratorium on e-commerce transactions, a vital step in simplifying and accelerating online shopping.
10. In 1998, the Internet Corporation for Assigned Names and Numbers (ICANN) was incorporated in California as a nonprofit, formalizing a critical Internet function, while keeping control within the U.S. until 2009.

All of the above were pro-innovation policies that helped the digital world move forward. They stemmed from the belief that information technology is important, and that government can accelerate its progress. However, since the Clinton administration, digital policies have been much less ambitious and supportive, as summarized below.

- The most relevant tech policy of the Bush administration was the passage of the Patriot Act, which greatly expanded the government's surveillance powers in both the online and offline worlds. In the aftermath of 9–11, national security concerns clearly trumped any worries about what was good or bad for the Internet.
- Although the Obama administration was often seen as tech savvy, its most high-profile policy effort was a failure. After often bitter debate, the FCC

embraced so-called *net neutrality*. Although treating all Internet traffic equally sounds fair and was intended to help the Internet continue to flourish, in practice it has proved unnecessary. It was quickly scrapped by the Trump administration with little vocal opposition.

- For reasons that had nothing to do with the future of the digital economy, the Trump administration withdrew from the Trans-Pacific Partnership (TPP). Part of that agreement would have better protected global data flows by prohibiting national policies that confine data within a country's borders. While President Trump was and is a very active user of social media, technology policy was a low personal and administration priority.

- The Biden administration can be seen as the first *techlash presidency*. It has taken the most punitive stances against Big Tech, sometimes calling for the abolition of Section 230 and a fundamental transformation of antitrust policy based on the premise that big is bad. It pressured technology firms to either ban or suppress content, especially information about Covid-19, a major statement that the traditional openness of the Internet was no longer wanted. It is also seeking to strongly regulate AI and restore unneeded net neutrality regulations. Internationally, it has abandoned trade efforts supportive of cross-border data flows, and done little to defend American tech firms from foreign government attacks. The 2018, 2020, and 2022 Congresses were similarly hostile, holding many emotionally charged and accusatory Big Tech hearings, seemingly designed more to attack than learn.

On the other hand, the August 2022 passage of the CHIPS and Science Act might someday be seen as marking the beginning of the end of the techlash, as a bipartisan group of legislators recognized that semiconductor manufacturing capabilities are vital to America's future, and that serious policy actions are required to make this happen. The challenge from China might prove to be a techlash tipping point, forcing policymakers to put their anti-tech concerns into a more realistic national interest perspective. We surely hope so, but there is a long way to go, especially given the many challenges in making chips in the United States, and China's dominance of key parts of today's technology industry value chain.

Missed Opportunities

In addition to these individual administration actions, policymakers have often come up short in areas where supportive technology policies are needed. To cite just four examples:

- **Privacy**. Privacy laws in the United States are a hodge podge of state rules, and no meaningful national standards have been established. This failure has essentially ceded the privacy field to Europe, especially its General Data Protection Regulation (GDPR) adopted in 2016, which has raised costs, slowed innovation, and put significant burdens on small businesses.[1] Europe continues to take a precautionary approach to the digital world in its more recent legislation, especially its Digital Services Act and Digital Markets Act, which are aimed mostly at Big Tech *gatekeepers*, who just happen to be overwhelmingly American. The U.S. has done little to push back against these policies, in large part because factions within the Biden administration agree with them.
- **Data Protectionism**. American firms benefited greatly from the global Internet. But in recent years, the Internet has been splintering. Support for *digital sovereignty* and local protectionism has risen sharply in authoritarian and democratic nations alike. Although some pushback along these lines was inevitable, it's been made easier by a growing abandonment of free trade by both the Biden and Trump administrations.
- **Censorship**. American executives and government officials have long complained about how U.S. social media firms are blocked in China, Russia, and elsewhere. But the rest of the world can now say that America has engaged in extensive censorship too. The global implications of this will be long-lasting, even if the censorship of the 2020–2022 period is reduced going forward.
- **Antitrust**. The Biden administration, and in particular, FTC Chair Lina Khan, has shown a particular animus toward large technology companies. It has unsuccessfully sought to block pro-innovation mergers like those between Microsoft and Activision, and between Facebook and the fitness app Supernatural,[2] while also trying to rewrite merger rules to make venture capital exits through acquisition more difficult. Most symbolically, it has launched major antitrust cases against Apple, Google, and Amazon.

The contrast between the pro-innovation policies of the twentieth century vs those of the twenty-first is striking. Both recent administration actions and shifting global dynamics have contributed to an anti-innovation climate, where America has often lost both global leadership and the moral high ground. This does not bode well for the smart policy decisions needed for the future, be they about artificial intelligence, facial recognition, cryptocurrencies, spectrum and satellite oversight, electronic voting systems, autonomous vehicles, robotics, AR/VR, quantum computers, prosthetics, synthetic biology, and the free flow of scientists, information and ideas.

Clearly, a new generation of pro-innovation policy leadership is needed and long overdue. America can't look to either Europe or China for guidance; it must rediscover its long history of pro-innovation political support.

A Pro-innovation Policy Agenda for the 2020s

It's no secret how to restore robust rates of innovation and productivity growth, and try to stay ahead of China in the tech race. It's mostly a matter of national will and execution. The federal government should develop and support pro-innovation policies in five main policy areas: trade, taxation, usage, R&D, and regulatory philosophy.

- **Nuanced Trade Policies**. Not all industries are the same. America should embrace free trade in low-wage industries that are not our competitive advantage. But it should allow some protectionism in high-wage industries that don't require global scale (e.g., motor vehicles and iron and steel). It should then push for more open markets for strategic U.S. industries that require global scale for competitiveness, such as in aerospace, software and information, computing and semiconductors, and biopharmaceuticals. We need more free trade and deeper integration with allies, and more strategic protectionism and less integration with China. Overall, we should insist on reciprocity, meaning that unless other nations open their markets for U.S. goods and services, the United States will reduce their access to U.S. markets.
- **Pro-innovation Taxation**. The current debate on taxes is one where the right wants lower taxes on pretty much everything and everyone, while the left wants the opposite, especially higher taxes on the wealthy and corporations. In reality, corporate taxes harm innovation more than individual ones, and within corporate taxes, it's better to boost incentives for investing in innovation than to simply lower the corporate rate across the board. This means, among other things, significantly increasing the R&D tax credit, allowing it to be used for advanced skill development, and restoring the ability of companies to expense capital investments in the first year, especially for machinery and software.
- **Public Sector Leadership**. The federal government needs to raise its digital game. Many of the innovations of the future—smart cities and grids, autonomous vehicles, electronic voting systems, digital payments, electronic healthcare records, etc.—will take place within or closely adjacent to

the public sphere. But the sad reality is that the U.S. government does little to support such transformations. It can't even modernize its own woefully out of date systems. If we want "smart everything" anytime soon, Congress must fund pilot projects, help establish effective standards, and require the federal government to be a much smarter digital customer and service provider.

- **Increased R&D**. In the early 1960s, the federal government alone invested more in R&D than every other country (business and government combined).[3] Today, as a share of GDP, federal R&D is about one-third of 1960 levels.[4] Rather than cutting taxes on the rich or boosting spending on social services, America needs to invest much more in cutting-edge innovation, especially in partnership with industry. However, R&D alone is not enough, as China has learned to copy and produce our innovations. America needs to support the scale-up and production of advanced technology goods in the United States. One step would be an investment tax credit for advanced tech equipment, similar to those that semiconductor firms are now getting.

- **Supportive Regulation**. The fact that it's almost impossible to build a new nuclear reactor in the United States, upgrade the electric grid, move to more automated freight trains, and, until recently, get permits to build semiconductor factories in the United States speaks volumes about how the nation has become risk averse and tangled up in legal, especially environmental, restrictions. As venture capitalist and tech visionary Marc Andreessen writes, "it's time to build."[5] At the same time, policymakers must provide viable innovation-enabling alternatives to restrictive European regulatory initiatives in areas such as privacy, cross-border data flows, facial recognition, and AI.

Similarly, America needs a regulatory system that wants to innovate, and is not so afraid of a bad outcome, that it limits good outcomes. Congress should create a new Office of Innovation Policy within the White House Office of Management and Budget. This office would review all significant proposed regulations to determine how they might help or harm innovation. The Office of Technology Assessment should also be restored. This advisory agency, eliminated by Newt Gingrich in 1995, was staffed by scientists, engineers, and doctors (Atkinson worked there), and provided Congress with important information about tech and tech policy.

Pro-growth Politics

But all of the above policies will be hard to enact unless there are corresponding changes in American politics. As long as Washington is deeply divided between right-wing, anti-government libertarianism and left-wing, anti-corporate progressivism, little will get done. The number of Republicans that want to move away from libertarianism and laissez-faire is growing, and to the extent that they do not embrace anti-corporate views, they need air cover. After all, Ronald Reagan supported a wide array of industrial policies that helped American outcompete Japan. Freedom is just a slogan if it means a world in which the United States is dependent on China.

Likewise, forces within the Democratic Party that want to put growth, innovation, and competitiveness ahead of social policy and redistribution also need to be strengthened. Groups such as the House New Democratic Coalition should be more vocal and take a stronger stance in favor of technology, technology companies, and technology policy while pushing back against the anti-tech wings of the Party. Its *Economic Opportunity Agenda* barely mentions technology, except for the need for clean tech.[6] And with the exception of calling for the repeal of a 2017 measure that weakened the R&D tax credit, the New Democrat's middle-class agenda is short on innovation policy. It mostly includes proposals for various transfer payments. In short, America needs more pro-growth Democrats and more pro-tech policy Republicans.

Winning Back Old Media

To read today's mainstream media, you would think that technology is the source of most of America's problems, especially polarization, distrust, and misinformation. But it wasn't always this way. From 1995 to 2015, the leaders of the technology industry were the rock stars of Davos, and widely seen as societal visionaries and even the saviors of the American economy. Newspapers, magazines, and television produced the gushiest of profiles.[7] Today, these perceptions have shifted to the other extreme, with the very same set of leaders often described as *surveillance capitalists* and *greedy monopolists.*

The extent of this change is ironic because social media and traditional media increasingly have many things in common. Professionals in both new and old media routinely switch sides and face similar challenges in terms of truth, trust, misinformation, polarization, bias, AI, profiling, automation, advertising, free services, deep fakes, fact checking, censorship, the use of new technologies, and many other areas.

As we have shown throughout this book, traditional media is no better—and often worse—in many of these areas than social media. But it's new media that gets most of the blame. Indeed, an easy way to describe today's traditional media perspective is to simply say: "Old media agrees: new media is the problem." Why has this view taken hold? And more importantly, what can be done about it? In addition to the lingering effects of the 2016 election, there are four main theories as to why today's tech coverage is so negative:

1. Some editors sincerely believe that the problems that technology creates need more attention, and that they are serving the public by highlighting these concerns. The fact that many of the most valuable tech innovations are now relatively mature—and thus less newsworthy—contributes to this mentality. This explanation supports the view that if important and more positive news emerges from either tech companies or policymakers—such as significantly returning chip making to the United States—media coverage might noticeably improve.

2. New media and old media compete for advertising dollars, and new media has been winning decisively. It's not that editors sit around and say that "the internet is really hurting us; we should run more stories about all the problems it creates." But it's only human nature for resentments regarding online media's success to spill over into editorial decisions to at least some extent. This dynamic will be hard to change unless the financial situations of traditional media stabilize. Voluntary deals such as Google's 2023 agreement to pay the New York Times for content could prove to be an ameliorating factor over time.

3. Bad news and scary stories attract more eyeballs than happy ones. This attitude predates the Internet, as in the once common phrase "if it bleeds, it leads." A single Tesla self-driving crash gets much more coverage than thousands of *routine* car accidents, ditto for any ChatGPT or facial recognition errors. This dynamic occurs in new and old media alike and cuts to the core of society's willingness to accept the risks that come with any significant change. But as the bad news in the world shifts to the war in Ukraine, the Mideast, rising crime, mass migration, inflation, climate change, and other problems, today's tech concerns will likely seem less scary going forward.

4. The vast majority of the mainstream media is liberal leaning, and much of the American left has long had an anti-corporate, anti-bigness, and anti-profit outlook. These inclinations are supported by a vast network

of academics, foundations, and nonprofits. Gaining support for a pro-innovation, pro-American agenda from these groups will be among the toughest challenges of all. For example, a generation ago the ethos in academia was to be objective. Too often today, it's to be an effective advocate, usually against new technologies and/or big companies, ideally with a lot of social media followers. Restoring media and institutional objectivity is beyond the scope of this book, but it would certainly help foster more accurate and positive narratives.

A Twenty-First-Century Pro-innovation Narrative

The industry, government, and media dynamics described above can help us see the shape of a new and much more positive technology narrative. If the tech industry is seen as helping America compete with China, making *American* prosperity a priority, being politically neutral, solving its most serious consumer problems, and addressing critical societal needs such as health, education, and climate change, then positive media coverage will surely follow.

Similarly, if there are effective bipartisan pro-innovation government policies that support these developments, old and new media from both the left and the right are likely to provide more positive coverage and support. Technology's downsides will be seen in perspective, especially when compared to the challenge from China and the many other problems the world faces today.

In the end, companies, politicians, and media all serve the citizen/consumer, and the consumer is still on technology's side. People see the enormous value of: Google Maps and Search; Uber and Lyft; Airbnb and Tripadvisor; Facebook and LinkedIn; Amazon and eBay; iPhones and Androids; Netflix and YouTube; working and learning at home; and countless other major and minor offerings. They have also experienced how supposedly scary things like facial identification and voice recognition help them with their smart phones and smart speakers. While they may see AI, robots, and virtual reality as potentially creepy, they haven't yet experienced any serious downsides. Overall, consumers have not been a major part of the techlash and have largely ignored the many myths and warnings. This is a major reason for optimism.

Indeed, given the chance, consumers might vote to give Google Maps the Nobel Peace Prize. Has any recent person or thing done as much to reduce conflict (between driver and passenger) and minimize stress (being lost in traffic)? Over one billion people use this free and highly reliable service every month, an extraordinary business and technical achievement. But Maps is now taken for granted, as if it was always there and is now some sort of inevitable and inalienable right. The same can be said for countless other technology services—wondrous benefits, often at little or no cost. This should be the lead story of innovation—past, present, and, hopefully, future.

Notes

1. Ashley Johnson, "Restoring US Leadership on Digital Policy" (ITIF, July 2023), https://itif.org/publications/2023/07/31/restoring-us-leader ship-on-digital-policy/.
2. Federal Trade Commission, "FTC Seeks to Block Virtual Reality Giant Meta's Acquisition of Popular App Creator Within," Federal Trade Commission News Release, July 27, 2022, https://www.ftc.gov/ news-events/news/press-releases/2022/07/ftc-seeks-block-virtual-reality-giant-metas-acquisition-popular-app-creator-within.
3. Paul Scharre and Ainikki Riikonen, "Defense Technology Strategy" (New America, 2020), https://www.jstor.org/stable/pdf/resrep26976.4. pdf.
4. Richard J. Brody, *Effective Partnering: A Report to Congress on Federal Technology Partnerships* (Washington, DC: Department of Commerce, 1996), http://www.nist.gov/tpo/publications/upload/effect ive_partnering.pdf; National Science Board, "A Companion to Science and Engineering Indicators 2008," website of the National Science Foundation, http://www.nsf.gov/statistics/nsb0803/start.htm.
5. Marc Andreesen, "It's Time to Build," Blog Post, Andreesen Horowitz, April 2020, https://a16z.com/2020/04/18/its-time-to-build/.
6. New Democrat Coalition, "New Dems Unveil Economic Opportunity Agenda to Continue Lowering Costs, Fighting Inflation, and Growing the Middle Class," News Release, July 18, 2023, https://newdemocr atcoalition.house.gov/media-center/press-releases/new-dems-unveil-eco nomic-opportunity-agenda-to-continue-lowering-costs-fighting-inflat ion-and-growing-the-middle-class.
7. Doug Allen and Daniel Castro, "Why so Sad? A Look at the Change in Tone of Technology Reporting From 1986 to 2013" (ITIF, February 2017), https://itif.org/publications/2017/02/22/why-so-sad-look-change-tone-technology-reporting-1986-2013/.

Index